The Moral Problem

PHILOSOPHICAL THEORY

SERIES EDITORS
John McDowell, Philip Pettit and Crispin Wright

For Truth in Semantics
Anthony Appiah

Abstract Particulars
Keith Campbell

Tractarian Semantics
Peter Carruthers

Truth and Objectivity
Brian Ellis

The Dynamics of Belief
Peter Forrest

Abstract Objects
Bob Hale

Facts and Meaning
Jane Heal

Conditionals
Frank Jackson

Sense and Certainty
Marie McGinn

Reality and Representation
David Papineau

Facts and the Function of Truth
Huw Price

Moral Dilemmas
Walter Sinnott-Armstrong

Unnatural Doubts
Michael Williamson

Identity and Discrimination
Timothy Williamson

√27-59
130-181

The Moral Problem

MICHAEL SMITH

BLACKWELL
Publishers

First published 1994
First published in USA 1995
Reprinted 1995, 1996, 1997

Blackwell Publishers Ltd
108 Cowley Road
Oxford OX4 1JF, UK

Blackwell Publishers Inc
350 Main Street
Malden, Massachusetts 02148, USA

British Library Cataloguing in Publication Data
A CIP catalogue record for this book is available from the British Library

Library of Congress Cataloging in Publication Data
Smith, Michael (Michael A.)
The moral problem/Michael Smith
p. cm. — (Philosophical theory)
Includes bibliographical references and index.
ISBN 0–631–18941–6 (alk. paper) — ISBN 0–631–19246–8 (pbk)
1. Ethics. 2. Rationalism. I. Title. II. Series
BJ1031.S64   1994   94–6156
170—dc20   CIP

Typeset in Baskerville on 11/13pt
by Best-set Typesetter Ltd, Hong Kong
Printed and bound in Great Britain
by Athenæum Press Ltd, Gateshead, Tyne & Wear

This book is printed on acid-free paper

For my parents Phyl and Roy Smith

Acknowledgements

Grateful acknowledgement is made for permission to reprint extracts from the following previously published material by Michael Smith: 'Should We Believe in Emotivism?' in Graham Macdonald and Crispin Wright, eds, *Fact, Science and Morality: Essays on A. J. Ayer's Language, Truth and Logic*, 1986, Basil Blackwell; 'The Humean Theory of Motivation', *Mind*, 1987, Oxford University Press; 'Dispositional Theories of Value', *Proceedings of the Aristotelian Society*, Supplementary Volume, 1989; 'Realism' in Peter Singer, ed., *A Companion to Ethics*, 1991, Basil Blackwell; 'Valuing: Desiring or Believing?' in David Charles and Kathleen Lennon, eds, *Reduction, Explanation, and Realism*, 1992, Oxford University Press; and 'Objectivity and Moral Realism: on the Significance of the Phenomenology of Moral Experience' and 'Colour, Transparency, Mind-Independence', both in John Haldane and Crispin Wright, eds, *Reality, Representation and Projection*, 1993, Oxford University Press.

Contents

Preface

The ideas for this book began to take shape while I was still a student at Oxford in the early eighties. However the project of turning them into a book only began in earnest towards the end of my time teaching at Princeton, and has been completed only since my return to Monash. I would like to take this opportunity to thank all those who have helped me in various ways during this time.

Princeton University granted me a sabbatical leave during 1988 when work on the book commenced. The faculty and alumni of Princeton University gave me research support in the form of the Class of 1931 Bicentennial Preceptorship in 1988, which greatly helped the work to continue. I would like to thank all those at Princeton for their generosity. I was able to get back to the book when Monash University granted me a sabbatical leave during the first half of 1993 and a further period of absence during the second half of 1993 so that I could take up a Visiting Fellowship in the Philosophy Program at the Research School of Social Sciences, Australian National University. I am grateful both to Monash and to RSSS for giving me the opportunity to undertake research in such ideal conditions. The book has been completed while I have been a Visiting Fellow here at RSSS.

In writing this book I have drawn, to a greater or a lesser extent, on several previously published papers: 'Should We Believe in Emotivism?' in *Fact, Science and Morality: Essays on A. J. Ayer's Language, Truth and Logic*, edited by Graham Macdonald and Crispin Wright, (Blackwell, 1986), 289–310; 'The Humean Theory of Motivation' *Mind*, (1987), 36–61; 'Dispositional Theories of Value' *Proceedings of the Aristotelian Society*, Supplementary Volume, (1989), 89–111; 'Realism' in *A Companion to Ethics* edited by Peter Singer, (Blackwell, 1991), 399–410; 'Valuing: Desiring or Believing?' in *Reduction, Explanation, and Realism* edited by David Charles and Kathleen Lennon, (Oxford University Press, 1992), 323–60; and 'Objectivity and Moral Realism: On the Significance of the Phenomenology of Moral Experience' and 'Colour, Transparency, Mind-Independence', both in *Reality, Representation and Projection* edited by John Haldane and Crispin Wright, (Oxford University Press, 1993). Thanks to the editors and publishers for their permission to use this material, and thanks once again to all those who are mentioned in the footnotes.

As with any book, the process of writing has made me aware of some more special debts. I am happy to acknowledge these here as well.

Simon Blackburn was my supervisor both for the B.Phil. and the D.Phil. at Oxford, and this book has very much grown out of that work I did with him. I learned a great deal from Simon then, and have continued to do so since, most recently while we were Visiting Fellows together at RSSS. Also from my time in Oxford, I would like to acknowledge a special debt to Jay Wallace. Jay and I were B.Phil. students together, and, ever since that time, his comments on and criticisms of my work have been invaluable. I have tried everywhere to accomodate his concerns in this book.

One of the many great pleasures of life in Princeton was teaching such talented graduate students, students who gave you instant, often devastating, feedback on your work as it progressed week by week. Jamie Dreier, Mark Kalderon, Gideon Rosen, Jamie Tappenden, Nathan Tawil and Mark van Roojen were all especially helpful to me in this way. Conversations with David Lewis and Mark Johnston were another highlight of life in Princeton. Many of the views I now hold were first developed through a series of exchanges with them. Though we have not ended up with much in the way of agreement, I am more than happy to admit the impact on me of not just Lewis's and Johnston's views, but also their quite different ways of doing philosophy. I thank them both for their friendship and for their encouragement. Other faculty, both regular and visiting, who helped me while I was still at Princeton include John Burgess, Joshua Cohen, Stewart Cohen,

Gil Harman, Barbara Herman, Susan Hurley, Will Kymlicka, George Wilson and Crispin Wright.

Since returning to Australia I have had the great benefit and pleasure of philosophical conversations with Philip Pettit and Frank Jackson. Conversations with Philip have led to several jointly authored papers, many of which are referred to elsewhere in this book. Even more so than with David Lewis and Mark Johnston I now find it difficult to put my finger on which of the views I now hold were originally Philip's and which were originally mine – if they ever originated with either of us. I'm sure he couldn't care less, but let me apologize in advance to Philip in case it turns out that I have here bungled the presentation of ideas we hold in common in ways that impact negatively on our jointly authored work. Over the years Frank Jackson has made a great impression on my understanding of philosophical method. I would like to think that his influence on the book is as pervasive as Philip's.

Colleagues and students at Monash University have helped shape most of the material from the book in classes and seminars. I would especially like to thank John Bigelow, Richard Holton, Lloyd Humberstone, Jeanette Kennett, Rae Langton and Robert Pargetter for their various helpful comments. More generally, thanks to everyone in philosophy at Monash for the lively research environment they have helped to create.

Others who have either heard or read portions of the book and whose reactions have proved especially helpful to me include David Brink, John Broome, John Campbell (La Trobe), John Campbell (Oxford), Jonathan Dancy, Ben Grüter, R. M. Hare, Brad Hooker, Julie Jack, Christine Korsgaard, David McNaughton, Douglas MacLean, Michaelis Michael, Chris Parkin, Denis Robinson, Geoffrey Sayre-McCord, Steve Schiffer, Peter Singer, Paul Snowdon, Natalie Stoljar, Galen Strawson, David Velleman and Susan Wolf. Crispin Wright first invited me to contribute a book to the Philosophical Theory series. Philip Pettit has been extremely helpful with editorial advice. Alison Truefitt and Donald Stephenson made many useful suggestions when they copyedited the final manuscript. Thanks to all of them for their help and encouragement.

Finally, I owe my greatest debts to my wife Monica, and to my children Jeremy, Julian and Samuel. Life in Oxford, Princeton, and now back in Australia, has very much been the life of a family. Thanks to all of them for making these years so happy. Only so could this book have been written.

Michael Smith
Canberra, Australia
December 1993

1

What is the Moral Problem?

1.1 NORMATIVE ETHICS VS. META-ETHICS

It is a common fact of everyday life that we appraise each others' behaviour and attitudes from the moral point of view. We say, for example, that we did the *wrong* thing when we refused to give to famine relief, though perhaps we did the *right* thing when we handed in the wallet we found on the street; that we would be *better* people if we displayed a greater sensitivity to the feelings of others, though perhaps *worse* if in doing so we lost the special concern we have for our family and friends. Most of us take appraisal of this sort pretty much for granted. To the extent that we worry, we simply worry about getting it right.

Philosophers are ordinary folk. They too are concerned to get the answers to moral questions right. Indeed they have been so concerned that their attempts have found their way all the way into the philosophy classroom, as a casual glance at the philosophy offerings in almost any university will reveal. Subjects in normative ethics, subjects with names like 'Practical Ethics', 'Applied Ethics', 'Contemporary Moral Issues', 'Crime and Punishment', 'Ethics and the Environment', 'The Good Things of Life' and so on, are now taught nearly everywhere. Of course, philosophers tend to give more technical and systematic answers to normative ethical questions than ordinary folk. I doubt that anyone seeking advice from a friend has been taken through the standard utilitarian, deontological, or virtue theory line – unless, of course, the friend is a professional philosopher or a philosophy student. But this is only because philosophers tend to construct moral theories to answer moral questions, whereas ordinary folk are happy to give and receive one-off answers. The important point, however, is that philosophers' theories do not generate answers that are different in kind to the answers ordinary folk give to moral questions. They are *merely* more technical and more systematic.

Despite their interest in normative ethics, however, philosophers have not tended to think that these sorts of questions are of the first importance in moral philosophy (though contrast Singer, 1973). Rather they have thought that we should do normative ethics only after we have given satisfactory answers to certain questions in meta-ethics. But why?

In meta-ethics we are concerned not with questions which are the province of normative ethics like 'Should I give to famine relief?', or 'Should I return the wallet I found in the street?', but rather with questions *about* questions like these. What does the 'should' in such questions mean? Does it signal that these questions are about some matter of fact? If so, then how do we justify giving one answer rather than another? In other words, what sort of fact is a moral fact? In what sense is moral argument simply a species of rational argument? And if the 'should' does not signal that moral questions are about a matter of fact then, again, how do we justify giving one answer rather than another to such questions? In other words, what is moral argument about? What is its point or function? What is the standard against which a good moral argument is to be measured?

As perhaps the final questions make clear, philosophers have surely been right to give meta-ethical questions a certain priority over questions in normative ethics. If moral argument is not simply a species of rational argument, then that calls into question the very role of moral argument in everyday life. For in everyday life such argument plays an integral role in decisions about how we are to distribute benefits and burdens. If these distributions of benefits and burdens cannot be *rationally* justified, then we must ask ourselves by what means, if any, they can be justified at all.

In terms of this distinction between normative ethics and meta-ethics I should now say that this book is unashamedly devoted to answering certain questions in meta-ethics. I defend two main claims. The first is that questions like 'Should I give to famine relief?', and 'Should I return the wallet I found in the street?', are questions about a matter of fact, and that moral argument is therefore simply a species of rational argument, argument whose aim is to discover the truth. This first claim is argued for in an analytic spirit, by way of an analysis of what the 'should' in such questions means, an analysis that in turn depends on my second claim, which I will mention shortly. By way of anticipation, one striking feature of the analysis is that it not only legitimates the interest that philosophers take in normative ethics, but also makes taking such an interest crucial for the final resolution of meta-ethical questions.

1.2   META-ETHICS TODAY

Before saying anything else, however, it seems to me best to begin by acknowledging, and attempting to diagnose, the difficulties involved in giving any convincing answers at all to meta-ethical questions. For if one thing becomes clear by reading what philosophers writing in meta-ethics today have to say, it is surely that enormous gulfs exist between them, gulfs so wide that we must wonder whether they are talking about a common subject matter. Here is a sample.

We are told that engaging in moral practice presupposes that there exist moral facts, and that this presupposition is an error or mistake akin to the error of presupposition made by someone who engages in a religious practice when there is in fact no God (Mackie, 1977). And we are told that moral commitment involves no such error of presupposition; that moral talk happens inside a perfectly kosher practice (Brink, 1984; Blackburn, 1985a; McDowell, 1985; Nagel, 1986).

We are told that moral facts exist, and that these facts are ordinary facts, not different in kind from those that are the subject matter of science (Harman, 1986; Railton, 1986; Jackson, 1992). And we are told that moral facts exist, and that these facts are *sui generis* (Moore, 1903; McDowell, 1979; Sturgeon, 1985; Boyd, 1988; Brink, 1989; Dancy, 1993).

We are told that moral facts exist and are part of the causal explanatory network (Railton, 1986; Boyd, 1988; Sturgeon, 1985; Brink, 1989). And we are told not just that moral facts play no role in the causal explanatory network, but that there are no moral facts at all (Ayer, 1936; Hare, 1952; Mackie, 1977; Blackburn, 1984; Gibbard, 1990).

We are told that there is an internal or necessary connection between moral judgement and the will (Hare, 1952; Nagel, 1970; Blackburn, 1984; McDowell, 1985; Korsgaard, 1986). And we are told that there is no such connection, that the connection between moral judgement and the will is altogether external and contingent (Frankena, 1958; Foot, 1972; Scanlon, 1982; Railton, 1986; Brink, 1986).

We are told that moral requirements are requirements of reason (Kant, 1786; Nagel, 1970; Darwall, 1983; Korsgaard, 1986). And we are told that it is not necessarily irrational to act immorally, that moral evaluation is different in kind from the evaluation of people as rational or irrational (Hume, 1888; Foot, 1972; Scanlon, 1982; Blackburn, 1984; Williams, 1985; Railton, 1986; Harman, 1985; Lewis, 1989).

We are told that morality is objective, that there is a single 'true' morality (Kant, 1786; Nagel, 1970; Darwall, 1983; Korsgaard, 1986; Brink, 1989). And we are told that morality is not objective, that there is not a single true morality (Ayer, 1936; Mackie, 1977; Harman, 1975, 1985; Williams, 1985).

Nor should it be thought that this account of the deep disagreements that exist is misleading; that though there are disagreements, there are certain dominant views. The situation is quite otherwise. There are no dominant views. In their recent comprehensive review of a century of meta-ethics, Stephen Darwall, Alan Gibbard and Peter Railton remark that the 'scene is remarkably rich and diverse' (1992: 124). But even to the casual observer, this is surely an understatement. The scene is so diverse that we must wonder at the assumption that these theorists are all talking about the same thing.

1.3   THE MORAL PROBLEM

Why do meta-ethical questions engender so much disagreement? In my view, the reason can be traced to two of the more distinctive features of morality, features that are manifest in ordinary moral practice as it is engaged in by ordinary folk. The philosopher's task is to make sense of a practice having these features. Surprisingly, however, these features pull against each other, so threatening to make the very idea of morality altogether incoherent (Smith, 1991).

To begin, as we have already seen, it is a distinctive feature of engaging in moral practice that the participants are concerned to get the answers to moral questions *right*. And this concern itself seems to force certain meta-ethical conclusions. Such concern presupposes, for example, that there are correct answers to moral questions to be had. And the natural interpretation of that presupposition is that there exists a domain of moral facts; facts about which we can form beliefs and about which we may be mistaken.

Moreover, the way in which we conduct ourselves in living the moral life seems to presuppose that these facts are in principle available to all; that no one in particular is better placed to discover them than anyone else. That we have something like this conception of moral facts seems to explain our preoccupation with moral conversation and moral argument on the one hand, and novels and films in which the different reactions people have to moral questions are explored on the other. For what seems to give these preoccupations their point and poignancy is the simple idea that we are all in the same boat. A moral dilemma or issue faced by one person is a dilemma or issue that might be faced by another. Absent some relevant difference in their circumstances, what counts as an adequate response in one person's case must count as an adequate response in another's.

To put the point another way, we seem to think that the only relevant determinant of the rightness of an act is the circumstances in which the action takes place. If agents in the same circumstances act in the same way then either they both act rightly or they both act wrongly. Given that this is so we have the potential to learn something from each others' responses to the moral dilemmas and issues that we face. A careful mustering and assessment of the reasons for and against our particular moral opinions about such dilemmas and issues is therefore the best way to discover what the moral facts really are. If we are open-minded and thinking clearly then such an argument should result in a convergence in moral opinion, a convergence upon the truth. Individual reflection may of course serve the same purpose, but only when it simulates a real moral argument; for only then can we be certain that we are giving each side of the argument due consideration; that we aren't simply congratulating ourselves on our own blind prejudices and preconceptions.

We may summarize this first feature of morality in the following terms: we seem to think moral questions have correct answers; that the correct answers are made correct by objective moral facts; that moral facts are wholly determined by circumstances; and that, by engaging in moral conversation and argument, we can discover what these objective moral facts determined by the circumstances are. The term 'objective' here simply signifies the possibility of a convergence in moral views of the kind just mentioned. Let's call this the 'objectivity of moral judgement'.

A second and rather different feature of morality concerns the practical implications of moral judgement. Suppose we are sitting together one Sunday afternoon. World Vision is out collecting money for famine relief, so we are waiting to hear a knock on the door. I am wondering whether I should give to this particular appeal. We debate the pros and cons of contributing and, let's suppose, after some discussion, you convince me that I should contribute. There is a knock on the door. What would you expect? I take it that you would expect me to answer the door and give the collector my donation. But suppose I say instead 'But wait! I know I *should* give to famine relief. But what I haven't been convinced of is that I *have any reason* to do so!' And let's suppose that I therefore refuse to donate. What would your reaction be?

It seems to me that your reaction would be one of extreme puzzlement. The conversation we had was about whether or not I should give to famine relief. But this just seems equivalent to a conversation about whether or not I have a reason to give to famine relief. Given that I claim to have been convinced by that conversation, and given that reasons have motivational implications, my refusal will therefore quite rightly occasion serious puzzlement. Perhaps I will be able to explain myself: perhaps I think that there is a better reason to do something else; or perhaps I am suffering from weakness of will or some other such psychological failure and am claiming only that I haven't been convinced that I have been given any ulterior motive, a motive that will move me in the face of my own weakness. But absent some such explanation, the puzzlement will be such as to cast serious doubt on the sincerity of my claim to have been convinced that it is right to give to famine relief at all.

We can summarize this second feature of morality as follows: moral judgements seem to be, or imply, opinions about the reasons we have for behaving in certain ways, and, other things being equal, having such opinions is a matter of finding ourselves with a corresponding motivation to act. Let's call this the 'practicality of moral judgement'.

These two distinctive features of morality – the objectivity and the practicality of moral judgement – are widely thought to have both metaphysical and psychological implications. However, and unfortunately, these implications are the exact opposite of each other. In order to see why this is thought to be so, we need to pause for a moment to reflect more generally on the nature of human psychology.

According to the standard picture of human psychology – a picture we owe to Hume (1888) – there are two main kinds of psychological state. On the one hand there are beliefs, states that purport to represent the way the world is. Since our beliefs purport to represent the world, they are assessable in terms of truth and falsehood, depending on whether or not they succeed in representing the world to be the way it really is. And on the other hand there are desires, states that represent how the world is to be. Desires are unlike beliefs in that they do not even purport to represent the way the world is. They are therefore not assessable in terms of truth and falsehood. Hume concludes that belief and desire are therefore distinct existences: that is, that we can always pull belief and desire apart, at least modally. For any belief and desire pair that we imagine, we can always imagine someone having the desire but lacking the belief, and vice versa. If this were not so, if we had to imagine a particular belief bringing a particular desire with it, then desires would – contrary to fact – be assessable in terms of truth and falsehood, at least derivatively; for we could count the desire as true whenever the belief with which it was necessarily connected counted as true, false whenever the belief with which it was necessarily connected counted as false.

Indeed, according to the standard picture of human psychology that we get from Hume, not only are desires not assessable in terms of truth and falsehood, they are not subject to any sort of rational criticism at all. The fact that we have a certain desire is, with a proviso to be mentioned presently, simply a fact about ourselves to be acknowledged. It may be unfortunate that we have certain combinations of desires – perhaps our desires cannot all be satisfied together – but in themselves our desires are all on a par, rationally neutral. This is an important further claim about desires. For it suggests that though we may make discoveries about the world, and though these discoveries may rightly affect our beliefs, such discoveries should, again with one proviso to be mentioned presently, have no rational impact upon our desires. They may, of course, have some *non*-rational impact. Seeing a spider I may be overcome with a morbid fear and desire never to be near one. However this is not a change in my desires mandated by reason. It is a *non*-rational change in my desires.

Now for the proviso. Suppose, contrary to the example I just gave, that I acquire the desire never to be near a spider because I come to believe, falsely, that spiders give off an unpleasant odour. Then we would certainly ordinarily say that I have an 'irrational' desire. However the reason we would say this clearly doesn't go against the spirit of what has been said so far. For my desire never to be near a spider is *based on* a further desire and belief: my desire not to smell that unpleasant odour and my belief that that odour is given off by spiders. Since I can be rationally criticized for having the belief, as it is false, I can be rationally criticized for having the desire it helps to produce. The proviso is thus fairly minor: desires are subject to rational criticism, but only insofar as they are based on beliefs that are subject to rational criticism. Desires that are not related in some such way to beliefs that can be rationally criticized are not subject to rational criticism at all.

According to the standard picture, then, there are two kinds of psychological state – beliefs and desires – utterly distinct and different from each other. The standard picture of human psychology is important because it provides us with a model for explaining human action. Crudely, our beliefs tell us how the world is, and thus how it has to be changed, so as to make it the way our desires tell us it is to be. An action is thus the product of these two distinct existences: a desire representing the way the world is to be and a belief telling us how the world has to be changed so as to make it that way.

Let's now return to consider the two features of moral judgement we discussed earlier. Consider first the objectivity of such judgement: the idea that moral questions have correct answers, that the correct answers are made correct by objective moral facts, that moral facts are determined by circumstances, and that, by engaging in moral argument, we can discover what these objective moral facts are. The metaphysical and psychological implications of this may now be summarized as follows.

Metaphysically, the implication is moral realism: the view that, amongst the various facts there are in the world, there aren't just facts about (say) the consequences of our actions on the well-being of our families and friends, there are also distinctively moral facts: facts about the rightness and wrongness of our actions having these consequences. And, psychologically, the implication is thus cognitivism: the view that when we make a moral judgement we thereby express our beliefs about the way these moral facts are. In forming moral opinions we acquire beliefs, representations of the way the world is morally.

Given the standard picture of human psychology, there is a further psychological implication. For whether or not people who have a certain moral belief desire to act accordingly must now be seen as a further and entirely separate question. They may happen to have a corresponding desire, they may not. However, either way, they cannot be rationally criticized. Having or failing to have a corresponding desire is simply a further fact about a person's psychology. On this view, believing that, say, I should give to famine relief does not require that, other things being equal, I have a reason to give to famine relief.

But now consider the second feature, the practicality of moral judgement. We saw earlier that to have a moral opinion simply is, contrary to what has just been said, to find ourselves with a corresponding motivation to act. If we think it right to give to famine relief then, other things being equal, we must be motivated to give to famine relief. The practicality of moral judgement thus seems to have a psychological and a metaphysical implication of its own.

Psychologically, since making a moral judgement requires our having a certain desire, and no recognition of a fact about the world could rationally compel us to have one desire rather than another, our judgement must really simply be an expression of that desire, or perhaps a complicated disposition to have that desire. This is non-cognitivism. And this psychological implication has a metaphysical counterpart. For it seems to follow that, contrary to initial appearance, when we judge it right to give to famine relief we are not responding to any moral fact: the rightness of giving to famine relief. Indeed, moral facts are an idle postulate. In judging it right to give to famine relief we are really simply expressing our desire, or disposition to desire, that people give to famine relief. It is as if we were yelling 'Hooray for giving to famine relief!' No mention of a moral fact there. Indeed, no factual claim at all. This is irrealism: the denial of the claim that there are any moral facts. But importantly it is irrealism in the form of expressivism: the view that in making moral judgements we do not even purport to make claims about how things are morally, but rather simply give expression to our non-cognitive states.

On this view, when I claim that I should give to famine relief, it does indeed follow that I have a reason to give to famine relief, at least other things being equal. That follows from the fact that I give expression to my desire, or disposition to desire. And when I claim that I should give to famine relief, it follows that I commit myself to judging that it is right for anyone in circumstances like mine to give to famine relief as well. That follows from the scope of my desire. But I need not think that these other people have any reason to give to famine relief. And, moreover, I should not think that the claim that people in circumstances like mine should give to famine relief is itself objective. For there is no reason to suppose that others could be brought to agree with me by means of a rational argument. A failure to elicit agreement from others would not necessarily be evidence of error or mistake

could say morality is about facts + we happen to usually be motivated by these facts. if we were not still moral facts. is why we have these desires a separate question? does this matter?

or confusion on someone's behalf. It would simply be evidence of the fact that they have different desires, or dispositions to have desires, from those that I have.

We are now in a position to see why meta-ethical questions engender so much disagreement. The task of the philosopher in meta-ethics is to make sense of ordinary moral practice. But the problem is that ordinary moral practice suggests that moral judgements have two features that pull in quite opposite directions from each other. The objectivity of moral judgement suggests that there are moral facts, wholly determined by circumstances, and that our moral judgements express our beliefs about what these facts are. This enables us to make good sense of moral argument, and the like, but it leaves it entirely mysterious how or why having a moral view is supposed to have special links with what we are motivated to do. And the practicality of moral judgement suggests just the opposite, that our moral judgements express our desires. While this enables us to make good sense of the link between having a moral view and being motivated, it leaves it entirely mysterious what a moral argument is supposed to be an argument about; the sense in which morality is supposed to be objective.

The idea of morality thus looks like it may well be incoherent, for what is required to make sense of a moral judgement is a strange sort of fact about the universe: a fact whose recognition necessarily impacts upon our desires (Mackie, 1977). But the standard picture of human psychology tells us that there are no such facts. Nothing could be everything a moral judgement purports to be. Perhaps we should therefore all be irrealists, and deny the existence of moral facts. But we should combine our irrealism with cognitivism: the view that our moral judgements purport to make claims about moral facts. In other words, we should all be moral nihilists, and simply acknowledge that moral practice is founded on a massive error of presupposition. Or so it may now seem.

This is what I call 'the moral problem' (Smith, 1989; 1994a). As I see it, the moral problem is in fact the central organizing problem in contemporary meta-ethics. It explains the massive disagreement that exists among philosophers about meta-ethical issues.

[handwritten marginal note:] stion: we have the beliefs we do because of our purposes (intentionality) so "seeing" a situation is such means we have certain motivations

This problem can be stated succinctly in the form of three apparently inconsistent propositions (see also McNaughton, 1988: 23).

1   Moral judgements of the form 'It is right that I φ' express a subject's beliefs about an objective matter of fact, a fact about what it is right for her to do.

2   If someone judges that it is right that she φs then, *ceteris paribus*, she is motivated to φ.

3   An agent is motivated to act in a certain way just in case she has an appropriate desire and a means-end belief, where belief and desire are, in Hume's terms, distinct existences.

The apparent inconsistency can be brought out as follows: from (1), the state expressed by a moral judgement is a belief, which, from (2), is necessarily connected in some way with motivation; that is, from (3), with having a desire. So (1), (2) and (3) together entail that there is some sort of necessary connection between distinct existences: moral belief and desire. But (3) tells us that there is no such connection. Believing some state of the world obtains is one thing, what I desire to do given that belief is quite another.

   In light of the moral problem it is easy to understand not just why meta-ethical questions engender so much disagreement, but also why these disagreements take just the form that they do. For those who offer answers to meta-ethical questions must now make a choice. If they are to remain faithful to the standard Humean picture of human psychology, then they must decide which of the two features of moral judgement – objectivity and practicality – to reject, and they then have to defend their choice. Thus it should come as no surprise that we find the expressivists rejecting (1), the claim that moral judgements express beliefs (Ayer, 1936; Hare, 1952; Blackburn, 1984, 1986, 1987; Gibbard, 1990), the externalists rejecting (2), the claim that there is a necessary connection of sorts between moral judgement and motivation (Frankena, 1958; Foot, 1972; Scanlon, 1982; Railton, 1986; Brink, 1986, 1989), and the anti-Humean theorists of motivation breaking ranks altogether and rejecting (3), the claim that motivation is to be explained in terms of a desire and means-end belief, where belief and desire are, in Hume's terms, distinct existences (Nagel, 1970; McDowell, 1978; Platts, 1981; McNaughton, 1988; Dancy, 1993). Moreover, it should come as no surprise that each of these theorists – the expressivists, the externalists, and the anti-Humean theorists of motivation – argue that the proposition that they reject, as opposed to the propositions the others reject, is a mere philosophical fantasy; something to be explained away. But, as is now I hope plain, no matter which proposition these philosophers choose to reject, they are bound to end up denying something that seems more certain than the theories they themselves go on to offer (Smith, 1989). Moral nihilism quite rightly looms (Smith, 1993a).[1]

1.4   TOWARDS A SOLUTION TO THE MORAL PROBLEM

The stage is thus set for this book. For in my view we are not forced to choose between accommodating the objectivity and the practicality of moral judgement in giving answers to meta-ethical questions. The correct solution to the moral problem allows us to accommodate both. Moreover, it does so without requiring us to give up the standard account of the explanation of action in terms of belief and desire and without plunging us into moral nihilism either.

I said earlier that I will defend two claims. The first is that questions like 'Should I give to famine relief?' are questions about a matter of fact, facts that we can discover through rational argument, argument whose aim is to discover the truth. The second claim is that, contrary to the Humean view, moral facts are indeed facts about the reasons that we all share. As I see it, we can accommodate both the objectivity and the practicality of moral judgement – propositions (1) and (2) that make up the moral problem – by defending these two claims. The trick is to show how these two claims, and the second in particular, can be made to square with the standard Humean account of the explanation of human action: that is, with proposition (3) that makes up the moral problem. How much of the whole psychological theory that we have inherited from Hume can we accept, how much must we reject? In essence that is, if you like, the major sub-plot of this book.

My argument will turn on a distinction between two kinds of reasons: motivating and normative. I will argue that we can and should accept Hume's claim that belief and desire are distinct existences, states with distinctive roles to play in the explanation of human action. For this is a true and illuminating claim about our motivating reasons: the reasons that motivate, and thus explain, our actions. However, I will argue, we cannot and should not accept Hume's claim that desires are themselves beyond rational criticism. For that amounts to a false claim about our normative reasons: the reasons that rationally justify our actions. It is therefore in the formulation of a distinctively anti-Humean theory of normative reasons that we will find room for the idea of moral facts as facts about the reasons we all share; it is here that we will find the solution to the moral problem. Or so I will argue.

1.5   SUMMARY AND PREVIEW

In this chapter I have explained what the difference is between normative ethical questions and meta-ethical questions. Moreover, I have defended the view, common among philosophers, that we should begin our study of ethics by focusing on meta-ethics, not normative ethics. For we cannot hope to do normative ethics without first knowing what the standards of correct argument in normative ethics are, and it is in meta-ethics that we discover these standards.

However, as we have seen, meta-ethical questions engender much disagreement. I have argued that this is because there is a central organizing problem in meta-ethics. Can we reconcile the objectivity and the practicality of moral judgement with the standard picture of human psychology that we get from Hume? This is what I call 'the moral problem'. My suggestion is to be that we can solve this problem by defending an analysis of what the 'should' means in moral questions, questions like 'Should I give to famine relief?' According to this analysis, a positive answer to this particular question implies that there is a reason for anyone in circumstances like mine to give to famine relief, a reason to be discovered through rational argument.

However, before giving my own view I begin by discussing the more standard solutions to the moral problem. In chapter 2, the expressivists' challenge to the claim that our moral judgements express our beliefs about an objective matter of fact is considered and rejected. In chapter 3, I consider and reject the externalists' challenge to the claim that there is some sort of necessary connection between moral judgement and motivation. And in chapter 4, I consider and reject the anti-Humean challenge to the standard, Humean, account of the explanation of action in terms of belief and desire, Hume's account of motivating reasons.

By the end of chapter 4, then, the standard solutions to the moral problem will all have been shown to be *bad* solutions. The claims that these standard solutions choose to reject should not be rejected at all. The remaining two chapters are more constructive.

In chapter 5, I develop an account of reasons – normative reasons – that allows us to say why certain desires are rationally required, and I explain why this account of normative reasons is not inconsistent with the Humean account of motivating reasons defended in chapter 4. And in chapter 6, I show how we can use this account of normative reasons to analyse our concept of rightness, and I explain how this analysis of rightness in terms of normative reasons enables us to provide a solution to the moral problem.

2

The Expressivist Challenge

2.1   DESCRIPTIVISM VS. EXPRESSIVISM

Expressivists deny that moral judgements represent the world as being one way rather than another. Moral judgements do not subserve a descriptive or fact-stating role at all, according to the expressivists, but rather serve to express the judger's attitudes of approval and disapproval (Ayer, 1936), or perhaps their more complicated dispositions to have such attitudes (Blackburn, 1984; Gibbard, 1990). My aim in this chapter is to outline the expressivists' case for this distinctive claim, and then to attempt a reply.

Note that my discussion of expressivism therefore differs from some in the philosophical literature (for example Hale, 1986, 1993; Wright, 1988, 1992; Horwich, 1992, 1994). For I am not inclined to question the coherence of any particular form of expressivism, once it gets spelled out in detail. Rather, conceding that, I am inclined to question whether expressivists have given us any convincing reason to accept one or another from the broad class of expressivist theories in the first place.

The basic argument to be considered is A. J. Ayer's classic defence of his own favoured form of expressivism, emotivism, in *Language, Truth and Logic* (1936), though various amendments and refinements of Ayer's argument, amendments inspired by R. M. Hare and Simon Blackburn, will be considered as well. Ayer's argument rightly deserves its classic status as it forces us to acknowledge an apparent dilemma for the descriptivist, a dilemma which, to my mind, descriptivists have not yet adequately explained their way around. If there are any moral facts then, Ayer tells us, these facts cannot be natural facts, in a sense of 'natural' to be characterized presently. And nor can they be 'non-natural' facts either. But since these exhaust the kinds of facts there could be, we must conclude that there are no moral facts at all. The appearance of factuality in morals is thus merely apparent.

This argument for expressivism raises large and difficult issues, issues that take us way beyond anything of interest merely to moral philosophers. In particular, in order to assess this argument we will need to take a stand on the extent to which moral terms can or cannot be analysed, and so will have to engage some thorny questions about the nature and method of conceptual analysis itself.

2.2   AN APPARENT DILEMMA FACING DESCRIPTIVISTS

In chapter 6 of *Language, Truth and Logic* A. J. Ayer sets out and defends emotivism, the view that moral judgements express certain non-cognitive attitudes: desires, preferences, or pro- and con-attitudes of some other kind.

He argues as follows (1936: 103–6). As ethical theorists, we are all trying to provide an 'analysis of ethical terms'. However, if we assume the analysis must preserve the apparently descriptive character that moral judgements have, then we are impaled on the horns of a dilemma. For we must say what moral judgements are supposed to be descriptive of, and no coherent answer is forthcoming. We are impaled on the first horn if we say that moral judgements describe *naturalistic* states of affairs: that is, states of affairs which are the subject matter of a natural or social science (the social sciences include psychology, and will therefore encompass facts about human wants, needs, and well-being quite generally).[1] We are impaled on the second horn if we say that they describe *non-naturalistic* states of affairs: that is, states of affairs which transcend the subject matter of the natural and social sciences. I will take the horns of Ayer's dilemma in turn.

Ayer considers two kinds of naturalistic theory. The first is subjectivism. Ayer tells us that subjectivism comes in at least two varieties. According to the first, which I will call 'general subjectivism', when I judge that my φ-ing is right I am saying that my φ-ing is approved of by the general masses. According to the second, which I will call 'first person subjectivism', when I judge that my φ-ing is right I am saying that I, at least, approve of my φ-ing. Ayer attempts to refute both theories by wielding Moore's Open Question Argument (Moore, 1903: 6–21).

As regards general subjectivism, he notes that 'it is not self-contradictory to assert that some things which are generally approved of are not good'. But if it is not self-contradictory, then, he concludes, it cannot be that what I am saying, when I say that my φ-ing is right, is that my φ-ing is generally approved of. And as regards first person subjectivism he similarly observes that 'a man who confessed that he sometimes approved of what was bad or wrong would not be contradicting himself'. Likewise, therefore, it cannot be that what I am saying, when I say that my φ-ing is wrong, is that I disapprove of my φ-ing.

The other kind of naturalistic theory Ayer considers is utilitarianism. According to Ayer, 'the utilitarian defines the rightness of actions, or the goodness of ends, in terms of the pleasure, or happiness, or satisfaction, to which they give rise'. And he then claims to refute this theory in much the same way as he claims to refute subjectivism. He tell us that 'it is not self-contradictory to say that some pleasant things are not good, or that some bad things are desired . . . and to every other variant of utilitarianism with which I am acquainted the same objection applies'.

What lies behind Ayer's argument in each case is, of course, the idea that there is a *naturalistic fallacy* – the idea that a fallacy is involved in attempting to define moral terms in naturalistic terms. The fallacy is supposed to be brought clearly into view when we see that there is no contradiction in claiming that an act has some moral property, but lacks the naturalistic feature which the naturalists tell us is, supposedly, definitive of it.

What if we take the second horn of the dilemma and hold instead that moral judgements describe some non-natural state of affairs; that moral properties are non-natural properties, properties that are neither constituted nor analysable naturalistically? The problem with this view, Ayer tells us, is that we must go on to give an account of how we come by knowledge of moral truths.

Though Moore was himself reluctant to adopt it, the epistemology non-naturalists tended to favour was intuitionism, the view that we possess a faculty of moral intuition akin to an ordinary perceptual faculty with which we intuit the presence of certain moral properties in the presence of certain natural properties.[2]

However, according to Ayer, if we embrace intuitionism then we are committed to the view that moral judgements are *unverifiable*. 'For it is notorious that what seems intuitively certain to one person may seem doubtful, or even false, to another. So that unless it is possible to provide some criterion by which one may decide between conflicting intuitions, a mere appeal to intuition is worthless as a test of a proposition's validity.' And, in light of the argument of *Language, Truth and Logic*, this is simply unacceptable, for 'considering the use which we have made of the principle that a synthetic proposition is significant only if it is empirically verifiable' it is clear that embracing intuitionism would 'undermine the whole of our main argument'. In other words, since intuitionism is inconsistent with the tenets of logical positivism, the doctrine that *Language, Truth and Logic* as a whole aims to elucidate and defend, so Ayer tells us that we must reject intuitionism, and non-naturalism with it.

Ayer's argument for emotivism may therefore be summed up as follows:

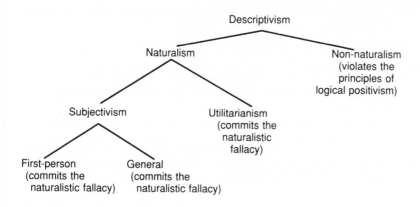

In brief, on the first horn we hold that moral judgements describe naturalistic states of affairs, and thus commit the naturalistic fallacy. On the second horn we hold that moral judgements describe non-naturalistic states of affairs, and thus violate the principles of logical positivism. Therefore, according to Ayer, we are impaled on the horns of a dilemma. What should we do?

Ayer recommends that we reject the assumption that generates the dilemma, the assumption that an analysis of moral terms must preserve the apparently descriptive character of moral judgements. He therefore concludes that a moral judgement is a species of non-descriptive judgement: an expression of certain pro- ('Hooray!') or con- ('Boo!') attitudes on the part of the speaker. Thus he is led to embrace his own favoured form of expressivism: emotivism – the view that moral judgements express our emotions.

What should we make of this argument? Let me take the horns of Ayer's dilemma in reverse order.

2.3　AYER'S OBJECTION TO NON-NATURALISM

Suppose we claim that moral properties are non-natural properties. According to Ayer we are then forced to embrace intuitionism, so impaling ourselves on the second horn of the dilemma. But what does the impaling? Ayer's answer is: logical positivism. However this is problematic.

Logical positivism is the view that a sentence is meaningful if and only if it is empirically verifiable, its meaning then being identical with its condition of verification. However, according to Ayer, because non-naturalism embraces intuitionism, moral claims turn out not to be empirically verifiable, and so they turn out to be meaningless. This all follows once we grant the tenets of logical positivism. However we have an objection here only if positivism is itself plausible. But, as is now generally agreed, logical positivism is implausible as a theory of meaning. All sorts of sentences that are not empirically verifiable seem yet to be meaningful. Consider, for example, the sentence 'Before the Big Bang all the objects in the Universe converged on a single point'. This sentence certainly seems to be meaningful. But, given that it is in the nature of the Big Bang to have destroyed all traces of what went on beforehand, it is not empirically verifiable – not even, as far I can tell, verifiable *in principle*. But if this sentence is meaningful, as it seems to be, Ayer's argument against non-naturalism is based on a faulty theory of meaning.

Should we therefore reject Ayer's argument on the second horn? That would be too swift. Despite appearances, positivism is not a crucial part of Ayer's argument against non-naturalism, something Ayer himself signalled in the Preface to the second edition of *Language, Truth and Logic*.

2.4 NON-NATURALISM AND EPISTEMOLOGY

Ayer's basic complaint is that the non-naturalist needs to tell us how we come by moral knowledge. The request is reasonable because, quite generally when we enrich our ontology, if the facts with which we enrich it are facts about which we are supposed to have knowledge, then we must be able to tell a story about how we *can* have knowledge of *those* facts. But it isn't at all clear how the non-naturalist is going to meet this request. Ayer fills in the details of this argument by appealing to logical positivism. However, as Simon Blackburn has shown, we can fill in the details in other ways (1987).

Consider how a non-naturalist might explain our coming to judge that an object with certain natural properties, N, say, has a certain moral feature, say M. The obvious strategy is to build on the idea that moral facts are known by intuition, where 'intuition' signifies a perceptual relation. The idea would be that we *perceive* the coinstantiation of certain natural properties, N, along with certain moral features, M. In this way, the non-naturalist might say, we come to have knowledge of the claim 'This object, with natural features N, has moral feature M'. But this cannot be the whole of the story.

Everyone agrees that the moral features of things *supervene* on their natural features (Blackburn, 1971, 1985b). That is, everyone agrees that two possible worlds that are alike in all of their natural features must also be alike in their moral features; that the moral features of things cannot float free of their natural features. Moreover, everyone agrees that this is a platitude; that it is an *a priori* truth. For recognition of the way in which the moral supervenes on the natural is a constraint on the proper use of moral concepts. If two possible worlds are alike in the kinds of individuals who occupy them, the motivations and aspirations they have, the extent to which the world lives up to their aspirations, their relative levels of well-being, and if the worlds are otherwise identical in natural respects as well, if they differ only in which *particular* individuals and objects have these various natural features, then there is a conceptual confusion involved in supposing that these worlds could differ in their moral standing – that one could be good and the other bad, for instance.

The situation is much the same as that we find with aesthetic properties like the beautiful or the ugly. Suppose two paintings are exactly alike with respect to the colour, the distribution, and the texture of the paint on their surface, the reactions they cause in those who look at them, and so on. These paintings could not differ in that one was beautiful and the other not. To suppose otherwise is to manifest a failure to understand the concepts of the beautiful and the ugly. For paintings are beautiful or ugly in virtue of the distribution, the colour and the texture of the paint on the surface of a canvas, the reactions they cause in those who look at them, and so on. This is a conceptual truth about the conditions under which it is appropriate to apply the words 'beautiful' and 'ugly'. Likewise, possible worlds are good or bad in virtue of their natural properties. This is a conceptual truth about the conditions under which it is appropriate to apply the words 'good' and 'bad'.

Now as I said, everyone agrees that it is an *a priori* truth that the moral supervenes on the natural. And this in turn presents a problem for the non-naturalist who embraces intuitionism. For such a non-naturalist has to be able to use the intuitionist, perceptual, account how we come by knowledge of the claim 'This object with natural features N has moral feature M' to somehow ground or explain the *a priori* truth that any object with exactly the same natural properties as this object, that is N, will have M as well. How might she do this?

She might suggest that, having perceived the coinstantiation of
N with M in this case, we generalize. If N is coinstantiated with M
in this case, then we conclude that N will be coinstantiated with M
in other cases as well. But there are two problems with this. First,
it doesn't explain why it is an *a priori* truth that the moral supervenes on the natural. It looks rather like an inductive argument
yielding a contingent and *a posteriori* conclusion. And second, as
Simon Blackburn points out, it is quite unconvincing to suppose,
as the non-naturalist is supposing, that moral knowledge is a
species of causal knowledge anyway.

> Literal talk of perception runs into many problems. One is that the
> ethical very commonly, and given its function in guiding choice,
> even typically, concerns imagined or described situations, not per-
> ceived ones. We reach ethical verdicts about the behaviour of the
> described agents or actions in light of general standards. And it is
> stretching things to see these general standards as perceptually
> formed or maintained. Do I see that ingratitude is base only on
> occasions when I see an example of ingratitude? How can I be sure
> of the generalization to examples I did not see (I could not do that
> with colour, for instance . . .)? Or do I see the timeless connection
> – but how? Do I have an antenna for detecting timeless property-to-
> value connections? Is such a thing much like colour vision? (1987:
> 365)

These observations are important, for they suggest that someone
who possesses moral concepts, and who is able to think about and
reflect upon natural properties in the abstract, is well enough
placed to work out that, for example, suffering is, at least *pro tanto*,
a bad thing. Seeing a particular instance of suffering may help
someone come by knowledge of this fact, but only because it gives
vivid knowledge of something that is not particular: the nature of
the suffering itself.

If this is right, however, if knowledge of the badness of suffering
does not itself require causal contact with someone suffering in
order to have knowledge of the coinstantiation of suffering with
badness, but merely reflection upon the general nature of suffering itself, then moral knowledge is not well explained via a causal
perceptual story. The idea that talk of 'intuition' signals a causal

perceptual story is thus misplaced. And that means in turn that talk of 'intuition' is all but empty.[3] If there are any non-natural moral properties, then, it seems that, whether or not such properties possess a causal role, their causal role is no part of the explanation of our coming to make judgements of the form 'Objects with natural feature N have moral feature M'. Mere reflection on N is enough to explain our making such judgements.

The upshot, then, is that the question we began by asking the non-naturalist remains in a more refined form. How can it be that *mere reflection* enables us to come by knowledge of which natural properties and which non-natural properties are coinstantiated, coinstantiated in a way that reflects the *a priori* supervenience of the moral on the natural? Given that, according to the non-naturalists, all we can say about non-natural moral properties *a priori* is that they are *simple* properties, neither constituted by nor analysable in terms of natural properties, it appears that they can give no answer. For them this must remain a mystery.

Note, by contrast, that expressivists have no such problems. Having eschewed all talk of moral knowledge they are able to give a straightforward explanation of how we come to make judgements of the form 'Objects with natural features N have moral feature M', an explanation that does adequate justice to the *a priori* supervenience of the moral on the natural (Blackburn, 1971).

Recall that, as expressivists see things, moral judgements are expressions of pro- and con-attitudes. But, they tell us, these attitudes count as 'moral' attitudes only if they are had towards particular people, actions or states of affairs in virtue of their natural features; they do not count as 'moral' attitudes if they are had towards people, actions or states of affairs in virtue of being the particulars that they are. Possible worlds which are identical in their natural features, though they differ in which particulars have these features, must therefore either both have, or both lack, the natural features towards which we have the pro- or con-attitudes that we express in moral judgements. It therefore follows that if one possible world is taken to be apt for the expression of a moral pro- or con-attitude, then any possible world that is identical to that world in naturalistic respects must also be taken to be apt for the expression of a moral pro- or con-attitude. According to the expressivists, then, this is why it is an *a priori* truth that the moral supervenes on the natural. The *a priori* supervenience of the moral on the natural is entailed by their account of what a *moral* attitude and a *moral* judgement are.

Note that expressivists also have a straightforward explanation of why we are able to make moral judgements on the basis of reflection alone. For we do not need to enter into causal contact with the particular people, actions or states of affairs who have the natural features towards which we have our pro- and con-attitudes in order to know which features we have these attitudes towards. We can tell what these features are by mere reflection on the features themselves. According to the expressivists, this explains why we can make moral judgements on the basis of reflection alone; this explains why it seems so wrong to suppose, as the non-naturalists might have it, that moral knowledge results from the perception of a good state of affairs or right act.[4]

To sum up: Ayer's official objection to non-naturalism is that it is inconsistent with the tenets of logical positivism. We can dismiss Ayer's objection in this form because it would make the argument against non-naturalism depend on a controversial theory of meaning. But the main thrust of Ayer's underlying objection to non-naturalism remains. Non-naturalists want to enrich our ontology with an extra property over and above those which earn their credentials in a natural or a social science, neither constituted by nor analysable in terms of such properties. Though there is no objection to this in principle, those who wish to enrich our ontology in this way do incur an epistemological debt. They owe us an account of how we come by knowledge of the relations the extra properties they posit stand in to natural properties. And this is just what non-naturalists fail to do in any plausible way. It follows that if we are describing things when we make moral judgements, then we cannot suppose, as the non-naturalists do, that we are describing the way things are in some non-natural respect.

2.5 AYER'S OBJECTION TO NATURALISM

On the first horn of Ayer's dilemma we embrace some form of naturalism: that is, as Ayer puts it, some form of either subjectivism or utilitarianism. However, before proceeding any further, it must be said that Ayer's discussion of naturalism is somewhat confusing and misleading. Let me therefore say a little about some distinctions within naturalism itself so that we can put these confusions to one side.

As I see it, Ayer thinks that naturalism comes in two forms: subjective and non-subjective naturalism. According to the subjective naturalists, when we say of some particular action, x, that it is right, then what we say means: 'x has the natural feature that is approved of by so-and-so'. Non-subjective naturalists are, however, different. They think that we can define rightness *directly* in terms of the natural properies that, according to the subjective naturalists, we merely approve of. Suppose, for example, that x has some natural property F, and that a subjective naturalist thinks that x is right because x has F and Fness is the property that is approved of by so-and-so. Then there will be a closely related version of non-subjective naturalism according to which x is indeed right, but not for the reason subjective naturalists give. Rather, according to the non-subjective naturalist, x is right because 'x is right' means 'x has natural property F'.

This distinction between these two forms of naturalism enables us to see a potentially misleading feature of Ayer's discussion. For when Ayer discusses utilitarianism, he is really only discussing one form of non-subjective naturalism. So even if we agree with Ayer that 'right' does not mean the same as 'conducive to happiness', in order to refute non-subjective naturalism *per se* he would need to consider a much wider range of theories. He would in fact need to consider every possible view about the natural features in virtue of which actions are right, and show that the claim to meaning-equivalence fails for each.

Moreover Ayer's discussion is misleading in another way as well. For, as is perhaps now clear, utilitarians need not embrace the theory Ayer discusses under the name 'utilitarianism'. For the theory Ayer discusses under that name is a distinctively *meta-ethical* theory, a form of non-subjective definitional naturalism, a theory about the meaning of moral terms. But those who hold a utilitarian *normative* ethic may, and of course often do, reject this meta-ethical theory in favour of some other: intuitionism

(Sidgwick, 1907) or expressivism (Hare, 1952), for example.[5] Indeed, they can even embrace *subjective* naturalism (Monro, 1967). For they can hold that 'x is right' means 'x has the natural property that is approved of by so-and-so', and so be subjective naturalists in meta-ethics, while yet thinking that the natural property that is approved of by so-and-so is the property of being conducive to happiness, and so be utilitarians in normative ethics. (Note that Mackie discusses a like potential confusion over 'subjectivism' (1977: 17).)

So much for preliminaries. Now that we better understand the views Ayer is arguing against, let's consider the merits of his objection. Ayer has a single objection to all forms of naturalism. He wields the Open Question Argument and concludes that there is no natural property F – whether F is characterized in subjective or non-subjective terms – such that it is self-contradictory to say that x has F but x is not right. How are we to reply to this objection? We have two options.

Since Ayer simply assumes that naturalists have to be in the business of giving definitions, we might reply by insisting that this assumption is false. We might say that naturalism is first and foremost a metaphysical doctrine rather than a definitional doctrine, and that though naturalists therefore have to be in the business of giving us property identities, they do not have to be in the business of giving us definitions. Or alternatively, we might accept Ayer's assumption that naturalists have to be in the business of giving us definitions, but deny that the Open Question Argument succeeds in refuting even definitional naturalism. I will consider these two strategies – that of retreating to metaphysical naturalism and that of defending definitional naturalism – in turn.

2.6 THE OPEN QUESTION ARGUMENT AND METAPHYSICAL NATURALISM

Consider the version of non-subjective naturalism Ayer discusses under the name 'utilitarianism'. The crucial feature of this theory that makes it naturalistic is that it identifies moral rightness with the natural property of being conducive to happiness. However note that Ayer does not object to this feature of the theory. Rather he objects to the fact that the non-subjective naturalists try to support this identity claim by turning it into a naturalistic definition. The question is therefore whether non-subjective naturalists are obliged to support the identity claim in this way. And the answer is that they are not. For, once we recognize the distinction between *a priori* and *a posteriori* necessities, we see that two concepts F and G may allow us to pick out the same property despite the fact that the claim 'x has F' is not analytically equivalent to the claim 'x has G'. We can have property identity without definitional equivalence (Harman, 1977: 19–20; Brink, 1989: 163–7; Darwall, Gibbard and Railton, 1992: 169–80; Railton, 1993b). Let me illustrate with an example, the example of colour terms.

According to at least one view about colours, though we can give no useful definitions of our colour concepts, we can and should none the less identify colours with certain surface reflectance properties (Smart, 1975; Kripke, 1980). Those who take this view owe us an account of how such identifications are to be made, of course. But this requires nothing so strong as a definition. It simply requires us to say about the word 'red' what we say about ordinary proper names. Thus, for example, if 'red' is used to refer to the surface property of objects that is causally responsible for our uses of the word 'red', then if surface reflectance property α is the property that is causally responsible for our uses of the word 'red', 'red' refers to surface reflectance property α (Tawil, 1987). We thus identify redness with surface reflectance property α without defining 'is red' as 'has surface reflectance property α'. We do so by first fixing the reference of the word 'red' via the description 'the surface property of objects that is causally responsible for our uses of the word "red"', and by then discovering, *a posteriori*, that that property is surface reflectance property α.

The idea, then, is that non-subjective naturalists in moral philosophy can eschew analysis in much the same way. They too can insist that though they identify rightness, say, with a certain natural property – perhaps conduciveness to happiness – they do not have to hold that it is true by definition that all and only those actions that are conducive to happiness are right. And in order to make this seem plausible they simply need to show how, via a plausible reference fixing description of rightness, we are able to discover, *a posteriori*, which natural property rightness is (this general idea is pursued by Boyd, 1988; Brink, 1989; Railton, 1986, 1993a, 1993b; and others).

However, popular though this reply to Ayer on behalf of the metaphysical-but-not-definitional naturalist is, it seems to me that the view that emerges is in fact quite problematic. In order to see what this problem is we need to pause for a moment to think more generally about the task of giving definitions, or analyses, of concepts. In doing so, it will be useful to focus on the case of colour and the claim that though our colour concepts elude definition or analysis, we can still, in the way just suggested, identify colours with surface reflectance properties. For, in opposition to this view, there is a well-known and popular analysis of colour terms, the dispositional analysis, according to which it is an analytic truth that redness is the property that causes objects to look red to normal perceivers under standard conditions (for discussion see Campbell 1993, Smith 1993b).[6] And, as we will see, once we are clear what a claim to definition or analysis amounts to, it is difficult indeed to see why we shouldn't accept this analysis, and therefore reject outright the claim that colour terms elude definition or analysis. A similar problem arises in the case of moral terms.

We need to begin by reminding ourselves of what is required for having mastery of a colour term, and the connections between these conditions for mastery and the project of analysis. To this end, then, note that there are all sorts of platitudes about colours and that these platitudes figure crucially in giving an account of mastery of colour terms. For example, there are platitudes about the phenomenology of colour experience, platitudes like 'Most everything we see looks coloured', 'The colours of objects cause us to see objects as coloured', 'There's no seeing a colour without seeing an extended coloured patch' and the like. There are platitudes about the nature of colours and the relations between them, platitudes like 'There's no such thing as transparent matt white', 'Red is more similar to orange than to blue' and so on. There are also corrective platitudes linking real as opposed to illusory colours to features of perceivers and their environments, platitudes like 'Unperceived objects are still coloured', 'If you want to know what colour something is, have a look at it', 'Things don't usually look the colour they really are in the dark', 'If you want to see what colour something really is, take it into the daylight', 'If your eyes aren't working properly you might not be able to tell what colour things really are' and the like. And there are platitudes about the way in which we learn colour terms by linking them up with features of the world, platitudes like 'If you want to teach someone what the word for red means, show her some red objects and then say the word for red', 'If you want to teach someone what the word for blue means, show her some blue objects and then say the word for blue', 'Teach what the word for red means at the same time as you teach what the other colour words mean', 'Teach what the word for blue means at the same time as you teach what the other colour words mean' and so on.

These platitudes about colour play a certain crucial role in our coming to master colour vocabulary, for we come to master colour vocabulary by coming to treat remarks like these *as platitudinous*. The point is not that if we have mastery of the word 'red' then we are able to produce a long list of remarks like these off the tops of our heads. That may or may not be true. The point is rather that these remarks capture the inferential and judgemental dispositions *vis-à-vis* the word 'red' of those who have mastery of that term, whether or not they are able to produce them off the tops of their heads. To have mastery of the word 'red' is to be disposed to make inferences and judgements along these lines. It is in this sense that the remarks constitute a set of platitudes.

To say that we make inferences and judgements along these lines is, of course, consistent with the possibility of our coming to think that it is wrong to do so. Our prereflective inferential habits are, after all, corrigible. We would, for example, change our inferential habits if we were shown that the judgements and inferences that we make as masters of the term 'red' – the platitudes themselves – were incompatible or inconsistent with each other. However it is to say that it would take something like such inconsistency to make us change our inferential and judgemental habits. And the reason why is easy enough to state. At the limit, to give up on the platitudes associated with colour terms is to give up on using colour terms altogether. For they themselves have a *prima facie a priori* status, and gain *a priori* status *simpliciter* by surviving as part of the maximal consistent set of platitudes constitutive of mastery of the term 'red'. That this is so should not be surprising if, as I have already suggested, they together constitute the pattern of inferences licensed by our colour concepts. For, other things being equal, these inferences are themselves valid *a priori*.

If this account of what it is to have mastery of colour terms seems on the right track, and if we are permitted to generalize on the basis of this example, then a certain natural picture emerges of how we might give an analysis of colour concepts like the concept of being red. Since an analysis of the concept of being red should tell us everything there is to know *a priori* about what it is for something to be red, it follows that an analysis should give us knowledge of all of the relevant platitudes about redness: that is, the maximal consistent set of platitudes constitutive of mastery of the term 'red'. Accordingly, we might suppose, an analysis is itself simply constituted by, or derived from, a long conjunction of these platitudes.

As the project of conceptual analysis is being thought of here, then, an analysis of a concept is successful just in case it gives us knowledge of all and only the platitudes which are such that, by coming to treat those platitudes as platitudinous, we come to have mastery of that concept. Given this way of thinking about conceptual analysis, the dispositional analysis would therefore seem to have a distinct advantage over the view that colour terms resist much in the way of conceptual analysis, being more like ordinary proper names. For the striking thing about the dispositional analysis is that, though the terms 'normal perceivers' and 'standard conditions' do not themselves occur in a statement of the platitudes, the platitudes do seem to tell us, more or less explicitly, about all sorts of ways in which perceivers and conditions of perception may be defective – by which I mean simply that they tell us when it would and would not be appropriate to use the colour experience of a perceiver of a certain sort in certain sorts of environmental conditions as a guide to the real colour of the objects perceived. And this suggests, in turn, that the dispositional analysis is perhaps best seen as an attempt to *encapsulate*, or to *summa-*

rize, or to *systematize*, as well as can be done, the various remarks we come to treat as platitudinous in coming to master the term 'red'. In this admittedly vague sense, it can therefore lay some claim to giving us knowledge of all the platitudes. And, accordingly, it can therefore lay some claim to constitute an analysis.

By contrast, the view that colour concepts elude analysis, being more like ordinary proper names, has a distinct disadvantage. For this view is committed to denying that we can analyse colour terms, and is therefore committed to denying that there are *any* interesting *a priori* truths about colours beyond the truism that our colour terms refer to the surface property of objects that are causally responsible for our uses of them. And this view surely stands refuted by the very fact that mastery of colour terms is constituted by coming to treat as platitudinous the rich set of platitudes about colour that we have just described. For they do constitute a rich set of *a priori* truths about the colours, a set that goes way beyond the single truism that colour terms refer to the surface properties of objects that are causally responsible for our uses of them. It is, for example, an *a priori* truth that red things look red to normal perceivers under standard conditions, an *a priori* truth that the view that colour terms are like ordinary proper names simply cannot accommodate or explain.

I said that the view that, though we cannot analyse our moral concepts, concepts like rightness, we can still identify rightness with natural features of acts faces a similar problem. The problem in this case is that, much as with our colour terms, there is in fact a rich set of platitudes about rightness that those who want simply to fix the reference of rightness by some minimal reference-fixing description simply fail to take into account. They are therefore unable to accommodate or explain these *a priori* truths.

In order to see this let's assume, with the metaphysical-but-not-definitional naturalists, that we use the word 'right' to refer to the property of acts that is causally responsible for our uses of the word 'right'. And now let's imagine that we come across a rather different community from ours in which they too use the word 'right' in a practice much like moral practice, and let's ask the metaphysical-but-not-definitional naturalists what we should say about the content of the judgements about the rightness and wrongness of actions made by those in this other community. The problem is, of course, that we cannot simply assume that the *same* property is causally responsible for their uses of the word 'right'. And if it is not, then we have not been given an account of the reference of the word 'right' that is consistent with one of the central platitudes governing our use of that word: namely, the platitude that when A says 'x is right' and B says 'x is not right' then A and B *disagree* with each other. We have not been given an account of what the word 'right' refers to that is consistent with the objectivity of morality.

This objection to metaphysical-but-not-definitional naturalism is in fact close to R. M. Hare's objection to naturalism in *The Language of Morals* (1952: 146–9), an objection that, he claims, forces us to admit that if moral language does have a descriptive function, then it must also have a more important non-descriptive function as well.

> Let us suppose that a missionary, armed with a grammar book, lands on a cannibal island. The vocabulary of his grammar book gives him the equivalent, in the cannibals' language, of the English word 'good'. Let us suppose that, by a strange coincidence, the word is 'good'. And let us suppose, also, that it really is the equivalent – that it is, as the Oxford English Dictionary puts it, 'the most general adjective of commendation' . . . If the missionary has mastered his vocabulary, he can, so long as he uses the word evaluatively and not descriptively, communicate with them about morals quite happily. They know that when he uses the word he is commending the person or object that he applies it to. The only thing they find odd is that he applies it to such unexpected people, people who are meek and gentle and do not collect large quantities of scalps; whereas they themselves are accustomed to commend people who are bold and burly and collect more scalps than the average.
>
> We thus have a situation which would appear paradoxical to someone who thought that 'good' . . . was a quality-word like 'red'. Even if the qualities in people which the missionary commended had nothing in common with the qualities which the cannibals commended, yet they would both know what the word 'good' meant. If 'good' were like 'red', this would be impossible; for then the cannibals' word and the English word would not be synony-

mous ... It is because in its primary evaluative meaning 'good' means neither of these things, but is in both languages the most general adjective of commendation, that the missionary can use it to teach the cannibals Christian morals.

In our terms, Hare's argument can be put like this: if the cannibals use their words 'good' and 'right' to refer to the causes of their uses of the words 'good' and 'right', and the missionaries use their words 'good' and 'right' to refer to the causes of their uses of the words 'good' and 'right', *and if no more can be said about the content of their respective judgements*, then a radical relativism is on the horizon. For we seem to have good reason to suppose that the causes of the cannibals' and the missionaries' uses of the words 'good' and 'right' are very different from each other. And in that case we cannot suppose that the cannibals and the missionaries disagree with each other about what is *really* good and right. It is as if speakers in both communities use the word 'Michael', but in the missionary community it is used to pick out one of the missionaries, whereas in the cannibal community it is used to pick out one of the cannibals. Once we are acquainted with the facts about the different causal origins of the missionaries' and the cannibals' uses of the word 'Michael' we are of course quite happy to admit that disagreements between the missionaries and the cannibals as to whether or not Michael has some feature are more apparent than real. The question is whether we can avoid drawing the same conclusion about the different communities' views about what is good and right.

According to Hare, the best we can get from a descriptive analysis of the meaning of the word 'good' is something that does indeed have this radically relativistic conclusion. He concludes that we should therefore reject descriptivism in favour of a non-descriptive account of the meaning of the words 'good' and 'right'. For he thinks that a non-descriptive account of the meaning of our moral judgements can explain why, for example, cannibals and missionaries really do disagree with each other when they talk about what is good and right. This seems to me to be a powerful argument indeed if the premise is true. If descriptive accounts of the meaning of 'good' and 'right' make our moral judgements inescapably relativistic, and non-descriptive accounts don't, then we surely have good reason to reject the idea that our moral judgements are descriptive. For such a relativism flouts core platitudes about moral disagreement; platitudes about the objectivity of morality (see also Brink, 1989: 24, 29–35; though contrast Harman, 1985). Everything therefore turns on whether or not the premise is true.

To sum up: Ayer's objection to non-subjective naturalism leaves the way open for naturalists to reformulate their theory so as to avoid any claim to be making a definition. They can advance a form of metaphysical-but-not-definitional naturalism. But even if they do it looks like they will run into trouble. For they must choose a description to fix the reference of the moral terms. And in doing this they must make sure that moral claims do not turn out to have different contents in different contexts. And yet this seems inevitable if they simply say that, for example, the word 'right' is used to refer to the feature of acts that is causally responsible for our uses of the term 'right'. For if the cause of A's and B's uses of the word 'right' are not the same, then, contrary to the platitude that if A says 'x is right' and B says 'x is not right' then A and B disagree, A and B are not disagreeing. A's judgement that x is right has a different content from B's judgement that x is right. Naturalists are therefore forced to pin their hopes on some form of definitional naturalism. Only so can they hope to build into the content of a moral judgement not just the purportedly objective status of moral claims, but also the other platitudes about morality: for example, the practicality of moral judgement.[7]

2.7 THE OPEN QUESTION ARGUMENT AND DEFINITIONAL NATURALISM

Definitional naturalism is the view that we can define moral terms exclusively in terms apt for describing the subject matter of the natural and social sciences. The catch-cry of definitional naturalists is therefore not just analysis, but *reductive* analysis. We must first define moral terms in non-moral terms, and then we must make sure that all of the non-moral terms in our definition are themselves thoroughly naturalistic.

Ayer's objection to definitional naturalism, following Moore, is that since for any natural property F it is possible to think that x has F while at the same time thinking that x is not right, it follows that, for no natural property F is it self-contradictory to claim that x has F but x is not right. But it would have to be self-contradictory, if it were possible to give a naturalistic definition of rightness. Therefore it is not possible to give a naturalistic definition of rightness. Does this argument succeed? I do not think so. The question is whether we should believe the premise that there is no natural property F such that it is self-contradictory to claim that x has F but x is not right. Here is why that premise is not, at any rate, *obviously* true.

The definitional naturalist seeks to give a definition or analysis, in naturalistic terms, of 'x is right'. But now, consider the enterprise of giving analyses quite generally. It is a familiar fact about analyses that a concept C* may constitute a correct analysis of a concept C despite the fact that it is possible to think that x falls under C* and yet also, apparently coherently, entertain the possibility that x does not fall under C. Consider, for example, the concept of being red and the concept of having the property that causes objects to look red to normal perceivers under standard conditions: that is, the dispositional analysis of colour concepts discussed earlier. Or consider the concept of knowledge and the concept of a justified true belief that meets the tracking condition (Nozick, 1981: 178). Or consider the concept of A's φ-ing intentionally and the concept of there being some ψ such that A has a desire to ψ, A's having the belief that she can ψ by φ-ing, and A's belief/desire pair's differentially explaining her φ-ing (Peacocke, 1979: chapter 2). The point I am making here does not require the assumption that we can correctly analyse the first in terms of the second in each case. The point is rather that the mere fact that it is an open question whether we can – something that can hardly be denied given the number of pages devoted to discussing these suggestions in the philosophical literature – is not already enough to show that we cannot. Indeed, ironically enough, Ayer himself

notes this fact about analyses when he tries to reconcile the fact
that mathematical claims can surprise us with his own favoured
reduction of mathematical claims to tautologies (1936: 85–7).

A first reaction to Ayer's argument against definitional naturalism is therefore that it simply overlooks the fact that there is such
a thing as the Paradox of Analysis (Darwall, Gibbard and Railton,
1992). The paradox is that, when we are looking for an analysis of
a concept C, we are looking for a concept C* that will tell us
something new and interesting about C, something we don't
already know. The claim that C is analytically equivalent to C*
must therefore be unobvious and informative in some way. But
C* must also, on the other hand, really be analytically eqivalent to
C. C* must therefore in some way already be contained in C. But
in that case it cannot tell us something that we don't know already, and cannot be informative. And that appears to be a contradiction. Ayer's argument, relying as it does on Moore's Open
Question Argument, insists upon the second part of the paradox
and, noting that naturalistic analyses are both unobvious and
informative, draws the conclusion that they cannot really be analyses at all. But when we remember the first part of the paradox, we
see that the conclusion is too hastily drawn. We could equally well
conclude that naturalistic analyses may be unobvious and informative, and yet be correct for all that.

Now it might be thought that the Paradox of Analysis shows
that there is something incoherent about the very idea of conceptual analysis. And, if so, then of course we have an even more
powerful argument against not just definitional naturalism, but
any philosophical theory erected on the basis of analyses or definitions. But in fact I think that this is not right. The Paradox of
Analysis is simply an artefact of bad views about the nature of
conceptual analysis. There is no paradox in the idea of conceptual
analysis.

According to the account of conceptual analysis sketched in the
previous section, in acquiring a concept C we come to acquire a
whole set of inferential and judgemental dispositions connecting
facts expressed in terms of the concept C with facts of other kinds.
A statement of all of these various dispositions constitutes a set of
platitudes surrounding C. And an analysis of a concept is then

best thought of as an attempt to articulate all and only these platitudes. An analysis of a concept C in terms of another concept C* is correct just in case knowledge of C* gives us knowledge of all and only the platitudes surrounding C: that is, knowledge of all and only the inferential and judgemental dispositions of someone who has mastery of the concept C.

This suggests a way of thinking about the analyses of being red, knowledge and intentional action described above. They are all best seen as attempts to encapsulate, or to summarize, or to systematize the platitudes surrounding the concepts of being red, knowledge and intentional action. And, seen in this light, it seems clear that, despite the fact that they are all controversial, they may still lay some claim to constitute analyses. For provided they are *good* encapsulations or summaries or systematizations, they can lay some claim to giving us knowledge of all and only the platitudes surrounding the concepts of being red, knowledge and intentional action.

This account of what conceptual analysis consists in enables us to make good sense of the phenomena associated with the Paradox of Analysis. Why are analyses unobvious and informative? Because even though someone who has mastery of some concept C must *have* certain inferential and judgemental dispositions, it may not be transparent to her what these inferential and judgemental dispositions are, and so, *a fortiori*, it need not be transparent to her what the best summary or systematization of the platitudes that describe these dispositions is. Whereas mastery of a concept requires knowledge-how, knowledge of an analysis of a mastered concept requires us to have knowledge-that about our knowledge-how. It might therefore take time and thought to see whether or not C* constitutes an analysis of C because it takes time and thought to figure out what the relevant inferential and judgemental dispositions are and what the best systematization of the platitudes describing these dispositions is.

Here, then, is the first part of our reply to Ayer's argument against definitional naturalism. Ayer wields the Open Question Argument against definitional naturalism, an argument whose force depends on the assumption that analyses cannot be correct if they are also unobvious and informative. But as the more plausible conception of conceptual analysis described above shows, analyses of concepts may be correct even though they are unobvious and informative. Indeed, it seem inevitable that they will be so.

Unfortunately, however, this cannot be the whole of our reply to Ayer. For though naturalistic analyses of moral terms, if there are any, are indeed unobvious, the claim that such analyses are to be had is not itself made plausible merely by showing that there can be unobvious analyses. We must therefore turn to consider the plausibility of the definitional naturalists' claim in its own right. We must begin by describing the inferential and judge-mental dispositions of those who have mastery of moral concepts. And then we must ask whether these can, as the definitional naturalist supposes, be reductively characterized in wholly natu-ralistic terms.

2.8   WHAT ARE THE PLATITUDES SURROUNDING OUR MORAL CONCEPTS?

To say that we can analyse moral concepts, like the concept of being right, is to say that we can specify which property the property of being right is by reference to platitudes about right-ness: that is, by reference to descriptions of the inferential and judgemental dispositions of those who have mastery of the term 'rightness'. Many of these platitudes have already been stated. Let me repeat some of them here, and then describe some others.

To begin with, as we saw from the outset, there are platitudes that give support to the idea that moral judgement is especially *practical*: 'If someone judges her φ-ing to be right, then, other things being equal, she will be disposed to φ'; 'Weakness of will, compulsion, depression and the like may explain why someone isn't moved in accordance with her moral beliefs'; 'Judgements about rightness and wrongness are judgements about our reasons for and against acting' and so on. There are platitudes that give support to our idea of the *objectivity* of moral judgement: 'When A says that φ-ing is right, and B says that φ-ing is not right, then at most one of A and B is correct'; 'Whether or not φ-ing is right can be discovered by engaging in rational argument'; 'Provided A and B are open-minded and thinking clearly, an argument between A and B about the rightness or wrongness of φ-ing should result in A and B coming to some agreement on the matter'; 'The rightness of someone's φ-ing is determined by the circumstances in which that person acts, circumstances that might be faced by another', and so we could go on. And there are platitudes that support the *supervenience* of the moral on the natural: 'Acts are right or wrong in virtue of their ordinary everyday non-moral features, features like being an act of loyalty or disloyalty to a friend, being an act that is conducive to happiness or unhappiness, being an act that gives one person an advantage over or a disadvantage relative to another'; 'Acts with the same ordinary everyday non-moral features must have the same moral features as well', and so on.

As I said, these platitudes were all mentioned earlier. But there are other platitudes as well. For example, there are platitudes concerning the *substance* of morality: 'Right acts are often concerned to promote or sustain or contribute in some way to human flourishing' (Foot, 1958); 'Right acts are in some way expressive of equal concern and respect' (Dworkin, 1977: 179–83; Kymlicka, 1989: 13, 21–9; 1990: 4–5), and the like. What these platitudes about substance force us to admit, at the very least, is that there are limits on the kind of content a set of requirements can have if they are to be moral requirements at all, as opposed to requirements of some other non-moral kind (Dreier, 1990).

And there other platitudes as well, for example, platitudes concerning the *procedures* by which we can discover which acts are right. Rawls famously gave system to such platitudes when he described what he calls the method of 'reflective equilibrium' (Rawls, 1951). For not only is it a platitude that rightness is a property that we can discover to be instantiated by engaging in rational argument, it is also a platitude that such arguments have a certain characteristic coherentist form. Thus, for example, when we engage in moral argument we generally begin from a point of disagreement about some particular moral matter, and we generally attempt to resolve such disagreements by finding other matters on which we can agree. These are usually uncontroversial matters on which there is widespread agreement. Such arguments are most likely to lead to a resolution if the parties to the disagreement are open-minded and willing to follow the argument wherever it leads. For having found areas of agreement, our task is to find more general principles that explain and justify our judgements in the cases about which we agree, and then to apply these newly found more general principles to the areas of disagreement in order to bring agreement about. And when we do so apply them, if the argument has been successful, one or another of us will find that we have to revise our original judgement. For we will find that the more general principle we have found dictates answers contrary to those we gave initially, and these new answers, supported as they are by the more general principle, will strike us as more plausible than our original judgement about the particular case.

This is by no means an exhaustive list of the platitudes surrounding our moral concepts. But these various platitudes concerning practicality, supervenience, objectivity, substance and procedure should suffice to establish the point that there is indeed a rich set of platitudes surrounding our moral concepts, and they should suffice to give some idea of what these platitudes are like. An analysis of moral terms must in some way capture these various platitudes. It must do so on pain of not being an analysis of *moral* terms at all. This point is important. For, as we will see, it allows us to explain why the forms of definitional naturalism Ayer considers are indeed utter failures as definitions.

2.9 SUBJECTIVE VS. NON-SUBJECTIVE DEFINITIONAL NATURALISM

Remember that, according to the subjective definitional naturalists, 'x is right' means 'x has the natural property that is approved by so-and-so'. Non-subjective naturalists, by contrast, focus in on the natural properties of acts that subjective naturalists say we merely approve of and define rightness directly in terms of one of those properties. For example, non-subjective definitional naturalists who are utilitarians think that we can define 'x is right' as 'x is conducive to happiness'. But the platitudes about rightness just described suggest that though both of these definitions have something to be said in their favour, at the end of the day they must both be rejected on the grounds that they conflict with platitudes about rightness (Smith, 1986b).

On the merit side, for example, subjective definitional naturalism does entail that it is *a priori* that the moral supervenes on the natural. Suppose two possible worlds are identical in naturalistic features. Then if one contains actions with naturalistic features of which we approve, and so we deem those acts to be right, then the actions in the other world with the same naturalistic features must also be deemed right. This follows directly from the definition of rightness. Moreover, depending on the way in which the subjective definitional naturalist spells out the 'so-and-so' – provided, that is, that the speaker herself is part of the so-and-so – subjective definitional naturalism will capture the practicality of moral judgement as well. For if judgements about the rightness of an agent's ϕ-ing are, *inter alia* judgements to the effect that the agent herself desires to ϕ, and if desiring to ϕ is the only way we can be motivated to ϕ, then it surely comes as no surprise that, other things being equal, an agent who judges it right to ϕ is motivated to ϕ.

On the debit side, however, subjective definitional naturalism is completely unable to account for either the objectivity of moral judgement or the various procedures via which we come by moral knowledge. For if desires are beyond rational criticism, as Hume thought, then the idea of a moral argument – an argument about the rightness or wrongness of an action, as opposed to an argument about the other non-moral features that might be possessed by an act – simply doesn't make a great deal of sense. An agent either approves of some natural property of acts or she doesn't. Either way there is nothing much to argue about; nothing to argue about in the way, and to the extent that, we argue about the rightness or wrongness of actions. Moreover, if another agent disapproves, then it is simply isn't true that they express their disagreement with each other when the one says 'This act is right' and the other says 'This act is wrong'. Rather, each self-ascribes their different pro- and con-attitudes, a self-ascription that the other can and perhaps should agree to be correct.

Non-subjective definitional naturalism, for its part, also clearly captures the supervenience of the moral on the natural. Two acts that are identical in their natural features will of course agree in their moral features if their moral features are, by definition, just those natural features themselves. And, unlike subjectivism, it does give us something to argue about in arguing about the rightness of an act: specifically, it lets us argue about the *meaning* of the word 'right' (though whether or not this is an appropriate account of what we are up to when we engage in moral argument I do not know). To this extent, then, non-subjective definitional naturalism allows us to capture the objectivity of morality. For if one person says that an act is right, and the other says that it is wrong, they do indeed disagree; for the act can only either have or lack the relevant natural feature: conduciveness to happiness, say.

On the debit side, however, non-subjective definitional naturalism seems completely unable to explain why, when we know that someone believes an act to be right, we are, other things being equal, in a position to know what she is motivated to do. For if, as Hume taught us, beliefs and desires are distinct existences, and if, as Hume taught us, desires are beyond rational criticism, then no matter which non-subjective natural feature of acts we pick on, we can readily imagine agents who will be left entirely unmoved by their belief that an act has that feature.

We must therefore conclude that though he rejected them for the wrong reasons, Ayer was right to reject the forms of definitional naturalism he considered. However this does not show that definitional naturalism is *as such* inadequate, it *merely* shows that the forms of definitional naturalism Ayer chose to consider are inadequate. We must therefore consider the plausibility of definitional naturalism as such. Can we can turn the platitudes concerning practicality, supervenience, objectivity, substance and procedure into a naturalistic analysis of our moral concepts: that is, an analysis of our moral concepts in naturalistic, non-moral, terms?

2.10   DEFINITIONAL NATURALISM AS THE SEARCH FOR NETWORK ANALYSES OF OUR MORAL CONCEPTS

According to the account of conceptual analysis described earlier, the aim of an analysis is to give us knowledge of all and only the platitudes surrounding our use of the concept that is up for analysis. So far we have seen just one way in which this might be done. We might summarize the relevant platitudes in the style of the dispositional analysis of our colour concepts.

This is, however, only one way in which we might try to derive an analysis from a set of platitudes, and if our aim is to find out how we might give a naturalistic analysis of our moral concepts, it is not the most promising way either. For, crucially, the dispositional analysis is not a reductive analysis. The dispositionalist tells us, after all, that redness is the surface property of objects that causes them to look *red*. The concept being analysed – the concept of being red – is thus used in stating the summary of the platitudes surrounding the concept of being red. The dispositional analysis of our concept of being red thus cannot serve as an adequate model for a naturalistic analysis of our moral concepts. For a naturalistic analysis does aspire to be reductive. How, then, might such an analysis be given?

Building on work by Frank Ramsey (1931) and Rudolf Carnap (1963), David Lewis has described an alternative technique by which we can derive analyses from platitudes (Lewis, 1970, 1972, 1989), a technique that has been explored further, particularly in its application to the moral case, by Frank Jackson (1992, forthcoming). Analyses in the Ramsey-Carnap-Lewis-Jackson style differ from analyses like the dispositional analysis of our colour concepts in two ways. First, they purport to capture platitudes explicitly, rather than via a summary, and second, they purport to be reductive: that is, the concept being analysed is not used in stating the analysis itself.

As I see it, definitional naturalism is best understood as the view that we can come up with a Ramsey-Carnap-Lewis-Jackson style thoroughly explicit and reductive analysis of our moral concepts, a 'network' analysis, as I will call it from here on. In what follows I will first outline the general structure of network analyses, and I will then consider whether such analyses are, in the end, at all plausible in the moral case.

In providing a network analysis of our moral concepts, the first step is to rewrite all of the platitudes that surround our use of moral terms – the platitudes concerning practicality, super-venience, objectivity, substance and procedure – so that the moral terms mentioned in stating these platitudes all occur in property-name style. 'If someone judges her φ-ing to be right, then, other things being equal, she will be disposed to φ' becomes 'If some-one judges her φ-ing to have the property of being right, then, other things being equal, she will be disposed to φ'; 'Right acts are often other-regarding' becomes 'Acts which have the property of being right are often other-regarding', and so on.

The second step is to write down a statement consisting of a long conjunction of all these rewritten platitudes. We can rep-resent this as a relational predicate 'M' true of the various moral properties. Where the property of being right and the rest are represented by the letters 'r', 's', 't' and the like, the conjunction can be represented by:

$M[rst...]$

Once we have this long conjunction, the third step is to strip out each mention of a property-name of a moral property and replace it with a free variable:

$M[xyz...]$

And once we have done this we can say that, if there are any moral properties, then the following must be true:

$$\exists x\, \exists y\, \exists z \ldots M[xyz\ldots]\ \&\ (x^*)(y^*)(z^*)\ldots M[x^*y^*z^*\ldots]\ \text{iff}$$
$$(x=x^*,\ y=y^*,\ z=z^*\ldots)$$

In other words, if there are any moral properties, then there is a unique set of properties which are in fact related to each other and to the world in just the way that the big conjunction of platitudes says the moral properties are related to each other and the world.

Moreover, if this is right, and if (say) the variable 'x' replaced the property of being right when we stripped out all mention of the particular moral properties, then we can define the property of being right as follows:

the property of being right *is* the x such that $\exists y \exists z \ldots M[xyz\ldots]$ & $(x^*)(y^*)(z^*) \ldots M[x^* y^* z^* \ldots]$ iff $(x=x^*, y=y^*, z=z^* \ldots)$

For what we have here is a definition of the property of being right in terms of the whole network of relations it stands in to the other moral properties, and to all of the other things that are mentioned in the platitudes about moral properties: motivation, action, circumstances of argumentation, acts of an other regarding kind, and so on.

This analysis of rightness thus has a very striking feature: the analysis itself mentions no moral terms at all. That is, no moral terms are needed to say what 'M' means, for these were all stripped out and replaced by variables at an earlier point in the analysis. Rightness is rather characterized in terms of the relations it stands in to the other moral properties and to the other things mentioned in the platitudes: motivation, action, the circumstances of argumentation, acts of an other regarding kind and the like. What we have here is therefore a definition of rightness in *non-moral* terms. Indeed, on the plausible assumption that the other things mentioned in the platitudes about moral properties are themselves natural features, it is a definition of the property of being right in entirely *naturalistic* terms.

Note that such an analysis might prove to be useful indeed. For armed with this definition we are now in a position to look for an argument of the following form in the attempt to vindicate, or perhaps to undermine, our right to talk descriptively about morals.

Conceptual claim: the property of being right *is* the x such that $\exists y \exists z \ldots M[xyz\ldots]$ &

$(x^*)(y^*)(z^*) \ldots M[x^* y^* z^* \ldots]$ iff
$(x=x^*, y=y^*, z=z^* \ldots)$

Substantive claim: the x such that $\exists y \exists z \ldots M[x y z \ldots]$ &
$(x^*)(y^*)(z^*) \ldots M[x^* y^* z^* \ldots]$ iff
$(x=x^*, y=y^*, z=z^* \ldots)$ *is* natural
property F

Conclusion: the property of being right *is* natural
property F

For, given the conceptual claim, it follows that there is indeed a
feature of rightness, possessed by acts, and this is in turn a natural
feature, just in case the substantive claim is true: that is, just in case
there is a natural feature that stands in all of the relations to other
natural features that the conceptual claim tells us rightness stands
in to motivation, action, the circumstances of argumentation, acts
of an other regarding kind and so on. And, correlatively of course,
if this substantive claim is false, then we have decisive reason to
conclude that all our moral thought and talk is in error. For there
would then be no natural feature that stands in all of the relations
to other natural features that the conceptual claim tells us rightness stands in; nothing in the world would deserve the name
'rightness'.

In summary, then, we have seen how we can give, in schematic
terms at least, a naturalistic definition of rightness. And we have
seen that such a naturalistic definition of rightness would be
useful indeed. For, armed with such a definition, we would be in
a position to show that morality can, or alternatively that it cannot,
be squared with a broader naturalism. We could vindicate, or
undermine, our right to talk descriptively about morals. It might
therefore be thought that this gives us ample reason to embrace
definitional naturalism. For haven't we just demonstrated that we
can define our moral concepts in wholly naturalistic terms? And
haven't we just seen what the benefits of such a definition are? In
my view it would, however, be far too hasty to draw either of these
conclusions. For as we shall see, the success of network analyses
depends upon the truth of an assumption, an assumption that we
have good reason to reject.

2.11 HOW NETWORK ANALYSES CAN BE DEFECTIVE: THE PERMUTATION PROBLEM

I said that the success of a network analysis depends on an assumption. The assumption is that, when we strip out all mention of the terms that we want analysed from a statement of the relevant platitudes there will still be enough left in the way of relational information to guarantee that there is a unique realization of the network of relations just in case the concepts we are analysing really are instantiated. But this assumption looks like it might well prove to be false in certain cases.

Since it may not be obvious that this is so, let's imagine ourselves trying to construct a network analysis of our colour concepts. Just as our aim in giving a network analysis of moral terms is to construct an analysis in naturalistic terms, an analysis that we can potentially use to go on to square our moral talk with a broader naturalism, let's imagine that our aim in giving a network analysis of colour terms is to construct an analysis in physical terms, an analysis that we can potentially use to go on to square our colour talk with a broader physicalism. Just as we want to be able identify moral features, if there are any, with natural features, we want to be able to identify colours, if there are any, with physical features.

The task, then, is to collect together all of the platitudes about the colours. So focus for a moment on the platitudes about the property of being red. Remember, in doing so, that we ordinarily take the property of being red to occupy a certain place on a continuous colour wheel, a colour wheel that fixes the similarity relations between the colours. The platitudes about the property of being red can then be seen to entail the following claims: the property of being red causes objects to look red to normal perceivers under standard conditions, and the property of being red is more similar to the property of being orange than it is to the property of being yellow, and so on. Now focus on the platitudes about the property of being orange. They entail the following claims: the property of being orange causes objects to look orange to normal perceivers under standard conditions, and the property of being orange is more similar to the property of being yellow than it is to the property of being green, and so on. And now focus on the platitudes about the property of being yellow. They entail the following claims: the property of being yellow causes objects to look yellow to normal perceivers under standard conditions, and the property of being yellow is more similar to the property of being green than it is to the property of being blue, and so on. And now focus on the platitudes about . . . And so we could go on.

Let's now make a further, and substantial, assumption. Let's assume that there are no platitudes about the colours that entail any claims beyond these about the properties of being red, or orange, or yellow, or the rest. I will have something to say about this assumption presently. However, with this assumption in place look at what happens if we construct network analyses of the various colour properties by simply conjoining all of the platitudes about these colours and following the Ramsey-Carnap-Lewis-Jackson procedure. Simplifying somewhat, we find that:

the property of being red *is*	the x such that $\exists y \exists z$ . . . objects have x iff they look x to normal perceivers under standard conditions, and x is more similar to y than it is to z . . . & . . . . (uniqueness conditions) . . .
the property of being orange *is*	the y such that $\exists z \exists v$ . . . objects have y iff they look y to normal perceivers under standard conditions, and y is more similar to z than it is to v . . . & . . . . (uniqueness conditions) . . .
the property of being yellow *is*	the z such that $\exists v \exists w$ . . . objects have z iff they look z to normal perceivers under standard conditions, and z is more similar to v than it is to w . . . & . . . . (uniqueness conditions) . . .

and so on. But now look at the network of relations specified by the definitions on the right hand side. In each case it is the *very same* network of relations. And what this means is, in essence, that in our definitions we have lost any distinction between the properties of being red, being orange, being yellow and the rest. The uniqueness requirement thus cannot be satisfied.

If this is right, then note that it has a quite disastrous effect on our ability to use network analyses of our colour concepts as premises in arguments that allow us to go on to identify colours with physical properties. For we lose any reason to make the second, substantive, claim in such arguments, the claim that the properties picked out by our definitions *are* certain physical properties. True enough, α might be a physical property that stands in a set of relations isomorphic to the relations that the property of being red stands in; but so does β, the property we might have hoped would turn out to be the property of being orange; and so does . . . and so on and so forth.

In short, then, because the claim to uniqueness is false, we lose any reason to believe that our network analyses of colour concepts allow us to pick out a unique set of physical properties to identify with the colours. Moreover, the problem here lies not with the world – we have not just demonstrated that there are no colours! – but rather with the network analyses themselves. Thoroughly explicit and reductive network analyses of our colour concepts lose *a priori* information about the *differences* between the colours. They are therefore defective, as analyses.

Let's call this the 'permutation problem'.[8] I said at the outset that the the success of network analyses depends on an assumption. The assumption is, in essence, that when we give a network analysis of a particular concept the analysis is not going to be vulnerable to the permutation problem. In the case of colours, for example, the assumption is that, if indeed there are colours, then when we strip out all mention of colour terms from the long conjunctive statement of the platitudes about colours, we will still be left with *enough* in the way of relational information to fix on a *unique* physical property with which to identify each of the various colours.

For that to be true there would have to be some extra platitudes about colours that we could use to discriminate the colours from each other. But it is, at any rate, not obvious that such platitudes can be found. To be sure, claims like 'Red is the colour of blood', 'Orange is the colour of ripe oranges', 'Yellow is the colour of a new born chicken', 'Blue is the colour of the sky on a cloudless day in summer, provided there is no pollution', and the like are widely believed to be true. And these truths are indeed platitudes, in one sense of that term. But the trouble is that they are not platitudes in the *relevant* sense. For though these claims are widely believed, they are still contingent and *a posteriori* truths about the colours, truths whose rejection, in relevant circumstances, would be neither here nor there with respect to whether or not we possess and are capable of using colour concepts. They are there-fore not truths whose internalization is in any way constitutive of mastery of the colour terms. They do not constitute a statement of a set of inferences or judgements licensed by our colour concepts *themselves*. Thus, since it is not even *prima facie a priori* that red is the colour of blood, yellow is the colour of a new born chicken, and so on, we cannot use these platitudes to enrich our defi-nitions of the colours. These truths cannot be used to supplement the first premise of the two-stage argument we envisaged giving in attempting to identify colours with physical properties, because they are not *conceptual* truths.

Colour terms thus seem to elude analysis in the thoroughly explicit and reductive style of network analyses. There should, I think, be no real surprise here. For we learn colour terms in part by being presented with paradigms of the various colours, para-digms which, for us, fit within a natural visual similarity space. In acquiring mastery of colour terms, we then acquire a dispo-sition to judge visually presented cases of particular colours to be the particular colours that they are (Peacocke 1985). Having mastery of colour terms is thus, in part, a matter of having our use of colour terms directly 'hooked up' with the colours those colour terms pick out. For this reason, the conditions for mastery cannot be fully spelled out without stipulating that these direct links are in place.

This is not to downplay the relevance of the various inferential dispositions required for having mastery of colour terms in giving an analysis. It is indeed a necessary condition of mastery of the concept of being red that someone is disposed to judge that red is more similar to orange than to blue; that a red object would look red under appropriate conditions; and so on. But it is to explain why, when we focus on the various inferential dispositions in the way that network analyses encourage us to, we will find ourselves focusing on a tight-knit set of platitudes, a set of platitudes that seem too tightly knit and interconnected to allow us to distill out of them a definition of the various colours that will distinguish the colours from each other.

But even if colours do elude analysis in the network style, it does not follow that they elude analysis altogether. For, as we have already seen, colour terms can be given a summary-style, non-reductive characterization in the style of the dispositional analysis. If the goal of an analysis is simply to give us knowledge of all of the platitudes surrounding our use of the concept up for analysis, then the mere fact that such an analysis is summary-style and non-reductive is, of course, no objection to it. Analyses are simply not required to be thoroughly explicit and reductive. Indeed, the non-reductive character of the dispositional analysis may now seem to be a distinct advantage. For its non-reductive character can be seen to reflect the fact that in having mastery of colour terms, our use of those terms must be directly 'hooked up' with the colours that those terms pick out, something a thoroughly reductive analysis seems bound to ignore, or to capture only inappropriately, to its peril (Smith, 1986a). This is why the permutation problem that faces network-style analyses of colour concepts is no problem at all for non-reductive analyses like the dispositional analysis.

Moreover, if our aim in giving analyses of colour terms is to be able to go on and use them in showing how colour talk can, or perhaps cannot, be squared with a broader physicalism, then the dispositional analysis looks like it will itself suffice for that task as well. For, much as with network style analyses, note that we can readily construct a two-stage argument of the following kind using the dispositional analysis.

Conceptual claim:	the property of being red *is* the property that causes objects to look red to normal perceivers under standard conditions
Substantive claim:	the property that causes objects to look red to normal perceivers under standard conditions *is* surface reflectance property α
Conclusion:	the property of being red *is* surface reflectance property α

In this argument, as in the earlier argument using a network analysis, we appeal to a conceptual truth about colours in order to find out whether there are any physical properties that deserve to be called 'colours'. Thus, according to the first premise of this argument, a physical property deserves the name 'redness' only if it is the surface property of objects which causes those objects to look red to normal perceivers under standard conditions. If there is such a physical property, then talk of redness can be squared with a broader physicalism because redness is a physical property. And if there isn't, then that is tantamount to a proof that nothing is red. For if there is no property of objects that causes those objects to look red to normal perceivers under standard conditions then nothing does deserve the name 'redness'.[9]

To be sure, someone who did not already possess the concept of being red would be in no position to endorse the first and second premises of this two-stage argument. To have good reason to believe the premises of this two-stage argument we have to draw upon our prior understanding of the concept of being red, and our prior beliefs about which objects would look red to normal perceivers under standard conditions. But, of course, that is neither here nor there given that our epistemic situation is one in which we do have such prior knowledge, and given that our interest in putting forward such an argument is squaring colour talk with physical talk.

The discussion of colour concepts is meant to have illustrative significance only. It is meant to give us a concrete example of a set of concepts that seem to elude thoroughly explicit and reductive, network-style, analysis. And it is meant to offer an explanation of why this is the case. It therefore gives us an issue on which to focus in considering network style analyses of our moral concepts. Are network analyses of our moral concepts vulnerable to a permutation problem?

2.12   CAN WE PROVIDE NETWORK ANALYSES OF MORAL TERMS?

So far we have the following schematic account of how to analyse our concept of rightness in non-moral, naturalistic terms.

the property of being right *is* the x such that $\exists y \exists z \ldots M[xyz \ldots]$ &
$$(x^*)(y^*)(z^*) \ldots M[x^* y^* z^* \ldots] \text{ iff}$$
$$(x=x^*, y=y^*, z=z^* \ldots)$$

According to this definition, the property of being right is the natural property of acts that stands in a certain distinctive network of relations to the natural features mentioned in the platitudes concerning objectivity, practicality, supervenience, substance and procedure, and of course to the other moral properties which themselves are characterized in terms of such relations as well.

But, of course, nothing said so far shows that when we strip out all mention of moral features from the long conjunction of platitudes concerning objectivity, practicality, supervenience, substance and procedure, leaving only mention of natural features, we will be left with enough in the way of relational information to *uniquely* specify the moral properties. For all we have said here, then, once we delve into the details of this definition, we may be left with a permutation problem; we may be unable to distinguish the various moral properties from each other. We may, for example, be unable to distinguish the right from the wrong, the good from the bad, the values from the disvalues, or whatever. How might we decide whether this is, or is not, the case, short of embarking on the superhuman task of collecting together all of the platitudes concerning practicality, objectivity, supervenience, substance and procedure, writing them down in a long conjunction, and then seeing whether the permutation problem arises?

In the case of our colour concepts the permutation problem arises for two related reasons. It arises because, first, we acquire mastery of colour terms *inter alia* by being presented with paradigms of the colours and by having our use of particular colour terms directly 'hooked up' with the particular colours these terms pick out, and because, second, as a consequence, the platitudes surrounding our use of colour terms therefore form an extremely tight-knit and interconnected group. The permutation problem arises because our colour concepts are not defined in terms of *enough* in the way of relations between colours and things that are not themselves colours – or, at any rate, things that are not themselves characterized in terms of colours.

Now, as I see it, our moral concepts are just like our colour concepts in this regard. We learn all our normative concepts, our moral concepts included, *inter alia* by being presented with paradigms. Just as we learn what the colours are by being presented with paradigmatic instances of the colours, we learn what a good argument is by being presented with paradigmatic cases of good arguments, we learn what rightness is by being presented with paradigmatic cases of right actions, we learn what wrongness is by being presented with paradigmatic cases of wrong actions, and so on. The platitudes surrounding our use of normative terms generally, and thus moral terms as well, therefore form an extremely tight-knit and interconnected group. Such terms are largely interdefined. Perhaps the most striking way of bringing this out, in the case of moral terms, is by focusing on the various platitudes about procedure: that is, the various descriptions of the ways in which we justify our moral beliefs, what Rawls calls the method of 'reflective equilibrium'. For it is hard to believe that, once all normative terms are stripped out of these platitudes, there will be any determinate content left to them at all. And the loss of such content is just what makes for a permuation problem.

Moreover it seems to me that there are other, inductive, reasons for thinking that network analyses of moral terms are vulnerable to a permutation problem as well. For it is surely a quite remarkable feature of the history of moral philosophy that attempts at giving naturalistic definitions have all been such failures. Ayer considers and rightly rejects – though not for the right reasons – versions of subjective and non-subjective definitional naturalism. But half a century later more recent attempts at giving naturalistic definitions do not seem to be faring any better (Wiggins, 1987; Johnston, 1989; Railton, 1993a, 1993b; Wiggins, 1993a, 1993b; and, especially, Blackburn, 1994). Surely the most plausible explanation of these failures is that such analyses are impossible. And the vulnerability of network analyses to a permutation problem is just what is required to establish this conclusion.

It seems to me that we therefore have good reason to reject the idea that we can give network analyses of our moral concepts. And, if I am right that the plausibility of definitional naturalism is tied to the plausibility of network analyses of our moral concepts – if network analyses offer the best hope for definitional naturalism – then it follows that we have good reason to reject definitional naturalism as well. We should therefore join Ayer in rejecting definitional naturalism outright.

2.13   CAN WE AVOID AYER'S DILEMMA?

We have in effect been considering a reconstructed form of Ayer's dilemma. Our results can be summarized as follows.

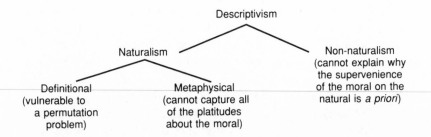

That is, very briefly, on the horn of the dilemma where we take moral judgements to be describing how things are in some non-natural respect we are left unable to explain moral knowledge in a way consistent with the fact that the supervenience of the moral on the natural is an *a priori* truth. And on the horn of the dilemma where we take moral judgements to be describing how things are in some natural respect we fare no better, for we must then choose between two equally unappealing alternatives: saying that this is so because we can give a thoroughly explicit and reductive network-style analysis of our moral concepts in naturalistic terms, or saying that this is so because, though we cannot give such an analysis, our moral concepts none the less refer to natural features. Both are equally unappealing because, if we say the first, we run up against the permutation problem, and if we say the second, then we have no guarantee that our favoured account of the content of a moral judgement, or the reference of moral terms, will respect the various platitudes concerning objectivity, practicality, supervenience, substance and procedure that we take to be definitive of the moral. If these exhaust our alternatives then in taking moral judgements to be descriptive we do indeed seem to be impaled on the horns of a dilemma. The question to ask is therefore whether these really exhaust our alternatives. And, as the discussion of our colour concepts makes clear, the answer is that they do not.

In order to make coherent the idea that moral judgements are descriptive, we do indeed need an analysis of our moral concepts that respects the various platitudes concerning objectivity, practicality, supervenience, substance and procedure. But in giving such an analysis, we do not have to take the reductive route; we do not have to give an explicit and reductive network-style analysis. As in the case of our colour concepts, we can rest content with summary-style, non-reductive analyses. In my view, this is how we will avoid Ayer's dilemma.

In giving such analyses we must not, of course, fall into the trap of simply positing the existence of non-natural properties all over again, for there are no non-natural properties. Our summary-style, non-reductive analyses of moral concepts must therefore make the legitimacy of moral talk depend on squaring such talk with a broader naturalism. If there are any moral properties, such properties must just be natural properties. But in this regard, our discussion of colour concepts is once again helpful. For, much as we saw in that case, summary-style, non-reductive analyses of our moral concepts should be able to figure as premises in arguments that permit us either to vindicate, or to undermine, all our moral talk, depending on whether or not they permit us to identify moral properties with natural properties.

We therefore end with a promise. The promise is that in the chapters that follow we will indeed find that we can give a sum-mary-style, non-reductive analysis of our moral concepts, an analy-sis that adequately captures the platitudes concerning objectivity, practicality, supervenience, substance and procedure. Moreover, the promise is that this analysis will allow us to square our moral talk with a broader naturalism. To anticipate, the analysis will do so because it will tell us that our moral concepts, like rightness, are themselves concepts of reasons for action, reasons that can in turn be identified with natural features of our circumstances.

2.14   SUMMARY AND PREVIEW

In this chapter we have considered in some detail Ayer's classic argument for the claim that moral judgements do not have de-scriptive content, and so do not express our beliefs; that rather moral judgements express our pro- or con-attitudes, and so have non-descriptive content. Ayer's argument has the form of a di-lemma: if moral judgements are descriptive then they must either describe a naturalistic or a non-naturalistic state of affairs. Since it is incoherent to suppose that they describe either, we must con-clude that they are not descriptive at all.

Against Ayer I have argued that, though a form of the argument he gives on the 'non-naturalistic' horn of his dilemma succeeds, the arguments he gives on the 'naturalistic' horn fail altogether. A moral judgement describes a naturalistic state of affairs just in case an analysis of moral terms allows us to square morality with a broader naturalism; just in case, for example, we can use the analysis in an attempt to identify the moral features of acts with their natural features. Ayer thinks that such analyses are imposs-ible. But his reasons for thinking this depend on his own quite implausible conception of what is involved in coming up with an analysis of our moral concepts; his assumption that analyses must be reductive.

We therefore leave Ayer's argument with a promise, a promise that we will indeed be able to provide an analysis of our moral concepts in summary-style, non-reductive terms, an analysis that does indeed vindicate the descriptive form of moral judgements. The argument is to be that we can analyse moral facts as facts about our reasons for action, and that such an analysis allows us to square morality with a broader naturalism. In the next chapter I take the first step towards providing such an analysis. I tackle head-on those who are skeptical about the connection between morality and reasons for action.

3

The Externalist Challenge

3.1 INTERNALISM VS. EXTERNALISM

Suppose we debate the pros and cons of giving to famine relief and you convince me that I should give. However when the occasion arises for me to hand over my money I say 'But wait! I know I *should* give to famine relief. But you haven't convinced me that I have any *reason* to do so!' And so I don't.

I suggested earlier that such an outburst would occasion serious puzzlement. Having convinced me that I should give to famine relief you seem to have done everything you need to do to convince me that I have a reason to do so. And having convinced me that I have a reason to give to famine relief – absent weakness of will or some other such psychological failure – you seem to have done everything you need to do to motivate me to do so. Puzzlement would thus naturally arise because, having convinced me that I should donate, you would quite rightly expect me to hand over my money. *Believing I should* seems to bring with it *my being motivated to* – at least absent weakness of will and the like.

This idea, that moral judgement has a practical upshot, is generally referred to as 'internalism' (Falk, 1948; Frankena, 1958; Davidson, 1970; Williams, 1980; Railton, 1986; Korsgaard, 1986; Brink, 1986; Wallace, 1990; Darwall, Gibbard and Railton, 1992). Unfortunately, however, 'internalism' is a vague label in the philosophical literature, used to refer to several quite different claims about the connection between moral facts or judgements on the one hand, and having reasons or being motivated on the other (as noted by both Brink and Wallace). Let me begin by spelling out some of these rather different claims.

Sometimes the idea behind internalism is that there is the following conceptual connection between moral judgement and the will (Nagel, 1970; McDowell, 1978, 1979, 1985; Platts, 1979, 1981).

> If an agent judges that it is right for her to φ in circumstances C, then she is motivated to φ in C.

In other words, moral judgement brings motivation with it *simpliciter*. This is a very strong claim. It commits us to denying that, for example, weakness of the will and the like may defeat an agent's moral motivations while leaving her appreciation of her moral reasons intact. And for this very reason it is, I think, a manifestly implausible claim as well. However I will not have anything more to say about it here; rather I defer discussion of this version of internalism until the next chapter, when it re-emerges as a consequence of one sort of anti-Humean theory of motivation.

More plausibly, then, the idea behind internalism is sometimes that though there is a conceptual connection between moral judgement and the will, the connection involved is the following *defeasible* one (Blackburn, 1984: 187–9, forthcoming; Johnston, 1989; Pettit and Smith, 1993a).

> If an agent judges that it is right for her to φ in circumstances C, then either she is motivated to φ in C or she is practically irrational.

In other words, agents who judge it right to act in various ways are so motivated, and necessarily so, absent the distorting influences of weakness of the will and other similar forms of practical unreason on their motivations. I will have more to say about this idea in what follows.

And sometimes the idea behind the internalism requirement is not, or at least is not primarily, that there is a conceptual connection of some sort between moral judgement and motivation, but that there is the following conceptual connection between the content of a moral judgement – the moral facts – and our reasons for action (Nagel, 1970; Korsgaard, 1986).

> If it is right for agents to φ in circumstances C, then there is a
> reason for those agents to φ in C.

In other words, moral facts are facts about our reasons for action;
they are themselves simply requirements of rationality or reason.

This last internalist claim might be offered as an explanation of
the previous one, for it plausibly entails the previous claim. The
proof of this will be spelled out in some detail later (chapter 5),
but in general terms the idea can be put like this. It is a platitude
that an agent has a reason to act in a certain way just in case she
would be motivated to act in that way if she were rational
(Korsgaard, 1986). And it is a consequence of this platitude that
an agent who judges herself to have a reason to act in a certain way
– who judges that she would be so motivated if she were rational
– is practically irrational if she is not motivated to act accordingly.
For if she is not motivated accordingly then she fails to be rational
by her own lights (Smith, 1992). But if this is right then it is clear
that the third form of internalism entails the second. For, according to the third form, the judgement that it is right to act in a
certain way is simply equivalent to the judgement that there is a
reason to act in that way.

The reverse does not hold, however. The second internalist
claim does not entail the third. Expressivists, for example, agree
that someone who judges it right to act in a certain way is either
motivated accordingly or practically irrational in some way, but
deny that moral requirements are requirements of rationality or
reason. They thus accept the second internalist claim because
they think that a moral judgement is the expression of a preference, or perhaps the expression of a disposition to have a preference; but they reject the third because they think that fully
rational creatures may yet differ in the preferences that they have,
or are disposed to have.

Let me give the second and third internalist claims names. I will
call the second, the one that may be accepted even by those who
deny the third internalist claim, 'the practicality requirement on
moral judgement'. And, for obvious reasons, I will call the third
internalist claim 'rationalism'. These two forms of internalism
allow us to distinguish corresponding forms of externalism.

One form of externalism amounts to a denial of rationalism. This kind of externalism is consistent with the practicality requirement. Expressivists are typically both externalists and internalists in this sense (Ayer, 1936; Hare, 1952; Blackburn, 1984). They are externalists in so far as they are anti-rationalists, and yet they are also internalists in so far as they accept the practicality requirement on moral judgement. But the other kind of externalism, the stronger form, amounts to a denial of the practicality requirement. Since rationalism entails the practicality requirement, this form of externalism therefore excludes rationalism as well. Many of those who think, against the expressivists, that moral judgements purport to be descriptive are externalists in this stronger sense (Foot, 1972; Sturgeon, 1985; Railton, 1986; Brink, 1986, 1989).

My task in the present chapter is to defend both these forms of internalism – both rationalism and the practicality requirement – against two recent externalist challenges. The first comes from David Brink (1986). Brink's challenge is directed primarily against the weaker internalist claim: that is, against the practicality requirement. The second comes from Philippa Foot (1972). Her challenge is directed primarily against the stronger internalist claim: that is, against rationalism.

In what follows I will begin by clarifying the kind of rationalism to which we are committed by the stronger internalist claim. I then consider Brink's and Foot's challenges in turn. As a matter of fact both Brink and Foot accept the stronger form of externalism, the form that excludes both rationalism and the practicality requirement. However, as we will see, being an externalist of either kind involves far more controversial and counter-intuitive commitments than either Brink or Foot seem to realize.

3.2 RATIONALISM AS A CONCEPTUAL CLAIM VS. RATIONALISM AS A SUBSTANTIVE CLAIM

John Mackie draws a distinction between two quite different claims a rationalist might make (Mackie, 1977: 27–30). As I see it, it is Mackie's appreciation of this distinction that allows him to argue for his 'error theory': the view that all moral thought and talk is infected with an error of presupposition; the presupposition that the world contains objectively prescriptive features (Smith, 1993a).

We can best introduce this distinction by way of an analogy. Suppose we are interested in whether or not there are any witches. How are we to go about answering our question? First we must ask a *conceptual question*. What is our concept of a witch? Let's suppose we answer this conceptual question as follows. Our concept of a witch is the concept of a person who exploits his or her relationship with a supernatural agency in order to cause events to happen in the natural world. Then, second, we must ask a *substantive question*. That is, having now fixed on what our concept of a witch is, we must ask whether there is anything in the world instantiating our concept of a witch. If we do not think that there are any supernatural agencies for anyone to have a relationship with, then we will answer this substantive question in the negative. We will say that there are no witches.

Mackie's idea is that, when we ask whether there are any moral facts, we have to follow exactly the same procedure. We must first of all ask a conceptual question. What is our concept of a moral fact? Mackie answers that our concept of a moral fact is the concept of an 'objectively prescriptive' feature of the world. And then, according to Mackie, we must go on to ask a substantive question. Is there anything in the world answering to our concept of a moral fact? Mackie's answer to this question is, famously, that once we are clear about what it is that we are looking for, we see that there are no moral facts. For we see that our concept of an objectively prescriptive feature is not instantiated anywhere in the world.

I said that Mackie draws our attention to two different claims a rationalist might make. This is because, in light of his distinction between conceptual claims and substantive claims, rationalism might now be taken to be a conceptual claim: the claim that our concept of a moral requirement is the concept of a reason for action; a requirement of rationality or reason. Or alternatively, rationalism might be taken to be a substantive claim. That is, rationalists might be telling us that there are requirements of

rationality or reason corresponding to the various moral requirements. Taken in the first way, rationalism is a claim about the best
analysis of moral terms. Taken in the second way, rationalism is a
claim about the deliverances of the theory of rational action.

As I see it, when Mackie tells us that our concept of a moral fact
is the concept of an objectively prescriptive feature of the world,
he is telling us that the rationalists' conceptual claim is true. And
when he tells us that there are no objectively prescriptive features
in the world, he is telling us that the rationalists' substantive claim
is false. That is, as I see it, Mackie's argument for the error theory
may be reconstructed as follows.

Conceptual truth: If agents are morally required to φ in circumstances C then there is a requirement of
rationality or reason for all agents to φ in
circumstances C

Substantive claim: There is no requirement of rationality or
reason for all agents who find themselves in
circumstances C to φ

Conclusion: Agents are not morally required to φ in circumstances C

That we are able to reconstruct Mackie's argument in this way is
important, for it shows that in defending the rationalists' conceptual claim we do not thereby beg any questions. Even if we accept
the rationalists' conceptual claim, we must still go on to defend
the rationalists' substantive claim. And conversely, even if we
deny the rationalists' substantive claim, we must still engage with
the rationalists' conceptual claim.

This distinction between rationalism as a conceptual claim and
rationalism as a substantive claim is to be central in what follows.
For note that the stronger internalist claim – what I have called
'rationalism' – is simply a claim about our concept of rightness: it
is a claim about the content of an agent's judgement that her
action is right, not a claim to effect that judgements with such
contents are *true*. Moreover, note that it is this conceptual claim
that entails the practicality requirement. The *truth* of the substantive claim is simply not required for that entailment to hold.

It is thus rationalism as a conceptual claim that is to be at issue in the present chapter, not rationalism as a substantive claim. Rationalism as a substantive claim will come up for discussion in later chapters, but for now the focus is to be purely conceptual.

3.3   BRINK'S 'AMORALIST' CHALLENGE

In 'Externalist Moral Realism' David Brink argues that we must reject the practicality requirement. Since the rationalists' conceptual claim entails the practicality requirement, his argument thus threatens to refute rationalism as well. Here is Brink.

> Much moral skepticism is skepticism about the objectivity of morality, that is, skepticism about the existence of moral facts. But another traditional kind of skepticism accepts the existence of moral facts and asks why we should care about these facts. Amoralists are the traditional way of representing this second kind of skepticism; the amoralist is someone who recognizes the existence of moral considerations and remains unmoved.
>
> The . . . [defender of the practicality requirement] . . . must dismiss the amoralist challenge as incoherent . . . We may think that the amoralist challenge is coherent, but this can only be because we confuse moral senses of terms and 'inverted commas' senses of those same terms . . . Thus . . . apparent amoralists . . . remain unmoved, not by what they regard as moral considerations, but only by what others regard as moral considerations.
>
> The problem . . . is that . . . [this] . . . does not take the amoralist's challenge seriously enough . . . We can imagine someone who regards certain demands as moral demands – and not simply as conventional moral demands – and yet remains unmoved . . . [If] . . . we are to take the amoralist challenge seriously, we must attempt to explain why the amoralist should care about morality. (1986: 30)

Brink's argument is simple enough.

According to defenders of the practicality requirement, it is supposed to be a conceptual truth that agents who make moral judgements are motivated accordingly, at least absent weakness of will and the like. But far from this being a conceptual truth, it isn't any sort of truth at all. For amoralists use moral terms to pick out the very same properties we pick out when we use moral terms. Their use of moral terms may therefore be reliably guided by the moral facts in the same way as our uses of those terms. But amoralists differ from us in that they see no reason at all to do what they thus take to be morally required. In other words, amoralists make moral judgements without being motivated accordingly, and without suffering from any sort of practical irrationality either. The practicality requirement is thus false.

As Brink notes, defenders of the requirement have generally not responded to this challenge by boldly denying that amoralists exist. And nor could they with any credibility, for amoralists are among the more popular heroes of both philosophical fantasy and non-philosophical fiction. Brink mentions Plato's Thrasymachus and Dickens's Uriah Heep. But nor are amoralists confined to the world of make-believe. There are, after all, real-life sociopaths like Robert Harris, the thrill-killer whose story is faithfully retold and analysed by Gary Watson (1987). Harris claims that he knew that what he was doing was wrong and that he simply chose to do it anyway; that he felt no conflict. It therefore seems quite wrong to suppose that he suffered from weakness of will, or, perhaps, from any other kind of practical irrationality either.

What defenders of the requirement have tended to insist is therefore rather that, properly described, the existence of amoralists is not inconsistent with the practicality requirement. For, they claim, amoralists do not *really* make moral judgements at all. Even if they do use moral words to pick out the same properties that we pick out when we use moral words, they do not really judge acts to be right and wrong; rather they judge acts to be 'right' and 'wrong'. That is to say they use moral words in a different sense; in the inverted commas sense Brink mentions.

According to Hare, for example, the sentence 'φ-ing is right' as used by an amoralist does not mean 'φ-ing is right'; but rather means 'φ-ing is in accordance with what other people judge to be right' (Hare, 1952: 124–6, 163–5). And, as such, the fact that an amoralist may judge it 'right' to φ without being either motivated to φ or suffering from weakness of will is no counter-example to the requirement. For the requirement tells us that those who judge it right to φ are motivated accordingly, absent weakness of will, not that those who judge is 'right' to φ are motivated accordingly, absent weakness of will.

Now Brink thinks that this inverted commas response doesn't take the amoralist challenge 'seriously' enough. And I must confess that I share his misgivings, at least as regards the details of Hare's version of the response. For, as Brink points out, there seems to be nothing incoherent about the idea of an amoralist who claims to have special insight into what is *really* right and wrong; an amoralist whose judgements about what it is right and wrong to do are therefore, even by her own lights, out of line with the judgements of others. But if this is right, then the judgements of amoralists can hardly be thought of as judgements about what other people judge to be right and wrong.

Despite these misgivings, however, I think that the inverted commas response to the amoralist challenge is along exactly the right lines. In what follows I want therefore to give a two part reply to Brink. First I will say what the inverted commas response really amounts to; how it differs from what Hare says. And second I will say why defenders of the requirement are right to think that the requirement is a conceptual truth.

3.4 REPLY TO BRINK'S CLAIM THAT AMORALISTS REALLY MAKE MORAL JUDGEMENTS

As I see it, defenders of the practicality requirement are right to say that amoralists do not really make moral judgements, they simply go wrong in trying to say more than this. The point is not that amoralists really make judgements of some other kind: about what other people judge to be right and wrong, for example. The point is rather that the *very best* we can say about amoralists is that they try to make moral judgements but fail. In order to see why this is not *ad hoc*, consider an analogy.

There is a familiar problem about the conditions under which we should say of someone that she really makes colour judgements (Peacocke, 1985: chapter 2; Tawil, 1987). The problem can be brought out by reflecting on the case of someone, blind from birth, who has a reliable method of using colour terms. We might imagine that she has been hooked up to a machine from birth that allows her to feel, through her skin, when an object has the appropriate surface reflectance properties.

Now such a person certainly has a facility with colour terms, a facility that allows her to engage in many aspects of the ordinary practice of colour ascription. For she uses terms with the same extension as our colour terms, and the properties of objects that explain her uses of those terms are the very same properties as those that explain our uses of colour terms. (This is similar to what we said earlier about the amoralist's use of moral language.) And we can even imagine, if we like, that her colour judgements are far more accurate and reliable than those made by sighted folk. When she makes colour judgements, she is therefore not appropriately thought of as making judgements about what other people judge to be red, green and the like. (This is again similar to what we have said about the amoralist.)

However, despite the facility such a blind person has with colour language, many theorists have thought that we should still deny that she possesses colour concepts or mastery of colour terms. For, they say, the ability to have the appropriate visual experiences under suitable conditions is partially constitutive of possession of colour concepts and mastery of colour terms (Peacocke, 1985: 29–30, 37–8). And what such theorists thereby commit themselves to saying is that, despite her facility with colour terms, such a blind person does not *really* make colour judgements at all. They do not have to say that she is really making judgements of some other kind, of course. Rather they can insist that though she is trying to make colour judgements, because she doesn't count as a possessor of colour concepts, she fails. When she says 'Fire-engines are red', 'Grass is green' and the like, she is therefore best interpreted as using colour terms in an inverted commas sense: she is saying that fire-engines are 'red', grass is 'green' and so on.

It is, I hope, clear that the structure of this debate over the conditions for mastery of colour terms is in crucial respects identical to the structure of the debate we are engaged in with Brink.

One side says that a subject has mastery of colour terms (moral terms), and thus really makes colour judgements (moral judgements), only if, under certain conditions, being in the psychological state that we express when we make colour judgements (moral judgements) entails having an appropriate visual experience (motivation). The other side denies this holding instead that the ability to use a term whose use is reliably explained by the relevant properties of objects is enough to credit her with mastery of colour terms (moral terms) and the ability really to make colour judgements (moral judgements). Having the appropriate visual experience (motivation) under appropriate conditions is an entirely contingent, and optional, extra. The debate is a real one, so how are we to decide who wins?

Imagine someone objecting that those who say that the capacity to have certain visual experiences is partially constitutive of mastery of colour terms do not take 'seriously' enough the challenge posed by people who can reliably say 'Grass is green', 'Fire-engines are red', and so on, while yet being completely blind. Suppose the objector insists that since blind people can reliably use colour terms in this way, it just follows that they have full mastery of colour terms. Would the objection be a good one? I do not think so. For the objection simply assumes the conclusion it is supposed to be arguing for. It assumes that blind people have mastery of colour terms, something that those who think that mastery requires the capacity to have the appropriate visual experiences under the appropriate conditions deny.

It seems to me that Brink's amoralist challenge is flawed in just this way. He puts a prejudicial interpretation on the amoralist's reliable use of moral terms. He assumes that the amoralist's reliable use is evidence of her mastery of those terms; assumes that being suitably motivated under the appropriate conditions is not a condition of mastery of moral terms. But those who accept the practicality requirement do not accept the account of what it is to have mastery of moral terms that makes this prejudicial interpretation of the amoralist's use of moral terms appropriate.

What this suggests is that, in order to adjudicate the debate with Brink, what we really need is an independent reason for accepting one or the other account of mastery. In what follows I want therefore to provide such an independent reason. The argument is to be that the account of mastery offered by those who defend the practicality requirement is to be preferred because it alone is able to provide a plausible explanation of the reliable connection between moral judgement and motivation in the good and strong-willed person.

3.5   AN ARGUMENT FOR THE PRACTICALITY REQUIREMENT

All we have said so far about the strong externalists' account of moral motivation is that, by their lights, it is a contingent and rationally optional matter whether an agent who believes that it is right to act in a certain way is motivated to act accordingly. But more quite evidently needs to be said.

By all accounts, it is a striking fact about moral motivation that a *change in motivation* follows reliably in the wake of a *change in moral judgement,* at least in the good and strong-willed person. A plausible theory of moral judgement must therefore explain this striking fact. As I see it, those who accept the practicality requirement can, whereas strong externalists cannot, explain this striking fact in a plausible way.

Suppose I am engaged in an argument with you about a fundamental moral question; a question about, say, whether we should vote for the libertarian party at some election as opposed to the social democrats. In order to make matters vivid, we will suppose that I come to the argument already judging that we should vote for the libertarians, and already motivated to do so as well. During the course of the argument, let's suppose you convince me that I am fundamentally wrong. I should vote for the social democrats, and not just because the social democrats will better promote the values that I thought would be promoted by the libertarians, but rather because the values I thought should and would be promoted by libertarians are themselves fundamentally mistaken. You get me to change my most fundamental values. In this sort of situation, what happens to my motives?

Though the precise answer to this question will of course depend, *inter alia*, on the very point at issue, this much at least can be accepted by defenders of the practicality requirement and strong externalists alike. If I am a good and strong-willed person then a new motivation will follow in the wake of my new judgement. So let's add in the assumption that I am a good and strong-willed person. Then, since I no longer judge it right to vote for the libertarians, I will no longer be motivated to do so. And since I have come to judge it right to vote for the social democrats, I will now be motivated to do that instead. The question is: how are we to explain the *reliability* of this connection between judgement and motivation in the good and strong-willed person? How are we to explain why, under a range of counterfactual circumstances, the good and strong-willed person's moral motivations will always fall in line behind her newly arrived at moral judgements?

As I see it, there are only two possible answers. On the one hand we can say that the reliable connection between judgement and movitation is to be explained *internally*: it follows directly from the content of moral judgement itself. The idea will then be either that the belief that an act is right *produces* a corresponding motivation (this is the rationalists' alternative), or perhaps that the attitude of accepting that an act is right is itself *identical* with the state of being motivated (this is the expressivists'). Or, on the other hand, we can say that the reliable connection between judgement and motivation is to be explained *externally*: it follows from the content of the motivational dispositions possessed by the good and strong-willed person. Those who defend the practicality requirement opt for the first answer, strong externalists opt for the second.

Consider the first answer. Since those who defend the practicality requirement think that it is in the nature of moral judgement that an agent who judges it right to φ in circumstances C is motivated to φ in C, at least absent weakness of will or some other such psychological failure, they will insist that it comes as no surprise that in a strong-willed person a *change* of moral motivation follows in the wake of a *change* in moral judgement. For that is just a direct consequence of the practicality requirement.

Moreover, and importantly, note that defenders of the requirement are in a position to insist that what an agent is thus motivated to do when she changes her moral judgement is precisely what she judges it right to do, where this is read *de re* and not *de dicto*. Thus, if an agent judges it right to φ in C, and if she has not derived this judgement from some more fundamental judgement about what it is right to do in C, then, absent weakness of will and the like, defenders of the practicality requirement can insist that she will be motivated non-derivatively to φ in C. This is because, on the rationalist alternative, a non-derivative desire to φ in C is what her judgement that it is right to φ in C causes in her, or because, on the expressivist alternative, the judgement that it is right to φ in C is itself just the expression of such a non-derivative desire. In the example under discussion, then, in deciding that it is right to vote for the social democrats, defenders of the practicality requirement can insist that I acquire a non-derivative concern for social democratic values.

But now consider the second answer, the answer favoured by the strong externalist. She will say that the defender of the practicality requirement has conveniently overlooked a crucial part of the story: namely, the stipulation that I am a *good* and strong-willed person. She will therefore insist that what explains the reliable connection between judgement and motivation is a motivational disposition I have in virtue of which I count as a good person. In other words, what explains the reliability of the connection is the *content of my moral motivation*. But what exactly *is* the content of my moral motivation, according to the strong externalist?

Before the argument began I was motivated to vote for the libertarians. Could it be that it was my having a non-derivative concern for libertarian values that made me count as a good person, when I judged it right to vote for the libertarians? Evidently not. After all, as a result of the ensuing argument I have come to reject my earlier judgement that it is right to vote for the libertarians in favour of the judgement that it is right vote for the social democrats. But since, on this way of seeing things, my initial motivation was not itself rationally mandated by my earlier judgement – since it was just a wholly contingent and rationally optional extra – so the mere fact that I have found reason to change my judgement gives me no reason to change this motive. I may therefore quite rationally continue to be have a desire to vote for the libertarians; though of course I would have to judge that in so doing I am motivated to do something that I now judge wrong. Having a non-derivative concern for liberatarian values while judging it right to vote for the libertarians is thus not what makes me a good person. For it cannot explain why I change my motivation when I change my judgement.

What this forces the strong externalist to admit is that, on their way of seeing things, the motive in virtue of which I am to count as a good person must have a content capable of explaining not just why I am motivated to vote for the libertarians when I judge it right to vote for the libertarians, but also why I stop being motivated to vote for the libertarians when I give up judging that it is right to do so. And the only motivational content capable of playing this role, it seems to me, is a motivation to do the right thing, where this is now read *de dicto* and not *de re*. At bottom, the strong externalist will have to say, having this self-conciously *moral* motive is what makes me a good person.[1]

Note that if this were the content of the good person's motivations, then the strong externalist would indeed be able to explain the reliability of the connection between moral judgement and motivation. A change in the good person's motivations would follow a change in her moral judgements because her motivations would be derived from her judgements together with her self-conciously moral motive. Thus, according to this story, when I no longer believe that it is right to vote for the libertarians, I lose a *derived* desire to vote for them, and when I come to believe that it is right to vote for the social democrats, I acquire a *derived* desire to vote for them. But my motivations are in each case derivative because they are derived from my current judgement about what the right thing to do is together with my basic moral motive: a non-derivative concern to do what is right.

However, if this is the best explanation the strong externalist can give of the reliable connection between moral judgement and motivation in the good and strong-willed person then it seems to me that we have a straightforward *reductio*. For the explanation is only as plausible as the claim that the good person is, at bottom, motivated to do what is right, where this is read *de dicto* and not *de re*, and that is surely a quite implausible claim. For commonsense tells us that if good people judge it right to be honest, or right to care for their children and friends and fellows, or right for people to get what they deserve, then they care non-derivatively about these things. Good people care non-derivatively about honesty, the weal and woe of their children and friends, the well-being of their fellows, people getting what they deserve, justice, equality, and the like, not just one thing: doing what they believe to be right, where this is read *de dicto* and not *de re*. Indeed, commonsense tells us that being so motivated is a fetish or moral vice, not the one and only moral virtue.

It is worthwhile underscoring the present objection by comparing it to a related objection of Bernard Williams's to the kind of moral philosophy that emphasizes impartiality (1976). Williams asks us to consider a man who, when faced with a choice between saving his wife or a stranger, chooses to save his wife. Many moral philosophers think that, even in such a case, a morally good person would be moved by impartial concern; that this man's motivating thought would therefore have to be, at best, 'that it was his wife, and that in situations of this kind it is permissible to save one's wife'. But, Williams objects, this is surely wrong. It provides the husband with 'one thought too many'. And in order to see that this is so he asks us to consider matters from the wife's perspective. She would quite rightly hope that her husband's 'motivating thought, fully spelled out' is that the person he saved was *his wife*. If any further motivation were required then that would simply indicate that he doesn't have the feelings of direct love and concern for her that she rightly wants and expects. He would be alienated from her, treating her as in relevant respects just like a stranger; though, of course, a stranger that he is especially well placed to benefit (Williams, 1976: 18).

The present objection to externalism is like Williams's objection to the kind of moral philosophy that emphasizes impartiality, only more powerful still; for it does not require the assumption, controversial by the lights of some, that morality itself embraces partial values like love and friendship. For the objection in this case is simply that, in taking it that a good person is motivated to do what she believes right, where this is read *de dicto* and not *de re*, externalists too provide the morally good person with 'one thought too many'. They alienate her from the ends at which morality properly aims. Just as it is constitutive of being a good lover that you have direct concern for the person you love, so it is constitutive of being a morally good person that you have direct concern for what you think is right, where this is read *de re* and not *de dicto*. This is something that must be conceded even by those moral philosophers who think that the only right course of action is one of impartiality. They too must agree that a morally good person will have a direct and non-derivative impartial concern; her concern for impartiality must not itself be derived from a more basic non-derivative concern *de dicto* to do the right thing.

We have therefore found a decisive reason to reject the strong externalists' explanation of the reliable connection between moral judgement and motivation in the good and strong-willed person. For, in short, the strong externalists' explanation commits us to false views about the content of a good person's motivations; it elevates a moral fetish into the one and only moral virtue. And the remedy, of course, is to retreat to the alternative, internalist, explanation of the reliability of the connection between moral judgement and motivation. But if we do that then, of course, we have to accept that the practicality requirement is a constraint on the content of a moral judgement after all.

The conclusion is important. For it means that we now have the independent reason we needed for giving an account of mastery of moral terms according to which the practicality requirement is itself a condition of having mastery. Only so can we explain the reliable connection between moral judgement and motivation in the good and strong-willed person. Brink's 'amoralist' challenge thus collapses. For despite the facility they have with moral language, amoralists do not have mastery of moral terms, and they therefore do not really make moral judgements. The fact that they make 'moral' judgements without being motivated or suffering from practical irrationality thus provides us with no challenge to the practicality requirement.

3.6 FOOT'S 'ETIQUETTE' CHALLENGE

Should we accept not just that there is a conceptual connection between moral judgement and motivation, but that there is also a conceptual connection between facts about the rightness of actions and facts about what we have reason to do? In other words, should we accept the rationalists' conceptual claim as well? Philippa Foot argues that we should not.

In 'Morality as a System of Hypothetical Imperatives' Foot has two main aims. First, she wants to explain why we should reject Kant's claim that moral facts are facts about our reasons for action. And second, she wants to set out, in schematic form at least, her own preferred alternative: an anti-rationalist, institutional account of moral facts. In what follows I will first consider Foot's arguments against Kant, and I will then say, more positively, why I think we should accept, with Kant, the rationalists' conceptual claim.

Foot begins by reminding us of Kant's distinction between categorical and hypothetical imperatives: that is, the distinction between requirements that are binding on someone conditionally on her having a certain desire, and requirements that are binding on someone unconditionally, that is whether or not she has a certain desire. The first are the hypothetical imperatives, the second are the categorical imperatives. This distinction is important for Kant because he claims that moral requirements are categorical imperatives, not hypothetical, and he seems to think that granting this is tantamount to the admission that moral requirements are, just as the rationalist supposes, reasons for action binding upon rational creatures as such. However, according to Foot, when we try to make Kant's claim more precise, it becomes either uncontroversial, and so useless as a defence of the rationalists' conceptual claim, or else it becomes unacceptable, *inter alia* because simply equivalent to a statement of that claim. Let me take the horns of this dilemma in turn.

Foot thinks it should be agreed on all sides that moral judgements are appropriately expressed by judgements employing a categorical, rather than a hypothetical, use of 'should'. She explains this distinction by example (1972: 159). Suppose a man wants to go home and in order to do so he has to catch the noon train. We therefore tell him 'You should catch the noon train.' However suppose further that, just before noon, he stops wanting to go home. According to Foot it would then be false for us to tell him that he should catch the noon train. The claim that was earlier true is now false. Here we have the hypothetical use of 'should'. For the truth of the 'should' claim just before noon is defeated by the fact that the man has no desire then that will be served by his doing what we said he should do.

Contrast this use of 'should' with the case in which a man behaves contrary to some moral requirement. Suppose he is cruel. As Foot points out, it is true to say of him that he behaved as he shouldn't even if his being cruel in these circumstances is precisely what he has to do if he is to act in a way that serves *his* interests and desires. But in that case it follows that moral requirements are, in one important sense at any rate, categorical. Since we are not obliged to withdraw the moral 'should' when we find out that acting morally serves no interest or desire of the agent, moral requirements are appropriately expressed by a categorical, as opposed to a hypothetical, use of 'should'.

What is the ground of the categorical use of 'should'? Foot tells us that it has to do with the kinds of consideration required to support the 'should' claim. More specifically, whereas hypothetical 'should' claims can be supported only by showing that the action in question serves a desire or interest of the agent, categorical 'should' claims have to be supported by mentioning some relevant feature of the agent's circumstances. It is the circumstances an agent faces, circumstances that might be faced by another agent with different desires and interests, that makes an action morally required.

However, as Foot reminds us, though in this sense moral requirements are indeed categorical, they are like many other more mundane requirements: for example, requirements of etiquette. Suppose someone acts contrary to a requirement of etiquette. He replies in the first person to a letter written to him in the third. Then, as Foot notes, it is true to say of him that he has acted as he shouldn't even if he tells us (truly) that acting in accordance with the requirements of etiquette in no way serves any interest or desire of his; that in order to achieve what he wants he must reply in the first person. For, as with requirements of morality, 'should' claims of etiquette are supported by citing some relevant feature of the agent's circumstances, circumstances that might be faced by someone with different desires and interests. What makes a requirement a requirement of etiquette is not that acting in the relevant way serves an interest or desire of the agent.

The fact that requirements of etiquette and requirements of morality seem in this respect to be on all fours provides Foot with the materials to complete her argument on the first horn of the dilemma. For no one holds that requirements of etiquette are requirements of reason. Someone who fails to live up to the requirements of etiquette is not, for that reason, deemed to be irrational. But in that case we have an example of a set of requirements appropriately expressed by a categorical use of 'should' that are not themselves requirements of reason. And once this is seen, it follows that admitting that moral requirements are categorical in the uncontroversial sense of being appropriately expressed using a categorical 'should' is thus insufficient to show that moral requirements are requirements of reason.

This gives Foot the materials to argue her case on the second horn of the dilemma, for those who insist that moral requirements are categorical imperatives in the further sense of being requirements of reason have to say what reason they have for supposing this to be so. They can, of course, simply *assert* that this is so. But, according to Foot, such an assertion is evidently controversial and, for that very reason, unacceptable. It runs counter to the orthodox philosophical view of practical rationality, a view she sums up in the following terms.

> Irrational actions are those in which a man in some way defeats his own purposes, doing what is calculated to be disadvantageous or to frustrate his ends. (Foot, 1972: 162)

In other words, practical rationality is a system of hypothetical imperatives, not a system of categorical imperatives. And she therefore draws the inevitable conclusion: 'Immorality does not *necessarily* involve any such thing' (1972: 162). According to Foot, we should therefore reject the rationalists' claim that moral requirements themselves provide us with reasons for action.

But what should we say instead? Foot suggests that the analogy with etiquette goes all the way down. In her view moral facts are, like facts about what etiquette requires of us, *institutional facts* (Foot, 1977). This explains why both sorts of requirement are categorical in the uncontroversial sense. For someone falls within the scope of an institutional norm simply in virtue of the circumstances in which she finds herself; her falling within the scope of the institutional norm is in no way conditional upon the desires that she happens, contingently, to find herself with in those circumstances. And it therefore also explains why neither sort of requirement is a requirement of reason or rationality. For someone who falls within the scope of an institutional norm requiring her to act in a certain way may or may not have a desire that would be satisfied by her acting in that way.

In what follows I want to begin by making some remarks about Foot's own positive view about the nature of moral requirements, her view that there is a substantial and illuminating analogy to be found between moral requirements on the one hand, and requirements of etiquette on the other. In my view, once we spell out the analogy it becomes evident that it breaks down in certain fundamental respects. The upshot is that we must reject Foot's view that moral facts are a kind of institutional fact. I will then consider in some detail her argument against the rationalists' conceptual claim.

3.7 REPLY TO FOOT'S CLAIM THAT MORALITY AND ETIQUETTE ARE ANALOGOUS

Foot does not tell us how exactly we should work out the institutional account of morality in detail, but it is reasonable to assume that it should be worked out along the lines of H. L. A. Hart's account of legal rules (1961). For Hart's is certainly the best and most thoroughly worked out account of institutional norms in the philosophical literature.

Hart's question is: 'What makes for the existence of a legal system?', and he wants an answer to this question that will account for the normativity of law: that is, an account of how the coercive measures of a legal system differ from the mere use of coercive force. His answer is that a legal system is comprised by a set of institutions of a certain kind. More precisely, his answer is that a legal system exists just in case there exists a system of rules that guide conduct, a system of rules that is in turn picked out by a supreme rule of recognition. The existence of a supreme rule of recognition, Hart tells us, is in turn constituted by a pattern of activity amongst a sub-group of those to whom the system of rules as a whole applies, those responsible for formulating the rules, implementing them and enforcing them.

The important feature of this sub-group that makes their activity constitutive of the existence of the rule of recognition, in Hart's view, is the fact that they accept the system of rules as a whole from 'the internal point of view': that is, they are moved by what they take its rules to be, and they want others to be so moved as well, because they think of the system of rules as a whole as justifiable and authoritative. It is this last feature that Hart thinks accounts for the normativity of the law. It explains how the coercive measures of a legal system differ from the mere use of coercive force (Hart, 1961: esp. 97–107).

As I see it, Hart's account of what makes for the existence of a legal system tells us something important about institutional norms, but what it tells us is bad news for the idea that moral requirements are such norms. For though it turns out to be a conceptual truth that institutional norms exist only if the members of a certain sort of sub-group of those to whom the norms apply are motivated in accordance with their beliefs about what the norms require, it is a wholly contingent fact about any particular member of the group to whom the norms apply – members of the sub-group included – whether or not she is motivated to act in accordance with her beliefs about what the norms require.

It follows that it is therefore possible for someone to believe that there exists an insitutional norm requiring her to act in a certain way without being motivated to act accordingly. Not only that, it is also possible that her lack of motivation signals not practical irrationality, but principled hostility to the system as a whole. For she may come to her belief by, say, seeing that those in the special sub-group accept, from the internal point of view, a supreme rule of recognition that entails that there is a certain norm that applies to her, and yet, as an outsider to this sub-group, she might think that their activity is positively unjustifiable. Perhaps, because she hasn't consented to those in the sub-group making up rules that apply to her, she thinks that they should mind their own business. In this way she might not only not accept the system of rules as whole from the 'internal point of view', but accept from the 'internal point of view' a system of norms that sets itself against the institution.

In short – and this may now seem all too obvious – on Hart's account of institutional norms an agent's judgement that there is an institutional norm requiring her to act in a certain way *is not* subject to the practicality requirement. Her motivation to do what she is institutionally required to do must therefore be *externally related* to her judgements about what the institutional norms require of her. Thus, for example, someone who is reliably motivated to act in accordance with the law must desire to do what she is legally obliged to do, where this is read *de dicto* and not *de re*. She must have this motivation because an independent source of motivation would not explain why the connection is *reliable*. Hart embraces this conclusion, of course. For he is a positivist, and so he thinks that it is always possible to raise the question whether or not we should be law-abiding citizens. According to Hart, there may be no reason at all for someone to do what she believes herself legally required to do.

As I see it, Hart's account of institutional norms is well-suited to explaining both the conditions under which norms of etiquette exist and our motivations to do what etiquette requires of us. For the existence of norms of etiquette, like the existence of legal rules as Hart sees things, does seem to be constituted by the activity of a sub-group which makes, changes, and enforces these norms, a sub-group of people who are moved by norms of etiquette because they accept them from the 'internal point of view':

that is, because they think of them as justifiable and authoritative. These are the people who think that it is a good thing that we all mind our manners, and who therefore censure us for our lapses, and praise us for keeping faith: Miss Manners and her kind. Without the activity of this sub-group, the system as a whole would simply collapse.

Moreover our judgements about what etiquette requires of us are at best only externally related to our motivations to act accordingly. Those who reliably do 'the done thing' – insiders to the sub-group, people like Miss Manners – do seem to desire to do what etiquette requires of them where this is read *de dicto*, and not *de re*; those who do not reliably do 'the done thing' do seem to have, at best, some independent source of motivation for doing what they believe etiquette requires of them. The independence of their motivation explains why, if what they are motivated to do is sufficiently at odds with what etiquette requires of them, they may even become actively hostile to doing what etiquette requires of them.

But now, by contrast with this institutional account of requirements of etiquette, the institutional account of moral requirements seems to have no plausibility whatsoever. For a consequence of an institutional account of moral requirements would have to be that our moral judgements too are only *externally related* to our motivations. Morally good people, those who reliably do what they believe they should, would therefore have to be thought of as being motivated to do what they believe they are morally required to do, where this is read *de dicto* and not *de re*. But we have already seen that this is just false. Morally good people are indeed reliably motivated to do what they believe they should, but only if we read this *de re* and not *de dicto*.

In short, the institutional account of moral requirements entails that moral judgements are not subject to the practicality requirement; entails that morally good people are motivated to do what they believe they should, where this is read *de dicto* and not *de re*. But both of these conclusions are false. For reasons we have already seen, we have to think of good people as motivated to do what they believe they should, where this is read *de re* and not *de dicto*, and the only way in which we can do this is by seeing moral judgements as subject to the practicality requirement. But if this is right then it follows that we must reject the institutional account of moral requirements. Foot's own favoured form of anti-rationalism is thus a non-starter. There is no illuminating analogy to be found between morality and etiquette.

3.8   REPLY TO FOOT'S OBJECTION TO THE RATIONALISTS' CONCEPTUAL CLAIM

So far I have focused on Foot's positive claims about the nature of moral requirements. Let me now focus on her negative claims, her explicit argument against Kant. As we will see, her argument turns on an assumption we have no reason to accept.

By all accounts, claims about what we are morally required to do are categorical imperatives: that is, if true, they are made true by facts about the circumstances in which we find ourselves; they cannot be defeated by the simple observation that acting in the way required will not serve any desire or interest that we happen to have. And, according to the rationalist, it is a conceptual truth that claims about what we are morally required to do are claims about our reasons; claims about what we are required by rationality or reason to do. But – and now here is Foot's objection – it is a conceptual truth that requirements of rationality or reason are hypothetical imperatives: that is, they *can* be defeated by the simple observation that acting in the way required does not serve any desire or interest that we happen to have. The rationalists' conceptual claim is therefore false; for a categorical imperative can hardly be analysed in terms of a hypothetical imperative.

My reply to this argument is simple. For note that Foot simply asserts that it is a conceptual truth that requirements of rationality or reason are hypothetical imperatives. She gives no defence of this claim. Perhaps she thinks that no defence is required given that it is philosophical orthodoxy. It is, after all, the view of practical rationality we have inherited from Hume. But it still seems quite wrong to me. As far as I can tell, it is in fact a conceptual truth that requirements of rationality or reason are categorical imperatives, not hypothetical imperatives.

My argument for this claim – that requirements of rationality or reason are categorical imperatives – will be given later (chapter 5). Here, however, I want to show how, on the assumption that requirements of rationality are categorical imperatives, we can clinch the argument for the rationalists' conceptual claim. Note that an extra argument is certainly needed; that the fact that categorical moral requirements are requirements of rationality does not follow *immediately* from the premise that requirements of rationality are categorical imperatives. For, for all that that premise tells us, moral requirements might even be institutional facts: that is, the analogy with etiquette might hold good. What is needed is thus an *argument* for the claim that morality connects in some fundamental way with the categorical requirements of rationality. And such an argument can, I think, be provided.

3.9 AN ARGUMENT FOR THE RATIONALISTS' CONCEPTUAL CLAIM

It seems to me that there is single, powerful, line of argument in support of the rationalists' conceptual claim. The argument trades on the truism that we expect agents to do what they are morally required to do. The argument can be stated as follows.

Moral requirements apply to rational agents as such. But it is a conceptual truth that if rational agents are morally required to act in a certain way then we expect them to act in that way. Being rational, as such, must therefore suffice to ground our expectation that rational agents will do what they are morally required to do. But how could this be so? It could be so only if we think of the moral requirements that apply to agents as themselves categorical requirements of rationality or reason. For the only thing we can legitimately expect of rational agents as such is that they do what they are rationally required to do.

The crucial step in this argument is the premise that we expect rational agents to do what they are morally required to do. It might be thought that this premise trades on a pun on 'expect'; that to say we expect someone to do something can mean either that we believe that they *will*, or that we believe that they *should*.

For the argument to work, the premise has to be interpreted in the former way; but, it might be said, for the premise to be true it has to be interpreted in the latter way. However I think that this is just a mistake. The premise is true when we interpret the claim that we expect rational agents to do what they are morally required to do as the claim that we believe they will.

In order to see this, note that we certainly expect rational agents to do what they *judge* themselves to be morally required to do: that is, we certainly believe not just that they should, but that they will, other things being equal. For this follows directly from the practicality requirement, and, as we have seen, we have no alternative but to accept that: absent practical irrationality, agents will do what they judge to be right, at least other things being equal. However it might be thought this is also the most that we can expect in that sense, and that, because of this, the argument doesn't go through. For even if, other things being equal, rational agents will do what they judge themselves morally required to do, the argument provides us with no reason to think that rational agents will all come up with the same judgements about what they are morally required to do. Rational agents may therefore differ in their moral judgements, differ without being in any way subject to *rational* criticism (Blackburn, 1984; Price, 1988). But if agents may differ in their moral judgements without being subject to rational criticism, then it cannot be that their judgements are about what they are required to do by the categorical requirements of rationality. This is the view taken by expressivists. It is the reason why, even though they accept the practicality requirement, they none the less reject the rationalists' conceptual claim. It is, if you like, the reason why they are expressivists.

In fact, however, the objection backfires. For, as we have seen, it is a platitude that our moral judgements at least purport to be objective (chapters 1 and 2). Thus if A says 'It is right to φ in circumstances C' and B says 'It is not right to φ in circumstances C' then we take it that A and B *disagree*; that at most one of their judgements is true. And that means, in turn, that we take it that we can fault at least one of A's and B's judgements from the rational point of view, for it is false. But if this is right then it follows that, just as the argument says, we do in fact expect *rational* agents to do what they are morally required to do, not just what they judge themselves to be morally required to do. For we can and do expect rational agents to judge *truly*; we expect them to *converge* in their judgements about what it is right to do. Our concept of a moral requirement thus turns out to be the concept of a categorical requirement of rationality after all.

Indeed, to the extent that we do not expect an agent to do the right thing, but perhaps only what she believes to be right, it can now be seen that our lesser expectation reflects our view of the agent as to some extent irrational; as someone who fails to live up to the requirements of reason to the extent that she should. For it reflects our view of her as someone who will not correct her false belief about what she is morally required to do before she acts. And this in turn suggests a range of other reasons why we might not expect an agent who is morally required to φ in fact to φ. For there are all sorts of ways in which agents can fail to live up the requirements of reason; all sorts of ways in which they can be practically irrational. They may suffer from weakness of will, or compulsion, or any of a range of other forms of practical un-reason (Pettit and Smith, 1993a). Importantly, however, none of these reasons for modifying our expectation shows that there is anything wrong with the crucial premise in the argument: the premise that we expect *rational* agents to do what they are morally required to do, in the sense of believing that they will, at least other things being equal. Indeed, all of these reasons for modify-ing our expectations *presuppose* the truth of that crucial premise, for they suggest that a modification of our expectation requires some form practical irrationality or unreason.

As I see it, the argument given is therefore sound. Our concept of a moral requirement is indeed the concept of a categorical requirement of rationality or reason. Moreover, note that we can reach this same conclusion from another direction. For, as I see it, the appropriateness of a whole range of moral attitudes depends upon the truth of the rationalists' conceptual claim. Approval and disapproval, for example, must lie somewhere close to the heart of any account of morality. For it is a datum that we approve and disapprove of what people do when moral matters are at stake: we approve of those who do the right thing and disapprove of those who do the wrong thing. But, as I will now go on to argue, such attitudes themselves presuppose the legitimacy of our expectation that rational people will act rightly, and so, in turn, presuppose the truth of the rationalists' conceptual claim.

In order to see why this is so, we need to remind ourselves of the difference between approval and disapproval on the one hand, and mere liking and disliking on the other. Foot herself makes the following remarks about the difference.

> What anyone can want or like is not restricted, logically speaking, by facts about his relationship to other people, as for instance that he is a friend or a parent of one, and engaged in a joint enterprise with another. Such facts can, however, create possibilities of approving and disapproving that would otherwise not exist. (Foot, 1977: 194)

In other words, whereas we can like and dislike more or less what we please, we cannot just approve and disapprove of what we please. Certain relationships between those who approve or disapprove on the one hand, and those who are approved or disapproved of on the other, are presupposed by the attitudes of approval and disapproval.

> [T]he attitudes of approval and disapproval would not be what they are without the existence of tacit agreement on the question of who listens to whom and about what. (Foot, 1977: 198)
>
> [A]pproval and disapproval can, logically speaking, exist only against a background of agreement about the part that other people's views shall be given in decision making. (Foot, 1977: 199)

Thus, according to Foot, it makes sense to say that I disapprove of your behaviour only if we presuppose that you are to take account of that fact in deciding what to do. But in order for it to make sense that I merely dislike your behaviour, we need to presuppose no such thing. Consider an example by way of illustration.

Suppose you eat peppermint ice-cream, and that I just can't stand it when people do that. What would it be appropriate for me to say: that I dislike your eating peppermint ice-cream, or that I disapprove of your eating peppermint ice-cream? According to Foot, it only makes sense to say that I disapprove if you are to take account of that fact in deciding what to do. For to say that I disapprove of your behaviour, as opposed to merely dislike it, signals the fact that, as I see it, your behaviour transgresses the standards in terms of which you and I both acknowledge your behaviour is to be judged. In other words, disapproval presupposes that your behaviour is contrary to my legitimate expectations; my beliefs about how you will behave. Disliking your behaviour presupposes no such thing.

However, if this is right, then it follows immediately that approval and disapproval are only ever in place when there exist *grounds* for legitimate expectations about how someone will behave. One obvious area in which approval and disapproval are in place is therefore the area of rational decision-making. For we all expect of each other that we will decide what to do on rational grounds. As Foot notes, however, this is not the only area in which approval and disapproval are in place. The members of a chess club may well disapprove of a fellow member who moves his castle on the diagonal, for instance, and their disapproval may survive the discovery that, in the context, this is not an irrational thing for him to do. For even if he has good reasons for doing what he does, he still acts contrary to their legitimate expectations, for he acts in violation of an agreement he either tacitly or explicitly entered into by becoming a member of the club, the agreement to move his chess pieces in accordance with the rules. Their legitimate expectation is thus that those who do not want to play by the rules will not play at all.

I began by saying that it is a datum that we approve and disapprove of what people do when moral matters are at stake. But now, in light of our account of the preconditions for approval and disapproval, an obvious question presents itself. Consider, for instance, disapproval of those who act contrary to moral requirements. Such disapproval is ubiquitous. Yet how can this be? For, as we have seen, disapproval of those who do not do what they are morally required to do presupposes the legitimacy of our expectation that they will act otherwise; it presupposes that, as we see it, their decision is a bad one in terms of the commonly acknowledged standards by which their decisions are to be judged. But what provides grounds for the legitimacy of this expectation? In virtue of what are there commonly acknowledged standards by which their decisions are to be judged?

Note how implausible it would be to suppose that what grounds the legitimacy of this expectation is the fact that rational creatures have each entered into an agreement to act morally, an agreement on a par with the agreement the chess player either tacitly or explicitly enters into by becoming a member of a chess club. For no such agreements have ever been made. Perhaps we should say instead that what grounds our expectation is not an agreement rational creatures have in fact made, but rather an agreement they would make if they were . . . If they were what? If they were rational, of course! But in that case we have abandoned the idea that what grounds the legitimacy of our expectation is the fact of agreement in favour of the alternative. What grounds the legitimacy of our expectation is the mere fact that people are rational agents. Being rational suffices to ground the expectation that people will do what they are morally required to do. Given that moral approval and disapproval are ubiquitous, the truth of the rationalists' conceptual claim thus seems to be entailed by the fact that the preconditions of moral approval and disapproval are satisfied.

It is worth remarking that Foot acknowledges that her views about the preconditions for moral approval and moral disapproval are in apparent conflict with the institutional account of moral requirements she favours. She asks, for example:

> What . . . are we to say about those who altogether reject morality? Surely we think it possible to disapprove of their actions, although they do not agree to take any account of what we say? This is true, and it is an important fact about the phenomenon that we call 'morality' that we are ready to bring pressure to bear against those who reject it. But this no more shows that moral attitudes do not depend on agreement within human society than the possibility of asserting other kinds of authority against those who do not accept it shows that authority requires no agreement . . . [W]e will confront them with the confidence that we have the world with us – the world that pays at least lip service to morality. (Foot, 1977: 205)

But her reply entirely misses the point. For even if, on Foot's institutional account of morality, we in the special sub-group who get to set the standards, change them and enforce them, can in some way be said to enter into an agreement to make our decisions on moral matters in a certain way, those who reject morality are, by her account, not a party to this agreement. The 'world' we have with us when we confront 'them' is thus, for them, simply a mob forcing its commonly agreed standard on another group whose agreement they do not have. The institutions that Foot thinks suffice to undergird a shared standard of decision-making thus undergird no such thing. They provide no basis at all for the expectation that those who reject morality will make their decisions in the way 'we' will. That requires the truth of the rationalists' conceptual claim, a claim that Foot is in no position to endorse.[2]

3.10   SUMMARY AND PREVIEW

My aim in this chapter has been to consider and defend two forms of internalism: the practicality requirement on moral judgement and the rationalists' conceptual claim. In the course of doing so I have considered and rejected two powerful arguments for externalism: David Brink's 'amoralist' challenge to the practicality requirement, and Philippa Foot's 'etiquette' challenge to the rationalist's conceptual claim.

If my arguments in this chapter have been on the right track, then it follows that, contrary to both Brink and Foot, our judgements about what we are morally required to do are simply judgements about what the categorical requirements of rationality or reason demand of us. However this is bound to raise eyebrows. For it is commonly held that the standard account of human psychology, the account of belief and desire we get from Hume, is inconsistent with the very coherence of the claim that there are categorical requirements of rationality. In the next two chapters I therefore turn to consider Hume's psychological theory in its own terms. How much of Hume's theory should we keep, how much should we reject? I begin by considering Hume's views about human motivation.

4

The Humean Theory of Motivation

4.1 TWO PRINCIPLES

It has been argued that the Humean theory of motivation (here-after the 'Humean theory') is a dogma in philosophical psycho-logy, that the dogma is fundamentally incorrect, and that it should therefore be replaced in philosophical psychology with a more plausible theory of motivation. I am thinking in particular of recent work by Thomas Nagel (1970), John McDowell (1978, 1979, 1981) and Mark Platts (1979, 1981). But what is the Humean dogma?

The Humeans in fact seem committed to two claims about motivating reasons, a weaker and a stronger. However there is no agreement among anti-Humeans as to whether the weaker and the stronger are both equally unacceptable, or whether it is only the stronger that we have reason to reject. According to the stronger claim – the claim that is, as I understand it, crucial to the Humean theory – motivation has its source in the presence of a relevant desire and means-end belief. This claim finds more for-mal expression in the following principle (Davidson, 1963):

P1   R at t constitutes a motivating reason of agent A to φ iff there is some ψ such that R at t consists of an appropriately related desire of A to ψ and a belief that were she to φ she would ψ.

To say that the desire and belief must be 'appropriately related' is merely to acknowledge that in order for a desire and belief to constitute a motivating reason the agent must, as it were, put the relevant desire and belief together (Smith, 1988b).

Anti-Humeans are united in their rejection of P1. However P1 entails the weaker principle that motivation requires the *presence* of a relevant desire and means-end belief, a principle that is in turn consistent with denying the constitution claim made in P1. Thus we have the following weaker principle:

P2   Agent A at t has a motivating reason to φ only if there is some ψ such that, at t, A desires to ψ and believes that were she to φ she would ψ

and anti-Humeans are not at all united in their rejection of P2. Thus, for instance, whereas Nagel (1970: 29), and McDowell following him (1978: 15), have argued that P2 is acceptable because consistent with the claim that the desires and means-end beliefs that must be present whenever there is motivation are not themselves the *source* of such motivation – that is, because consistent with denying the constitution claim made in P1 – other anti-Humeans, such as Platts, have argued that P2 is also unacceptable because either 'phenomenologically false . . . or utterly vacuous' (1979: 256).

I am inclined to agree with the anti-Humeans that the Humean theory is a dogma in philosophical psychology, at least in the sense that both P1 and P2 seem to find a fair degree of uncritical acceptance. However, unlike the anti-Humeans, I do not believe that the Humean theory, as characterized by P1, is fundamentally incorrect, and thus I do not think that P2 is 'utterly vacuous'.

My task in this chapter is to offer an explicit argument for the Humean theory and to defend it against objections offered by Nagel, McDowell and Platts. If the argument offered here is correct then the Humean theory is the expression of a simple but important truth about the nature of motivating reasons, a truth that anti-Humeans have failed to appreciate either because they have failed to distinguish motivating reasons from other sorts of reasons, or because they have an inadequate conception of desire, or because they have overlooked the implications of the fact that reason explanations are teleological.

4.2 MOTIVATING REASONS VS.
NORMATIVE REASONS

P1 is a principle connecting *motivating* reasons with desires and beliefs. We must begin by emphasizing this fact, otherwise it will seem simply implausible to suppose that P1 provides individually necessary or jointly sufficient conditions for a state's constituting a motivating reason.

In order to see this, consider the following counter-examples to the claim that P1 provides necessary conditions:

(i)   Suppose I now desire to purchase an original Picasso, but I do not now believe that were I to purchase the painting before me I would do so – suppose I don't believe that it is a Picasso. If the painting before me is indeed a Picasso, then surely it would be appropriate for an outsider to say I have a reason to purchase the painting before me. But I lack the relevant belief.

(ii) Suppose I knowingly stand on someone's foot so causing that person pain. Surely we can imagine its being appropriate for an outsider to say I have a reason to get off the person's foot even though I lack the relevant desire, and, indeed, even if I desire to cause that person pain.

Consider now the following counter-example to the claim that P1 provides a sufficient condition:

(iii) Suppose I now desire to drink a gin and tonic and believe I can do so by mixing the stuff before me with tonic and drinking it (Williams, 1980). Suppose further that this belief is false; that the stuff before me is petrol rather than gin. Surely it would be appropriate for an outsider to say I have no reason to mix this stuff with tonic and drink it. Yet I have both the relevant belief and desire.

Do we have, in examples like these, the makings of an objection to P1, and hence to the Humean theory? We do not. The reason why was perhaps evident from the start. The outsider's perspective is not irrelevant to the examples.

Michael Woods argued some time ago that 'the concept of a reason for an action stands at the point of intersection, so to speak, between the theory of the explanation of actions and the theory of their justification' (1972: 189). Woods's idea was that reasons – *all* reasons – have both an explanatory and a justificatory dimension. I doubt very much that that claim is true, something I will argue for explicitly later (chapter 5). However Woods is surely right that our concept of a reason for action is loosely defined by these two dimensions of explanation and justification. Indeed, it seems to me that we work with two quite different concepts of a reason for action depending on whether we emphasize the explanatory dimension and downplay the justificatory, or *vice versa*. The claim 'A has a reason to φ' is thus itself ambiguous. It may be a claim about a *motivating* reason A has, when we emphasize the explanatory dimension and downplay the justificatory, or a claim about a *normative* reason A has, when we emphasize the justificatory dimension and downplay the explanatory. Let me say a little about the similarities and differences between these two sorts of reasons.

Motivating and normative reasons do have something in common in virtue of which they both count as reasons. For citing either would allow us to render an agent's action intelligible. This is essential. For there is an *a priori* connection between citing an agent's reasons for acting in a certain way and making her acting in that way intelligible: that is, specifying what there is to be said for acting in the way in question. In virtue of their differences, however, motivating and normative reasons make actions intelligible for quite different reasons.

To say that someone has a normative reason to φ is to say that there is some normative requirement that she φ's, and is thus to say that her φ-ing is justified from the perspective of the normative system that generates that requirement. As I see it, and as I will argue later, normative reasons are thus best thought of as truths: that is, propositions of the general form 'A's φ-ing is desirable or required' (chapter 5). These truths may well be many and varied, as many and varied as there are normative systems for generating requirements. Thus, for example, there may be normative reasons of rationality, prudence, morality, and perhaps even normative reasons of other kinds as well. The number of different kinds of normative reasons will ultimately depend on the extent to which we can reduce one kind of normative reason to another; for example, whether, as I will argue here, we can reduce moral requirements to rational requirements.

Motivating reasons are, however, different. The distinctive feature of a motivating reason to φ is that, in virtue of having such a reason, an agent is in a state that is *explanatory* of her φ-ing, at least other things being equal – other things must be equal because an agent may have a motivating reason to φ without that reason's being overriding. Given that an agent who has a motivating reason to φ is in a state that is in this way potentially explanatory of her φ-ing, it is thus natural to suppose that her motivating reason is itself *psychologically real*. For it would seem to be part of our concept of what it is for an agent's reasons to have the potential to explain her behaviour that her having those reasons is a fact about her; that the goals that such reasons embody are *her* goals. By contrast with normative reasons, then, which seem to be *truths* of the form 'It is desirable or required that I φ', motivating reasons would seem to be *psychological states*, states that play a certain explanatory role in producing action.[1]

If this way of marking the distinction between motivating and normative reasons seems right, then we are in a position to draw the following lessons. First, motivating reasons and normative reasons are of quite different *categories*. For whereas motivating reasons are psychological states, normative reasons are propositions of the general form 'A's φ-ing is desirable or required'. And, second, we have so far been given no reason to suppose that there is any general connection between the two sorts of reasons. For all we have seen so far, an agent may therefore have a motivating reason to φ without having any normative reason to φ, and she may have a normative reason to φ without having any motivating reason to φ. Given these lessons we must therefore emphasize the fact that P1 purports to give necessary and sufficient conditions for the existence of motivating reasons. P1 is silent about whether or not A has some normative reason.

Let's now return to the examples that were supposed to make trouble for P1 with this distinction between motivating and normative reasons in mind. What we see is that they simply confirm the idea that there is little connection between the two sorts of reasons. For the outsider's perspective draws our attention to a relevant normative requirement in each case. The examples thus in no way challenge the claim that an agent has a motivating reason if and only if she has a relevant desire and belief.

In (i), for example, it suffices for the truth of the claim that I have a reason to buy the painting in front of me that there is a requirement – in this case, in the broad sense, a requirement of rationality – that I buy the painting in front of me.[2] For I think that buying a Picasso is desirable and the painting in front of me is indeed a Picasso. But the existence of such a normative reason does not suffice for my having a motivating reason to buy the painting in front of me. This is because, since I do not believe that painting is a Picasso, I am not in a state that is potentially explanatory of my buying it. (I am, of course, in a psychological state that is potentially explanatory of my buying a Picasso, for I desire to buy a Picasso and believe that were I to buy a Picasso I would buy a Picasso. But this is not to have a motivating reason to buy the painting in front of me. It is rather to have a motivating reason to buy a Picasso. The Humean will thus regard an agent's desire to ϕ, together with the trivial belief that were she to ϕ she would ϕ, as the limiting case of having a motivating reason to ϕ.) The example thus in no way undermines the necessity of having a means-end belief for having a motivating reason. It merely draws our attention to the fact that I may have no motivating reason to do what I am rationally required to do.

A similar point applies in (ii), the case in which I have a reason to get off someone's foot when I am causing him pain. For it suffices for the truth of the claim that I have a reason to get off his foot that there exists a requirement – in this case moral – that I do not cause him pain, and that, in the present circumstances, in order to comply with that requirement I have to get off his foot. But, once again, the mere existence of this normative reason is consistent with the claim that I am not in a state that is potentially explanatory of my behaviour. Indeed, note that this must be conceded even if the argument of this book as a whole is right and moral reasons are themselves rational requirements on action.

For, as we have already seen, rational requirements are in turn simply further normative reasons, and may thus exist in the absence of motivating reasons. Thus this kind of example does not by itself show that having a desire is not a necessary condition for having a motivating reason.

Consider now (iii), the counter-example to the sufficiency of the condition. In what sense do I not have a reason to mix the stuff before me with tonic and drink it? Once again it seems that the reason is normative rather than motivating. For I am certainly in a state that is potentially explanatory of my mixing the stuff before me with tonic and drinking it. After all, I desire to drink a gin and tonic and believe that the stuff before me is gin. Moreover, if we did explain my doing so by citing that desire and belief my doing so would certainly be made intelligible. For I could be seen as aiming at a goal that I have. Thus, though there is a sense in which I do not have a reason to mix the stuff before me with tonic and drink it – prudence, for example, would counsel me against doing so – the reason I lack is a normative reason. It seems entirely correct to suppose that I now have a motivating reason to do just this. We thus have here no counter-example to the claim that P1 provides a sufficient condition for a state's constituting a motivating reason.

To sum up: in the light of the distinction between motivating and normative reasons, we have seen that the Humeans' is a theory about the nature of motivating reasons. The Humean theory may yet be false. But it is not shown to be false simply by showing that P1 fails to give necessary and sufficient conditions for the existence of a variety of normative reasons.

4.3   A PRELIMINARY OBJECTION FROM NAGEL

Note that the two claims just argued for – that there is a distinction between motivating and normative reasons, and that the Humean theory is a theory about the former, not the latter – suffice to undermine one of Thomas Nagel's main arguments against the Humean theory in *The Possibility of Altruism* (1970).

Nagel's objection centres on the Humeans' explanation of prudential motivation.

Prudential motivation is possible only if an agent's recognition of the fact that she will have a desire to φ in the future somehow gives her a reason now to take steps to promote her φ-ing then. The task of explaining this possibility takes on a particular form for the Humean. For, as we have seen, he holds that now having a motivating reason to φ requires currently desiring to φ. He must therefore explain how an agent's recognition that she will desire to φ in the future gives rise to a present desire to promote her φ-ing then. The Humean's answer is fairly predictable. He says that agents who are motivated by prudential considerations each have a quite general present desire to further their future interests.

Nagel offers the following objection to the Humean's explanation of prudence.

> The two features of the system to which I object are (a) that it does not allow the expectation of a future reason to provide by itself any reason for present action, and (b) that it does allow the present desire for a future object to provide by itself a reason for present action in pursuit of that object. (1970: 39)

Thus, as he points out, the following constitute possibilities under the Humean theory.

> First, given that any desire with a future object provides a basis for reasons to do what will promote that object, it may happen that I now desire for the future something which I shall not and do not expect to desire then, and which I believe there will then be no reason to bring about. Consequently I may have a reason now to prepare to do what I know I will have no reason to do when the time comes.
>
> Second, suppose that I expect to be assailed by a desire in the future: then I must acknowledge that in the future I will have a *prima facie* reason to do what the desire indicates. But this reason does not obtain now, and cannot by itself apply derivatively to any presently available means to the satisfaction of the future desire. Thus in the absence of any further relevant desire in the present, I may have no reason to prepare for what I know I shall have reason to do tomorrow. (1970: 39–40)

The response Nagel wants to elicit from us, faced by these examples, is that in the first case I have no reason to promote the future object despite my present desire, and that in the second, I do have a reason to promote the object of my future desire despite my lacking a relevant present desire.

We do have this response, and it seems to me that we are right to. But I do not think that this fact counts against the Humean theory. In order to see why, consider Nagel's own summary objection to the Humean theory's licensing such possibilities.

> A system with consequences such as this not only fails to require the most elementary consistency in conduct over time, but in fact sharpens the possibilities of conflict by grounding an individual's plottings against his future self in the apparatus of rationality. These are formal and extremely general difficulties about the system, since they concern the relation of what is rational to what will be rational, no matter what source of reasons is operative. (1970: 40–1)

Thus if we accept Nagel's own diagnosis of our response to these examples – and I think we should – it emerges that examples like these fail even to touch the Humean. For, to take just the first (the problem with the second is much the same), Nagel's objection to the Humean's claim that an agent may have a motivating reason now to promote her φ-ing in the future, despite the fact that she believes that she will have no motivating reason to φ then, is that it would now be irrational to do so; that she now has no reason from the perspective of rationality to do so (see also Nagel, 1970: 64–5). But this is to conflate the claim that an agent has a motivating reason to φ with the claim that she has a normative reason from the perspective of rationality to φ. The Humean is making only the first claim, not the second.

Moreover, if Nagel is right that it is irrational for an agent to promote her φ-ing in the future if she believes that she will then have no motivating reason to φ, then the Humean theorist of motivation can accept this on his own terms, perhaps by claiming that since there is a normative reason of rationality for agents to promote their future interests, so a theory of rationality requires agents to have the desire to promote their future interests (Parfit,

1984: 131–6). For, importantly, the tasks of constructing a theory of motivating reasons and a theory of the normative reasons are just different tasks.[3]

I therefore do not see that the rationality of prudence makes for a special difficulty with the Humean's theory of motivation. To think it does requires a conflation of the Humean theory of motivation with a theory of rationality.

4.4 WHY SHOULD WE BELIEVE THE HUMEAN THEORY?

We have seen that we will find no easy refutation of P1 – the claim that motivating reasons are constituted by appropriately related desires and means-end beliefs – by reflecting on those cases in which we would ordinarily say of someone that she has a reason to φ. But can we find some reason actually to believe this claim?

John McDowell has attempted to diagnose commitment to the Humean theory (1981). He begins by isolating what he takes to be the theory's distinctive feature, that 'to cite a cognitive propositional attitude', that is a belief, 'is to give at most a partial specification of a reason for acting; to be fully explicit, one would need to add a mention of something non-cognitive, a state of the will or a volitional event' (1981: 155): that is, in the terms in which we have put it, a desire. He continues:

> I suspect that one reason people find . . . [this claim] . . . obvious lies in their inexplicit adherence to a quasi-hydraulic conception of how reason explanations account for action. The will is pictured as the source of forces that issue in the behaviour such explanations explain. This idea seems to me a radical misconception of the sort of explanation a reason explanation is, but it is not my present concern. (1981: 155)

But what exactly is a 'quasi-hydraulic' conception of reason-explanation?

According to a quasi-hydraulic conception of reason-explanations, the mind is an arena where various forces or pressures

(McDowell says 'desires') get channelled (via beliefs) in certain directions and ultimately combine together to produce a result-ant force or pressure (an action). Perhaps McDowell is right that commitment to such a conception of reason-explanations has, in the past, explained why people accept the Humean theory. But even if we agree with McDowell that such a conception is a 'radical misconception', it is not clear how this would be supposed to cast doubt on the Humean theory. Indeed, to suppose it does sounds a lot like affirming the consequent. What would cast doubt on the Humean theory is not the fact that some people who accept it do so or have done so because they adhere to a mistaken conception of reason-explanation, but rather that adhering to the Humean theory itself *requires* adherence to such a mistaken conception of reason-explanation. But, as I now want to argue, this last claim is manifestly implausible. Far from being committed to a quasi-hydraulic conception of reason-explanations, the Humean is not even committed to a causal conception of reason expla-nations. Given that a quasi-hydraulic conception is one form a causal conception might take, it follows that the Humean is simply not committed to a quasi-hydraulic conception of reason-explanations.

In order to see this, consider the following argument causal theorists actually give for a causal conception of reason expla-nations (Davidson, 1963: 8–11). 'What is the feature that makes the difference between the case in which an agent φs *and* has a reason to φ and the case in which she φs *because* she has reason to φ? The only illuminating answer available' says the causal theorist, 'is that the reasons in the second case – the case in which the reason explains the action – *cause* her φ-ing.' Now I am not here concerned with the merits of this argument. Rather what I want to emphasize is the fact that the argument makes no substantial assumption about the nature of motivating reasons. Thus, for all that this argument tells us, motivating reasons may be constituted by beliefs or by desires or by some other kind of psychological state altogether. However, if this is right, it follows that we should be able to accept or reject this argument quite independently of our views concerning the theory of motivation.

Suppose, for example, that we reject Davidson's argument. It seems evident enough why we might do so. For we might think that there is something more basic and yet still illuminating to say about the 'because' in 'She φs because she has a reason to φ'. For, we might say, the 'because' here signals the availability of a *teleological* explanation of the agent's φ-ing in terms of her reason for φ-ing, an explanation that is not necessarily available when all we know is that the agent φs *and* has a reason for φ-ing (McGinn, 1982: 99–100; Wilson, 1985: 31–2). Moreover, we might say, it is controversial, and certainly not forced merely by the fact that we have to admit the difference between 'She φs and she has a reason to φ' and 'She φs because she has a reason to φ', to suppose that this teleological explanation can be further cashed out in *causal* terms. Importantly, however, note that this is something that the Humean and anti-Humean theorist of motivation may each *equally* say in response to the argument just given for the causal theory. For there is nothing in the debate about the theory of motivation *per se* that forces us to suppose that motivating reasons are causally, rather than merely teleologically, explanatory. Indeed, the causal theory is best thought of as a further, and perhaps optional, interpretation of the claim that reason explanations are teleological.

Now suppose that we accept Davidson's argument; that we think that the best interpretation of the teleological character of reason explanations is an interpretation in causal terms. Then, to be sure, we must conceive of some psychological states as possessing the causal power to produce behaviour. But, again, we need not think that desires are the only psychological state that possess such causal power. We might think instead that only certain beliefs, or some other psychological states altogether, possess such causal power. Whether we think of desires or beliefs or some other psychological state altogether as possessing causal power will, of course, depend on whether we accept a Humean or an anti-Humean theory of motivation. But that should now seem to be wholly independent of whether or not we should in addition accept a causal interpretation of the teleological character of reason explanations.

The upshot seems therefore to be that Humean and anti-Humean theorists of motivation are engaged in a debate that is both independent of and more fundamental than the debate over whether reason explanations are a species of quasi-hydraulic, or even simply causal, explanation. In short the difference is this. The causal and non-causal theorist can both accept that reason explanations are teleological explanations without enquiring further into what it is about the nature of reasons that makes it possible for reason explanations to be teleological explanations – that is, explanations that explain by making what they explain intelligible in terms of the pursuit of a goal. For their disagreement concerns the further question whether such teleological explanations are themselves in turn a species of causal explanation, a disagreement which may, as I have suggested, cut across disagreements concerning the nature of reasons themselves. But, as I see it, the Humean and anti-Humean are precisely engaged in a dispute concerning what it is about the nature of reasons that makes it possible for reason explanations to be teleological explanations.

If this is right, then it would seem that there will be only one reason to believe the Humean's theory, if indeed we should believe his theory at all, and that is that his theory alone is able to make sense of motivation as the pursuit of a goal. In what follows I will argue that this is indeed the case. I proceed by focusing on two different conceptions of desire. One of these gives no support to the Humean theory. I argue that this conception is anyway implausible. Perhaps unsurprisingly it seems to be the conception of desire held by many opponents of the Humean theory. There is, however, an alternative and more plausible conception. This conception enables us to see that desires must be constituents of motivating reasons given that an agent's motivating reasons must themselves be constituted by her having certain goals.

4.5   DESIRES AND PHENOMENOLOGY

What is a desire?

According to Hume, desires are a species of the passions, and passions are, in turn, a certain kind of feeling. Hume seems to hold that this is so not just in the trivial sense that passions are a species of perception and perceptions are a kind of feeling (1888:

190). Rather he suggests that when we desire something 'we feel an . . . emotion of aversion or propensity' (1888: 414). His view thus seems to be that we are 'directly aware' of the presence of the desires that we have; that desires are themselves phenomenologically salient (Stroud, 1977: 163).

Hume's suggestion is not entirely misguided. There is, after all, such a thing as the phenomenology of desire, as, for instance, to use one of Hume's own examples, 'when I am angry I am possest with the passion' (1888: 416). That is, we may agree with Hume that, on occasion, when I have a desire, I have certain psychological feelings, analogues of bodily sensations. This may suggest a way of elaborating Hume's view. For if we take up his suggestion that all desires are known by the way they make us feel, then, in an attempt to explain why this is so, we may be led to identify desires with such psychological feelings. And this may in turn lead us to endorse what I will call the 'strong phenomenological conception' of desires: the view that desires are, like sensations, simply and essentially states that have a certain phenomenological content.

Perhaps unsurprisingly, I think that the strong phenomenological conception of desire ought to be rejected. For it seems to me that there is no way such a conception can be married with a plausible epistemology of desire.

Now it might be thought that this objection doesn't even get off the ground. The strong phenomenological conception of desire makes the epistemology of desire unproblematic, it might be said, because on that conception the epistemology of desire becomes just like the epistemology of sensation. Just as it is plausible to hold that a subject is in pain if and only if she believes that she is in pain – for we take it that a subject is in a state with a certain phenomenological content if and only if she believes herself to be in a state with that content – so, if we think of desires on the model of sensations, it is plausible to hold that a subject desires to ϕ if and only if she believes that she desires to ϕ.

What exactly is wrong with this line of thought? There are two things wrong with it. To begin, and most straightforwardly, the principle 'Subjects desire to ϕ if and only if they believe they desire to ϕ' is simply false. I argue by counter-example.

Suppose each day on his way to work John buys a newspaper at a certain newspaper stand. However, he has to go out of his way to do so, and for no apparently good reason. The newspaper he buys is on sale at other newspaper stands on his direct route to work, there is no difference in the price or condition of the newspapers bought at the two stands, and so on. There is, however, the following difference. Behind the counter of the stand where John buys his newspaper, there are mirrors so placed that anyone who buys a newspaper there cannot help but look at himself. Let's suppose, however, that if it were suggested to John that the reason he buys his newspaper at that stand is that he wants to look at his own reflection, he would vehemently deny it. And it wouldn't seem to John as if he were concealing anything in doing so. However, finally, let's suppose that if the mirrors were removed from the stand, his preference for that stand would disappear.

If all this were the case, wouldn't it be plausible to suppose that John in fact desires to buy his newspaper at a stand where he can look at his own reflection; that, perhaps, he has a narcissistic tendency and buying his newspaper at that stand enables him to indulge it on the way to work? And wouldn't it also be plausible to suppose that he does not believe that this is so, given his, from his point of view, sincere denials? If this is agreed, then we have reason to reject the principle left to right: that is, we have reason to deny that if a subject desires to φ then she believes that she desires to φ.[4]

Consider another example. Suppose John professes that one of his fundamental desires is to be a great musician. However, his mother has always drummed into him the value of music. She is a fanatic with great hopes for her son's career as a musician, hopes so great that she would be extremely disappointed if he were even less than an excellent musician, let alone if he were to give up music altogether. Moreover, John admits that he has a very great desire not to upset her, though he would, if asked, deny that this in any way explains his efforts at pursuing excellence in music. However, now suppose John's mother dies and, upon her death, he finds all of his interest in music vanishes. He gives up his career as a musician and pursues some other quite different career. In such circumstances, wouldn't it be plausible to suppose that John was just mistaken about what he originally wanted to do and that, despite the fact he believed that achieving excellence in music was a fundamental desire of his, it never was? If so, then we have reason to believe that the principle is false right to left as well: that is, we have reason to deny that if a subject believes that she has reason to φ then she desires to φ.

If this is agreed, then any conception of desires that entails that a subject desires to φ if and only if she believes that she desires to φ is a conception to be rejected. It is to be rejected for the simple reason that the epistemology it provides is implausible. Thus, if the phenomenological conception entails such a principle, it ought to be rejected. And this in turn teaches us the following valuable lesson. It is an adequacy constraint on any conception of desire that the epistemology of desire it recommends allows that subjects may be *fallible* about the desires they have.

I said at the outset that there are two lines of objection to the strong phenomenological conception of desire. The second is even more powerful than the first. Let's suppose we grant that desires are like sensations in that they essentially have phenomenological content. Even so, it must be agreed that they differ from sensations in that they have, in addition, propositional content (Platts, 1981: 74–7). Ascriptions of desires, unlike ascriptions of sensations, may be given in the form 'A desires that p', where 'p' is a sentence. Thus, whereas A's desire to φ may be ascribed to A in the form 'A desires that she φs', A's pain cannot be ascribed to A in the form 'A pains that p'.

It is therefore ambiguous to claim that the epistemology of desire is like the epistemology of sensation. To be sure, if desires are essentially phenomenological states then the epistemology of the *phenomenological content* of a desire may be based on the epistemology of sensation. But what about the epistemology of the *propositional content* of desire? This cannot be based on the epistemology of sensation at all, for sensations have no propositional content.

It therefore turns out that we have an even stronger reason to reject the strong phenomenological conception of desire. For, according to this conception, there is no difference between desires and sensations. Each is a state that simply and essentially has phenomenological content. The strong phenomenological conception of desires is thus unable to account for the fact that desires have propositional content at all. Little wonder that it cannot provide a plausible epistemology of the propositional content of desires.

I suspect that, for this very reason, some will have thought the strong phenomenological conception of desire a strawman all along. But note that, with our objections to the strong phenomenological conception firmly in place, we are now in a position to argue against *all* versions of the phenomenological conception, even the more plausible weaker conceptions according to which desires are like sensations in that they have phenomenological content essentially, but differ from sensations in that they have propositional content as well. For we can now say this about all such conceptions. They in no way contribute to our understanding of what a desire as a state with propositional content is, for they cannot explain how it is that desires have propositional content. They therefore in no way explain the epistemology of the propositional content of desire. And they thus require supplementation by some independent and self-standing account of what a desire is that explains how it is that desires have propositional content and how it is that we have fallible knowledge of what it is that we desire.

The question that immediately arises with regard to weaker phenomenological conceptions is then why we should believe any such conception to be true. The only answer available is that a phenomenological conception is alone true to the phenomenology of desire. But is this answer plausible? Do we really believe that desires are states that have phenomenological qualities essentially? That is, do we believe that if there is nothing that it is like to have a desire, at a time, then it is not being had at that time?

I should say that, at least as far as commonsense opinion goes – and what else do we have to go by in formulating a philosophical conception of folk psychological states? – we evidently have no such belief. Consider, for instance, what we should ordinarily think of as a long-term desire: say, a father's desire that his children do well. A father may actually feel the prick of this desire from time to time, in moments of reflection on their vulnerability, say. But such occasions are not the norm. Yet we certainly wouldn't ordinarily think that he loses this desire during those periods when he lacks such feelings. Or consider more mundane cases in which, as we should ordinarily say, I desire to cross the road and do so, or in which I desire to write something down and so write it down. As Stroud points out, in such cases 'it is difficult to believe that I am overcome with emotion . . . I am certainly not aware of any emotion or passion impelling me to act'; rather 'they seem the very model of cool, dispassionate action' (Stroud, 1977: 163). However it would be grossly counter to our commonsense opinion to conclude that simply because I do not introspect the presence of desires in such cases so I incorrectly attribute desires to myself – that I cross the road and write things down even though I do not want to!

Of course, if we thought that there was nothing for a desire to be in the absence of its being felt then we might, in our role of philosophical theorist, feel ourselves forced into concluding that some of our commonsense desire attributions are mistaken, and hence feel ourselves forced to revise our commonsense opinions in favour of a phenomenological conception. But given we have seen that such a conception is unable to deliver an account of what a desire as a state with propositional content is anyway, so we should feel no such pressure in our role of philosophical theorist. Rather we should concede that a desire may be had in the absence of its being felt.

This is significant. For many anti-Humeans seem to work with a phenomenological conception of desire, and then use the fact that we do not introspect the presence of desires whenever there is motivation against the Humean theory. Consider, for instance, the following argument from Mark Platts:

The crucial premiss . . . is the claim that any full specification of a reason for an action, if it is to be a reason for the potential agent for action, must make reference to that agent's desires. At first sight, it seems a painful feature of the moral life that this premiss is false. We perform many intentional actions in that life that we apparently do not desire to perform. A better description of such cases appears to be that we perform them because we think them desirable. The difficulty of much of moral life then emerges as a consequence of the apparent fact that desiring something and thinking it desirable are both distinct and independent. The premiss can, of course, be held true by simply claiming that, when acting because we think something desirable, we do indeed desire it. But this is either phenomenologically false, there being nothing in our inner life corresponding to the posited desire, or utterly vacuous, neither content nor motivation being given to the positing of the desire. Nothing but muddle (and boredom) comes from treating desire as a mental catch-all. (1979: 256)

Thus, according to Platts, the Humean may hold that when we act believing something to be desirable we do desire it, but if he does, he is impaled on the horns of a dilemma. But consider the horns of Platts' dilemma.

If there is no reason why any theorist should accept a phenomenological conception of desire, as we have seen that there is not, then it can hardly be an objection to the Humean's theory that we are unable to introspect the presence of each and every desire he says we have. Thus we should not force upon the Humean the phenomenological falsehood on the first horn. Platts might agree. But, he would say, this merely forces the Humean on to the second horn of his dilemma.

Here Platts claims that if we do not accept a phenomenological conception of desire, then the positing of a desire must be 'utterly vacuous', or without 'content'. But, as we have seen, given just the assumption that desires are states with propositional content, an assumption that must be accepted even by those who endorse a phenomenological conception, the only way that we can give content to the concept of such a state, and hence to the positing of a desire, is precisely via some independent and self-standing non-phenomenological conception. So, far from non-phenomenological conceptions making ascriptions of desire 'utterly vacuous', non-phenomenological conceptions alone make the ascription of desires with propositional contents possible.

Indeed, even John McDowell, who himself rejects a phenomenological conception, covertly ascribes such a conception to the Humean when arguing against him.[5] This emerges in McDowell's defence of his own view that the virtuous agent may be motivated by her conception of the situation in which she finds herself, something that, according to McDowell, may properly be thought of as a cognitive state. He rightly supposes that the Humean would reply that, if someone who has such a conception is indeed motivated, then getting her to have such a conception must involve getting her to have a certain desire. But he then interprets this as the suggestion that

> 'See it like this' is really a covert invitation to feel, quite over and above one's view of the facts, a desire which will combine with one's belief to recommend acting in the appropriate way. (1978: 22)

And he rightly rejects this suggestion. But, if the Humean does not have to accept a phenomenological conception of desire, why give his reply that interpretation? To be sure, getting someone to have a certain view of the facts that will lead her to act in a certain way may not involve getting her to *feel* a desire, but it may involve getting her to *have* a desire none the less.

4.6 DESIRES, DIRECTIONS OF FIT AND DISPOSITIONS

We have seen that there must be an alternative to phenomenological conceptions of desire, an alternative that allows us to make sense of desires as states with propositional contents and that thus allows us to make sense of our commonsense desire attributions. But what is the alternative to be?

Surprisingly enough, Platts himself outlines the alternative I favour; a suggestion about the difference between beliefs and desires that he attributes to Anscombe (1957). Platts' own summary is so succinct and makes the idea sound so plausible that I will merely quote it. I consider below why Platts is himself subsequently so unsympathetic towards the idea.

> Miss Anscombe, in her work on intention, has drawn a broad distinction between two kinds of mental states, factual belief being the prime exemplar of one kind and desire a prime exemplar of

the other . . . The distinction is in terms of the direction of fit of mental states with the world. Beliefs aim at the true, and their being true is their fitting the world; falsity is a decisive failing in a belief, and false beliefs should be discarded; beliefs should be changed to fit with the world, not *vice versa*. Desires aim at realisation, and their realisation is the world fitting with them; the fact that the indicative content of a desire is not realised in the world is not yet a failing in the desire, and not yet any reason to discard the desire; the world, crudely, should be changed to fit with our desires, not *vice versa*. (1979: 256–7)

Myself I think that this characterization of the difference between beliefs and desires captures something quite deep in our thought about their nature. Moreover, I want eventually to argue that the idea that desires are states with which the world must fit allows us to bring out an important connection between our concepts of desire and motivation.

However, as Platts notes, talk of the direction of fit of a state is highly metaphorical. This is problematic. For it might be thought that we would be unjustified in appealing to the concept in characterizing desires, and in illuminating the connection between desires and motivation, if we had no way of understanding it in non-metaphorical terms. Moreover, as again Platts notes, if we take the characterization quite strictly, it is unclear whether it allows us to characterize desires at all. For, he claims, since 'all desires appear to involve elements of belief', desires are not states whose direction of fit is entirely of the second kind. The question arises whether there are any such states (Platts, 1979: 257).

It seems to me that Platts is right to highlight these problems with the metaphor, but that we would be wrong to think that the problems he raises are insurmountable. For I want to suggest that the metaphorical characterization of desires as states which are such that the world must fit with them meshes with another, and more plausible, suggestion about the epistemology of desires, a suggestion inspired by certain other remarks of Hume's.

Hume realized all too well that alongside the 'violent passions' that affect the subject who has them, there are 'calm passions', passions that lack phenomenological content altogether. He was therefore cognizant of the fact that his official line on the epistemology of desires – that they are known by their phenomenology – was totally inadequate as an account of the epistemology of the calm passions, and that he therefore needed an alternative account of the epistemology appropriate for them. As a result, Hume suggested that, by contrast with the violent passions, the calm passions 'are more known by their effects than by their immediate sensation' (1888: 417).

When Stroud considers this suggestion, he points out that it commits Hume to the view that desires are to be conceived of as the causes of actions (Stroud, 1977: 166). It might therefore be thought that Hume's suggestion should be of little interest to us. For I have argued that the only argument for the Humean theory, if there is to be one at all, will be that it alone is able to make sense of reason explanation as a species of teleological explanation, and that one may accept that reason explanations are teleological without accepting that reason explanations are causal. Yet if we accept this conception of desire we immediately lock ourselves into a causal conception.

However, though this makes acceptance of Hume's suggestion as it stands inappropriate, it seems to me that we would be wrong to abandon Hume's suggestion altogether. For if we are less interested in *Hume's* view than in a *Humean* view then it seems to me that we can find in Hume's suggestion about the epistemology appropriate for the calm passions the inspiration for a somewhat different conception of desires; a conception that allows us to remain neutral about whether desires are causes.

According to this alternative conception, desires are states that have a certain functional role. That is, according to this conception, we should think of desiring to ϕ as having a certain set of dispositions, the disposition to ψ in conditions C, the disposition to χ in conditions C′, and so on, where, in order for conditions C and C′ to obtain, the subject must have, *inter alia*, certain other desires, and also certain means-ends beliefs, beliefs concerning ϕ-ing by ψ-ing, ϕ-ing by χ-ing and so on. For Hume's suggestion about how the calm passions are known may then be translated into the thought that the epistemology of desire is simply the epistemology of dispositional states – that is, the epistemology of such counterfactuals. This does not commit us, as Humeans, to the thesis that desires are to be conceived of as the causes of actions. For it is a substantial philosophical thesis to claim that dispositions are causes (Prior, Pargetter and Jackson, 1982) – though let me here register my own view that dispositions, and so desires, are indeed causes (Jackson and Pettit, 1988).

A dispositional conception of desires enables us to solve many of the problems that we have confronted so far. For instance, a dispositional conception is precisely an account of what a desire is that explains how it can be that desires have propositional content; for the propositional content of a desire may then simply be determined by its functional role (Loar, 1981; Jackson and Pettit, 1988).

A dispositional conception of desires also meets the constraint on the epistemology of desire argued for earlier. It entails that the epistemology of desire must allow that subjects are fallible about the desires they have. For, given just the assumption that desires are dispositions to act in certain ways under certain conditions, it is implausible to suggest quite generally that if the counterfactuals that are thus true of a subject who desires to φ are true of her then she believes they are, and it is likewise implausible to suggest quite generally that if a subject believes that such counterfactuals are true of her, then such counterfactuals are true of her.[6]

Furthermore, a dispositional conception of desires is consistent both with the claim that certain desires have phenomenological content essentially and with the claim that certain desires lack phenomenological content altogether. For, according to this conception, desires have phenomenological content just to the extent that the having of certain feelings is one of the things that they are dispostions to produce under certain conditions. Some desires may be dispositions to have certain feelings under all conditions: these have phenomenological content essentially. Other desires, though they are dispositions to behave in certain ways, may not be dispositions to have' certain feelings at all: these lack phenomenological content altogether.

We are also able, given a dispositional conception of desires, to see why Platts is right that, in many ways, desires 'involve elements of belief'. For if the desire to φ is a certain sort of complex dispositional state of the kind described, then desiring to φ may 'involve' elements of belief in each of the following ways: the obtaining of the conditions in which the subject φs may require that she has certain beliefs, especially means-end beliefs; the truth of the counterfactual 'Were the subject in conditions C she would φ' may require that the subject has certain other beliefs due to holistic constraints on desire and belief attribution; and so on.

Finally, a dispositional conception enables us to see why, despite the fact that in these many ways desires may involve elements of belief, we may properly say of someone who has a desire that she is in a state with which the world must fit. For a dispositional conception of desires enables us to cash in non-metaphorical terms, and therefore in turn finds support from, the metaphorical characterization of beliefs and desires in terms of their different directions of fit. For the difference between beliefs and desires in terms of direction of fit can be seen to amount to a difference in the functional roles of belief and desire. Very roughly, and simplifying somewhat, it amounts, *inter alia*, to a difference in the counterfactual dependence of a belief that p and a desire that p on a perception with the content that not p: a belief that p tends to go out of existence in the presence of a perception with the content that not p, whereas a desire that p tends to endure, disposing the subject in that state to bring it about that p.[7] Thus, we might say, attributions of beliefs and desires require that different kinds of counterfactuals are true of the subject to whom they are attributed. We might say that this is what a difference in their directions of fit is.[8]

These are important results. For they serve to make a dispositional conception of desire attractive period, quite independently of the theory of motivation that we happen to favour. Moreover, they license us to talk unashamedly of desires as states with which the world must fit, for such talk, though metaphorical, captures the feature that distinguishes desires from beliefs. Such talk aptly describes the *kind* of dispositional state a desire is.

The Humean's reasons for believing P1 – the principle that a motivating reason is constituted by the presence of a desire and a means-end belief – may now be stated rather simply. Given that, as we have seen, all theorists should accept a dispositional conception of desire, and given that this conception licenses us to talk of desires as states with which the world must fit, the Humean's reasons are also, I think, both intuitive and compelling.

4.7 DESIRES, DIRECTIONS OF FIT, GOALS AND MOTIVATING REASONS

What is it for someone to have a motivating reason? The Humean says that we understand what it is for someone to have a motivating reason at a time by thinking of her as, *inter alia*, having a goal at that time (the '*alia*' here includes having a conception of the means to attain that goal). That is, having a motivating reason just is, *inter alia*, having a goal. But what kind of state is the having of a goal? Which direction of fit does this state have? Clearly, the having of a goal is a state with which the world must fit, rather than *vice versa*. Thus having a goal is being in a state with the direction of fit of a desire. But since all that there is to being a desire is being a state with the appropriate direction of fit, it follows that having a goal just is desiring.[9]

In short, then, the Humean believes P1 because P1 is entailed by the following three premises:

(a)   Having a motivating reason is, *inter alia*, having a goal

(b)   Having a goal is being in a state with which the world must fit

and

(c)   Being in a state with which the world must fit is desiring.

Simple though it is, this argument is, I think, really quite powerful. After all, which premise in the argument could plausibly be denied? Let's consider them in turn.

Given just the assumption that reason explanations are teleological explanations, (a) seems unassailable; indeed it has the status of a conceptual truth. For we understand what it is for someone to have a motivating reason in part precisely by thinking of her as having some goal. And (b) is likewise unassailable. For becoming apprised of the fact that the world is not as the content of your goal specifies suffices not for giving up that goal, it suffices rather for changing the world. The most vulnerable premise is perhaps (c), the claim that being in a state with which the world must fit is desiring. I can imagine two sorts of objection to this premise.

First, according to Platts, Anscombe claims only that desire is 'a prime exemplar' of those states with which the world must fit. But, he might say, there are other states that have this direction of fit as well: hopes, wishes, intentions and the like. Therefore, given (a) and (b), we should surely say that such states may constitute the having of goals as well. But, *ex hypothesi*, hopes, wishes and intentions are not desires.

However an attack on the Humean's argument of this kind is clearly not an attack on the *spirit* of his argument, it is rather an attack on the *details* of his argument. The Humean may, of course, choose to defend the details. He might argue that, though these states do in some sense have the direction of fit of a desire, insofar as they differ from desires, they differ because they also involve elements of belief. Thus he might suggest that such states are in fact composites of desire and belief: wishing that p is just desiring that p and believing that p is very unlikely; intending to ϕ is simply desiring most to ϕ and believing that you will therefore try to ϕ; and so on. Alternatively, the Humean might agree that, even after we analyse out the elements of belief in such states, it is implausible to suppose that the state that is left over is itself a desire. He might therefore choose to concede the details of the argument to the objector. For if 'desire' is not a suitably broad category of mental state to encompass all of those states with the appropriate direction of fit, then the Humean may simply define the term 'pro-attitude' to mean 'psychological state with which the world must fit', and then claim that motivating reasons are constituted, *inter alia*, by pro-attitudes (compare Davidson, 1963: 4).

A second objection to (c) concedes that beliefs and desires have only one direction of fit, but then tackles instead the assumption that there are only states having one or the other direction of fit; the assumption that we can always analyse out the belief-like elements of states having the direction of fit of a desire.[10] The objector wants to know why there couldn't be a state of some further kind having both directions of fit; a state which is both such that the world must fit with it and such that it must fit the world. If such a state were possible then, he might say, it could constitute the having of a goal. But given that it would not be a desire, nor even a pro-attitude, for it has been conceded that desires and pro-attitudes have only one direction of fit, we would then have to reject (c). Motivating reasons could be constituted by this further kind of state.

However, though it might sound like a coherent possibility that there be such a state, it isn't really, at least not if we take the suggestion quite literally. For, as we have understood the concept of direction of fit, the direction of fit of a state with the content that p is determined, *inter alia*, by its counterfactual dependence on a perception with the content that not-p. A state with both directions of fit would therefore have to be such that, both, in the presence of such a perception it tends to go out of existence, and, in the presence of such a perception, it tends to endure, leading the subject who has it to bring it about that p. Taken quite literally, then, the idea that there may be a state having both directions of fit is just plain incoherent.

A more subtle objector might find fault with this reply (McDowell, 1978; McNaughton, 1988). He might say that the reply works only if we take the suggestion to be that there is a state having both directions of fit with respect to the same content. But, he might well ask, why take the suggestion that literally? After all, why shouldn't we think that there are, in addition to states having one or the other direction of fit with respect to a single content, unitary states having both directions of fit, though with respect to two different contents? The objector might even offer us an example of such a state – unsurprisingly, an example that takes us back to the original moral problem, and to his own preferred solution to it.

Consider what we should ordinarily think of as the moral belief that it is right to φ. The objector might say that this is really better thought of as, to use J. E. J. Altham's excellent term, the *besire* that φ-ing is right – 'besire' because, as we shall see, though this state is belief-like, it is also desire-like (1986). The besire that φ-ing is right is appropriately described as being a state that must fit the world because it tends to go out of existence when the subject is confronted with a perception with the content that φ-ing is not right. This is why, in terms of the original moral problem, we were wrongly, even though understandably, disposed to say that moral judgements express beliefs. Moreover, he might point out, the besire that φ-ing is right is also appropriately described as being such that the world must fit with it. For a subject's having the besire that φ-ing is right disposes her to φ. Besires, a third unitary kind of psychological state alongside belief and desire, are thus *both* expressed in moral judgements of the form 'φ-ing is right' *and* constitute our moral motivations. How are we to reply to this more subtle objector?[11]

Let's be clear what is at issue. Humeans need not deny that agents may, for example, believe that it is right to φ and desire to φ: that is, they need not deny the contingent coexistence of beliefs and desires. And nor, as we will see in the next chapter, need they deny that if an agent believes that it is right for her to φ, then she rationally should desire to φ: that is, they need not deny that the contingent coexistence of certain beliefs and desires is rationally required (Smith, 1988a, 1988b). Rather, what Humeans must deny and do deny is simply that agents who are in belief-like states and desire-like states are ever in a *single, unitary, kind of state*. This is the cash value of the Humean doctrine that belief and desire are distinct existences. And their argument for this claim is really quite simple. It is that it is always at least possible for agents who are in some particular belief-like state not to be in some particular desire-like state; that the two can always be pulled apart, at least modally. This, according to Humeans, is *why* they are distinct existences.

In the particular case under discussion, then, the Humeans' claim must be that it is always at least *possible* for agents who are in a belief-like state to the effect that their φ-ing is right to none the less lack any desire-like state to the effect that they φ; that the two can always be pulled apart, at least modally. And, correspondingly, anti-Humeans must say precisely the opposite. They must claim that it is *impossible* for agents who are in a belief-like state to the effect that their φ-ing is right not to be in a desire-like state to the effect that they φ; that the two cannot be pulled apart, not even modally. As I see it, the disagreement between Humeans and anti-Humeans as to whether we are just believers and desirers, or rather besirers as well, amounts to no more and no less than a disagreement about these modal claims.

However once the issue is painted in these terms it becomes clear that the anti-Humean is on shaky ground. Everything turns on how we should interpret the idea that moral judgement is essentially practical. Is the idea that someone who judges it right to act in a certain way is motivated to act accordingly *simpliciter*? Or is the idea rather that someone who judges it right to act in a certain way is motivated to act accordingly, *ceteris paribus*? The anti-Humean needs moral judgement to be practical in the first sense. But moral judgement is quite evidently practical only in the second. (Remember again the first two versions of internalism described at the beginning of chapter 2.) Contrary to the first idea, practical irrationalities of various kinds – weakness of will and the like – can break the connection between moral judgement and motivation.

This point is well made by Michael Stocker in his 'Desiring the Bad: An Essay in Moral Psychology'.

> Through spiritual or physical tiredness, through accidie, through weakness of body, through illness, through general apathy, through despair, through inability to concentrate, through a feeling of uselessness or futility, and so on, one may feel less and less motivated to seek what is good. One's lessened desire need not signal, much less be the product of, the fact that, or one's belief that, there is less good to be obtained or produced, as in the case of a universal Weltschmerz. Indeed, a frequent added defect of being in such 'depressions' is that one sees all the good to be won or saved and one lacks the will, interest, desire or strength. (Stocker, 1979: 744)

And the same goes for the connection between believing an action to be right and being motivated to perform it. It is a commonplace, a fact of ordinary moral experience, that practical irrationalities of various kinds – various sorts of 'depression' as Stocker calls them – can leave someone's evaluative outlook intact while removing their motivations altogether. The anti-Humeans' claim that moral judgements are expressions of besires is inconsistent with this. The Humeans' claim that they are expressions of beliefs is not. The anti-Humeans' view must therefore be rejected in favour of the Humeans'.

At this point the anti-Humean will insist that we confront head-on John McDowell's account of the psychology of the virtuous person. For he famously insists that virtuous people have a distinctive way of conceiving of the situations that they confront. To conceive of situations in this way, McDowell tells us, is to be in a cognitive state whose 'possession entails a disposition of the possessor's will' (1978: 18). In other words, it is to have a besire. He argues for this claim by way of an example.

> [In] . . . urging behaviour one takes to be morally required, one finds oneself saying things like this: 'You don't know what it means that someone is shy and sensitive.' Conveying what a circumstance means in this loaded sense, is getting someone to see it in the special way in which a virtuous person would see it. In the attempt to do so, one exploits contrivances similar to those one exploits in other areas where the task is to back up the injunction 'See it like this': helpful juxtapositions of cases, descriptions with carefully chosen terms and carefully placed emphasis, and the like . . . No such contrivances can be guaranteed success, in the sense that failure would show irrationality on the part of the audience. That, together with the importance of rhetorical skills to their successful deployment, sets them apart from the sorts of thing we typically regard as paradigms of argument. But these seem insufficient grounds for concluding that they are appeals to passion as opposed to reason: for concluding that 'See it like this' is really a covert invitation to feel, quite over and above one's view of the facts, a desire which will combine with one's belief to recommend acting in the appropriate way. (1978: 21–2)

Now McDowell in fact does two things here. Let me separate these out. First, McDowell describes, in what seems to me to be more or less accurate terms, an ordinary process of moral argument. When we engage in such argument we do, as he suggests, engage in various forms of analogical reasoning. In this particular case, we try to get our audience to think of someone's being shy and sensitive as relevantly similar to other ways people might be, ways that our audience grants justify special or more sensitive treatment. Such reasoning lies at the very centre of the procedures via which we try to come by moral knowledge; it lies at the very centre of what we earlier described under the banner of 'reflective equilibrium' (chapter 2).

Second, however, and more controversially, McDowell offers us an *interpretation* of what we are up to when we engage in this sort of reasoning. Specifically, he suggests that we are trying to get our audience to have a besire. The real question is therefore whether his discussion of the example makes this interpretation seem plausible. Does he, in other words, provide us with a plausible example of a cognitive state whose possession entails a disposition of the possesser's will: the virtuous person's conception of someone as shy and sensitive? I do not think so.

McDowell is, I think, misled by the fact that, if we agree with the substantive moral assumptions he makes, then we will accept that a conditional along the following lines is true.

> (x) (If x is virtuous and x conceives of someone as shy and sensitive, then x is disposed to make that person feel comfortable when he is in company, to protect him from those who would embarrass him, and so on and so on.)

The list will of course be open-ended because there may be no limit to the different things that would have to be done in different circumstances. Now I agree that we will accept this conditional. But does accepting it require accepting as well that virtuous people have a special way of conceiving of the situations that they confront? Does it amount to accepting that being in a belief-like state to the effect that someone is shy and sensitive is to be in a desire-like state to the effect that he is to be made to feel comfortable when he is in company, to be protected from those who would embarrass him, and so on and so on? Is that what the conditional says? No. That is not what the conditional says. What the conditional says is that there is a necessary connection in the restricted case where the believer is a virtuous person. And if, as the Humean will claim, someone counts as a virtuous person only if she has certain desires – the desire to make someone who is shy and sensitive feel comfortable when he is in company, the desire to protect someone who is shy and sensitive from those who would embarrass him, and so on and so forth – then we see immediately that the necessary connection is an artefact of that restriction. The virtuous person is a regular believer and desirer after all.

Indeed, it seems to me that the Humean can give a knockdown argument for this claim (Wallace, 1983). For if the virtuous person's appreciation of the fact that someone is shy and sensitive really were a besire, it would have to be impossible to break the belief-like part of that state apart from the desire-like part; it would have to be impossible, for example, for the virtuous person to retain her appreciation of the fact that someone is shy and sensitive and yet not be in a desire-like state to the effect that that person be made to feel comfortable when he is in company. This is in effect to insist that those who were once virtuous who, through some mishap or other, suffer from weakness of the will on some occasion, mustn't any longer really appreciate the fact that that someone is shy and sensitive; that they must have some-how forgotten something that they used to know all too well (McDowell, 1979). But that is surely quite incredible. Stocker's observations about the effects of 'depression' are once again all too appropriate. It is a commonplace, a fact of ordinary moral experience, that when agents suffer from weakness of the will they may stare the facts that used to move them square in the face, appreciate them in all their glory, and yet still not be moved by them (Pettit and Smith, 1993a). That this is so is crucial for an understanding of how horrible it can be for people who are weak. McDowell's description of the virtuous person is simply inconsistent with this commonplace. If he is to make out his case, he therefore has to convince us that there is some fact or other that cannot be simply stared down in this way by someone suffering from weakness of will.

McDowell does face up to this difficulty. He admits that, by any ordinary test, virtuous and non-virtuous people entertain the very same propositions.

> Failure to see what a circumstance means, in the loaded sense, is of course, compatible with competence, by all ordinary tests, with the

language used to describe the circumstance; that brings out how loaded the notion of meaning involved in the protest is. (1978: 22)

But he thinks that this simply shows that the ordinary tests we have for individuating the propositions entertained by agents are inadequate.

To preserve the distinction we should say that the relevant conceptions *are not so much as possessed except by those whose wills are influenced appropriately* (1978: 23 – the emphasis is mine).

In other words, he thinks that we can simply define the propositions entertained by the virtuous person to be those propositions which are such that, if someone is in a belief-like state with respect to such a proposition, then she is in a desire-like state with respect to another corresponding proposition.

But while this manoeuvre is technically available, it only serves to lay bare how intractable the problem facing McDowell really is. For what we have already seen is that all of the ordinary tests by which we individuate propositions, and the facts of ordinary moral experience – that is, Stocker's descriptions of the various 'depressions' that sap motivation while leaving cognition intact – suggest that there are no such propositions. But in that case it is hard to see what possible reason McDowell could have for thinking that there are. Ironically enough, it seems that it is McDowell's anti-Humean view that has turned into a dogma, not the Humean view that it was supposed to replace.

This is a pleasant result. For it is because he thinks that there are certain propositions which are such that, if they are entertained at all, then the entertainer must be disposed to act in a certain way, that McDowell thinks he can concede P2 to the Humean – the claim that motivation requires the presence of a desire – while rejecting P1 – the claim that these desires constitute our motivations. His idea is this. Since, if an agent is in a besire state it is acceptable to ascribe a corresponding desire to her as well, so we can concede that motivation requires the presence of a desire, and thus P2 (1978: 25). But so long as we remember that the desire thus ascribed is merely 'consequentially ascribed' – that is, that its acceptable ascription is a mere consequence of the fact that the agent is in a besire state – we see that we are not thereby committed to thinking that the agent's desire constitutes her motivation: that is, we are not committed to P1. Rather we may say that her motivation is constituted by her besire.

However, if the argument given here has been right, it emerges that P2 is not a principle we have any reason to believe in its own right at all. There are no propositions of the kind McDowell imagines. Properly understood, then, our only reason for believing P2 is that it is entailed by P1. And, as we have seen, we have every reason to believe P1. Desires are indeed the only states that can constitute our motivating reasons.[12]

4.8   SUMMARY OF THE ENTIRE ARGUMENT SO FAR AND PREVIEW

In this chapter I have argued for the Humean theory of motivation. This theory is, I hope, beginning to look far more plausible than many have thought. The argument I have given has been really quite simple. Once we keep it firmly before our minds that the Humean's is a theory of motivating reasons, and equip ourselves with an adequate conception of desire, we see that only the Humean's claim that motivating reasons are constituted, *inter alia*, by desires is able to make proper sense of reason explanation as a species of teleological explanation.

Simple though it is this argument seems to have been entirely overlooked by those anti-Humean theorists of motivation who claim that an agent's having certain beliefs may constitute her having a motivating reason. Some have done so because they fail to distinguish motivating reasons from normative reasons. Others have done so because they hold a phenomenological, and hence inadequate, conception of desire. Most have done so because they have overlooked the implications of the fact that, since reason explanations are teleological, so having a motivating reason is therefore, *inter alia*, having a goal. For, as we have seen, only an agent's desires may constitute her having certain goals, and it follows from this that only her desires may constitute her motivating reasons.

In the next chapter we therefore leave the theory of motivating reasons behind and consider instead the theory of normative reasons. Doing so is crucially important, given the argument of the book as a whole. In order to see why, consider again the moral problem, and what we have so far learned about the standard solutions to it.

As we saw at the outset, the moral problem may be stated in the form of an apparent conflict between three plausible propositions (chapter 1).

1   Moral judgements of the form 'It is right that I φ' express a subject's beliefs about an objective matter of fact, a fact about what it is right for her to do.

2   If someone judges that it is right that she φs then, *ceteris paribus*, she is motivated to φ.

3   An agent is motivated to act in a certain way just in case she has an appropriate desire and means-end belief, where belief and desire are, in Hume's terms, distinct existences.

The three standard responses to this problem, and the reasons we have seen to reject them, may now be summarized as follows.

The first response is the expressivists'. As they see it, if moral judgement has an essential and necessary connection with action (as in (2)), and yet we accept the Humean view that desires are among the prime movers in the explanation of action (that is (3)), then we have no alternative but to reject the claim that our moral judgements express our beliefs about an objective matter of fact (that is (1)). Expressivists thus see the moral problem as giving support to their view that moral judgements express our desires, or dispositions to desire, rather than our beliefs about moral facts, objective or otherwise. The very idea of such facts is, they claim, incoherent for quite independent reasons.

We considered the expressivists' attack on moral facts in chapter 2. Their argument is that, since we cannot come up with a plausible analysis of our concept of a moral fact in naturalistic terms, so it follows that our moral concepts do not subserve a descriptive or fact-stating role. For natural facts are the only facts that there are, and naturalistic concepts are therefore the only coherent descriptive concepts that we can have. However, as we saw, the arguments expressivists give for the latter claim depend on a quite inadequate conception of both conceptual analysis and the way in which, via conceptual analysis, we might vindicate a broader naturalism. An analysis of moral facts must indeed capture certain core platitudes about morality on pain of not being an analysis of *moral* concepts at all. These include platitudes about the objectivity of moral judgement (and thus (1)), the practicality of moral judgement (and thus (2)), the supervenience of the moral on the natural (and thus a broader naturalism), the distinctive substance or subject matter of morality, and the procedures via which we arrive at moral knowledge. But in order to capture such platitudes, and so to vindicate a broader naturalism, it suffices that we give a summary-style, non-reductive analysis of moral facts, an analysis that enables us, *inter alia*, to identify moral features of actions and states of affairs with their natural features. A reductive definition of moral features in terms of natural features is simply not required.

This brings us to the second standard solution to the moral problem. If we think – perhaps for the reasons just given – that moral judgements do express our beliefs about an objective matter of fact (from (1)), a matter of fact that can be identified with some natural feature, but we accept as well that our beliefs cannot produce actions all by themselves (from (3)), then it might seem that we have no alternative but to reject instead the claim that moral judgements are essentially practical (that is (2)). This is the externalists' solution to the moral problem. They see the moral problem as giving support to their own view that the moral judgements we make bear no special relationship to the reasons for action that we have. The idea that they do bear such a relationship is, they claim, demonstrably false.

We considered externalism at some length in chapter 3. Though externalists give a variety of arguments against both the practicality requirement and the claim that our concept of a moral requirement is the concept of a reason for action we saw that these arguments all fail. Indeed, it emerged that externalism itself has two fatal flaws. First, though externalists admit that there is a reliable connection between the moral judgements that a morally good and strong-willed person makes and her motivations, they can only explain why this is so by assuming, implausibly, that what makes a person morally good is the fact that she is motivated to do what she believes to be right, where this is read *de dicto* and not *de re*. Externalism thus enshrines a form of moral fetishism. And second, we saw that externalism is unable to explain why we expect rational people to do what they are morally required to do. In order to explain this we need not just a conception of moral facts that embraces the practicality requirement, but a stronger conception of moral facts as facts about categorical requirements of rationality or reason.

This brings us to the third standard solution to the moral problem. If we think that we should accept both the claim that our moral judgements express our beliefs about an objective matter of fact (that is (1)), and the practicality of moral judgement (that is (2)), and we think that what this shows – perhaps for the reasons just given – is that there must be objective facts about the reasons for action that we all share, then it might be thought that we have no alternative but to reject Hume's idea that belief and desire are distinct existences (that is (3)). This is the response to the moral problem favoured by anti-Humean theorists of motivation. They think that Hume's characterization of the way in which belief and desire combine to produce action is a dogma in philosophical psychology, a dogma we have no good reason to accept.

We have considered the anti-Humean theory of motivation at length in this chapter. We have seen that anti-Humeans fail to appreciate a distinction between two kinds of reasons for action that we have: motivating reasons and normative reasons. And once this distinction is firmly in place it becomes clear that the anti-Humean's own theory of motivation faces formidable objections. For only a Humean theory of motivation can adequately explain why an explanation of an agent's action in terms of her motivating reasons is itself a species of teleological explanation. The Humean theory of motivation is thus on solid ground.

The three standard solutions to the moral problem are thus all *bad* solutions. We need a different approach. As I see it, the anti-Humeans were right that the solution to the moral problem lies in the rejection of a thoroughly Humean conception of human psychology. But they were wrong that what we have to reject is Hume's account of the distinct roles played by belief and desire in human motivation. Rather, what we have to reject is Hume's distinctive account of the rationality of desire: his theory of normative reasons. It is thus to the task of providing an anti-Humean analysis of normative reasons that I now turn (chapter 5). It is here that we will find our solution to the moral problem (chapter 6).

5

An Anti-Humean Theory of Normative Reasons

5.1 FROM MOTIVATING REASONS TO NORMATIVE REASONS

The Humean claims that motivating reasons are constituted by desires and means-end beliefs. I have argued we have good reason to accept this claim. However a theory of motivating reasons is not the whole of a psychological theory, for, as we have seen, alongside motivating reasons there are also normative reasons. A psychological theory therefore needs to tell us about those of our normative reasons which express norms of rationality or reason as well; about what it is and is not rational for us to do.

Hume's own view, of course, is that whereas our beliefs can be assessed in terms of truth or falsehood, and so can be deemed to be rational or irrational, our desires, which cannot be assessed in these terms at all, are beyond rational criticism altogether – at least provided that they are not themselves based on any false beliefs (chapter 1; Smith, 1988b). The distinctive Humean view of normative reasons, then, is that the rational thing for an agent to do is simply to act so as maximally to satisfy her desires, whatever the content of those desires. What it is rational for an agent to do is therefore relative to what she wants most to do. This is the so-called 'maximizing' conception of rationality (Gauthier, 1975). The question that naturally arises is whether we should accept some such version of a Humean theory of normative reasons as well.

Notwithstanding our earlier defence of the Humean theory of motivating reasons, my own view is that we should not accept a Humean theory of normative reasons. We should rather accept a radically *anti*-Humean theory. My task in the present chapter is to say why, and to spell out the version of an anti-Humean theory of normative reasons I favour. Such theories of normative reasons are controversial, however, and for good reason. As I see it, part of this controversy centres on a so-far unacknowledged puzzle about the explanation of action. I begin by bringing this puzzle out into the open.

5.2   THE INTENTIONAL AND THE DELIBERATIVE

Note that we can, in general, explain intentional action from two quite different perspectives: the *intentional* and the *deliberative* (Pettit and Smith, 1990; Pettit, 1993: 20–4). Though at first sight this seems unproblematic, on reflection it provides us with a puzzle. Let me explain the two perspectives.

From the intentional perspective, we explain an intentional action by fitting it into a pattern of teleological, and perhaps causal, explanation: in other words, we explain by citing the complex of psychological states that produce the action. Consider my typing these words. We explain this action from the intentional perspective when we cite my desire to write a book and my belief that I can do so by typing these words, for this is the desire/belief pair that teleologically, and perhaps causally, explains my typing these words. In terms of our distinction between two kinds of reasons, we explain by citing my *motivating reasons*.

From the deliberative perspective, by contrast, we explain an intentional action in terms of the pattern of rational deliberation that either did, or could have, produced it. Consider again my typing these words. In deciding whether or not to type these words I reflect on certain facts: that it would be desirable to write a book and that I can do so by typing these words. These are amongst the considerations I actually take into account in deciding what to do before I do it; they give my reasons; they constitute my rational justification. In terms of our distinction between two kinds of reasons, these considerations constitute my *normative reasons* for doing what I do, at least as those reasons appear to me. Of course, it would be wrong to suppose that we conciously go through such a process of reasoning each time we act, but, even when we don't, we can often reconstruct the pattern of reasoning that could have been explicit in our deciding to do what we did. In this case, *ex post facto* justification takes the form of constructing an 'as if' story, a story that may be more or less close to the truth.

At first sight, then, the distinction between the intentional and the deliberative may seem to involve a difference in *category*. For whereas, from the intentional perspective, we are interested which psychological states of the agent explain her actions, from the deliberative perspective we are interested in which propositions, from the agent's point of view, justify her actions. As such, it might be thought that there is no conflict at the level of explanation. However, on closer examination, we see that both perspectives commit us to claims about explanation and that they are therefore potentially in conflict with each other.

In order to see that the deliberative perspective is indeed a perspective on explanation, it suffices to note that to say otherwise is tantamount to supposing that the connection betweeen what we decide to do, on the basis of rational deliberation, and what we do do, is altogether contingent and fortuitous. And that is patently absurd. When we deliberate, and decide what we have a rational justification for doing, that very fact sometimes makes a difference to what we do. But if deliberation is, even if only sometimes, practical not just in its content but also in its issue, then we must suppose that our attitudes towards the propositions that figure in our deliberations are capable of figuring in an explanation of what we do. And now the potential for conflict arises.

Consider again our example. If I think that it is desirable that I write a book – or, equivalently, if I think that I have normative reason to do so – and I think that I can write a book by typing these words, then we can redescribe my attitudes in these terms: I *value* writing a book and *believe* that I can write a book by typing these words. We might say, then, that in our deliberative explanation the attitudes in question are valuing and believing. But now we must ask how this deliberative explanation in terms of *valuing* and believing relates to the intentional explanation of the very same action in terms of *desiring* and believing. The problematic attitude is valuing. What is valuing? And how does valuing relate to desiring?

5.3 SOME DIFFERENCES BETWEEN VALUING AND DESIRING

We want an answer to the question 'What is valuing?' In answering this question we must remain faithful to our ordinary thoughts about the relations between our valuings, on the one hand, and our desirings on the other. In other words we must remain faithful to various platitudes about the connection or slack that we find between what we take to be rationally justified and what we are motivated to do. I have already said why we must think that there is some connection. In this section I explain why we must also think that there is some slack.

Consider the following passage from Ayer's 'Freedom and Necessity'.

> The kleptomaniac does not go through any process of deciding whether or not to steal. Or rather, if he does go through such a process, it is irrelevant to his behaviour. Whatever he resolved to do, he would steal all the same. And it is this that distinguishes him from the ordinary thief. (Ayer, 1954: 20)

Ayer rightly takes it as given that the kleptomaniac steals intentionally; that is, that what he does is explicable in terms of what he wants to do. The problem he highlights, however, is that though the kleptomaniac's action is therefore explicable from the intentional perspective it need not be explicable from the deliberative. For there is, as Ayer notes, the potential for a gap between what the kleptomaniac 'resolves' to do as a result of deliberating and what he wants to do: a gap between what he takes himself to have a normative reason to do and what he has a motivating reason to do. This is important, for it suggests a gap between valuing and desiring. In particular, it suggests that an agent may desire to act in a certain way without valuing acting in that way: that is, without accepting that she has a rational justification for acting in that way.

Harry Frankfurt makes a similar point. He has us imagine a heroin addict who

> ... hates his addiction and always struggles desperately, although to no avail, against its thrust. He tries everything that he thinks might enable him to overcome his desires for the drug. But these desires are too powerful for him to withstand, and invariably, in the end, they conquer him. He is an unwilling addict, helplessly violated by his own desires. (Frankfurt, 1971: 87)

The heroin addict certainly wants to take the drug. However, as Frankfurt notes, we can imagine him saying that he 'does not "really" want to' take the drug; or even that he 'would rather die than' take it (1971: 83). Here, as elsewhere, talk of what we 'really want' is a surrogate for talk about what we value or think rationally justifiable. Frankfurt's point, like Ayer's, is thus that we may desire to act in a certain way without valuing acting in that way; without thinking that so acting is rationally justified.

Gary Watson makes a related point.

> Consider the case of a woman who has a sudden urge to drown her bawling child in the bath; or the case of a squash player who, while suffering an ignominious defeat, desires to smash his opponent in the face with the racquet. It is just false that the mother values her child's being drowned or that the player values the injury and suffering of his opponent. But they desire these things none the less. They desire them in spite of themselves. It is not that they assign to these actions an initial value which is then outweighed by other considerations. These activities are not even represented by a positive entry, however small, on the initial 'desirability matrix'. (Watson, 1975: 101)

Thus if the woman Watson describes in fact drowns her baby then, though she may act intentionally, she does not act in a way that she values; she acts without thinking that what she does is rationally justified at all. And the same goes for the angry and defeated squash player as well.

What the Ayer-Frankfurt-Watson cases all show, then, is that we may desire something without valuing it; without thinking that, if we act on our desire, we act with rational justification. But there are other cases as well, cases that suggest that we may think ourselves rationally justified in acting in a certain way without desiring to act in that way.

As we saw earlier, Michael Stocker observes that various emotional and physical factors – 'spiritual or physical tiredness', 'accidie', 'weakness of body', 'illness', 'general apathy or despair', 'inability to concentrate', 'a feeling of uselessness or futility' and so on; 'depressions', as he generically terms them – can sap our desire to do what we value doing (chapter 4; Stocker, 1979: 744). And what Stocker says here about the gap between our judgements of what is good and what we desire applies equally to cases in which what is at issue is what we have a rational justification for doing. In these cases too various 'depressions' can sap desire altogether. The depressive may thus know full well that the rational thing for her to do is, for example, to get up and get on with her life: to go to work, to visit a friend, to read a book, to cook a meal, or whatever. But the effect of her depression may be precisely to remove any desire at all that she has to do any of these things. Having no desire at all to get up and get on with her life, she may therefore simply do nothing – or, at any rate, nothing intentionally.

The significance of these cases should be clear. They remind us not just that our motivating reasons may come apart from the normative reason claims that we accept, but also that this kind of split occurs for certain characteristic sorts of reasons. Thus the Ayer-Frankfurt-Watson cases remind us that, as a result of psychological compulsions, physical addictions and emotional disturbances, we may have a motivating reason to act in a certain way without thinking that we can provide a rational justification for acting in that way. And the Stocker cases remind us that, as a result of spiritual tiredness, accidie, illness, and the like, we may lack any motivating reason to do what we think we have a rational justification for doing. Stocker himself thus sums up the point this way.

> Of course, citing the (believed) good may always be a reason in the sense of being a justifying reason. But this is only to say that what serves as a justifying reason may not help make an act intelligible, and what may help make an act intelligible may not be a justifying reason, but a 'dysjustifying' one. (Stocker, 1979: 746)

The cases in which splits of these kinds occur between the normative reason claims we accept and our motivating reasons are all deviant, to be sure. But ordinary thought tells us that such cases exist and are therefore not to be ignored when we come to give an account of the relationship between valuing or accepting normative reasons on the one hand, and desiring on the other.

5.4   THE PUZZLE

I said that the fact that intentional action can be explained from both the intentional and the deliberative perspectives provides us with a puzzle. We are now in a position to explain that puzzle more fully.

To the extent that reflection on our normative reasons moves us to act – that is, to the extent that we are effective deliberators – accepting that we have certain normative reasons must in some way be bound up with having corresponding motivating reasons. But the deviant cases just described remind us that our desires may come apart from our acceptance of corresponding normative reason claims, and so that we may be ineffective deliberators. The puzzle, then, is to explain how it can be that accepting normative reason claims can both be *bound up with* having desires and yet *come apart from* having desires. In other words, the problem is to explain how deliberation on the basis of our values can be practical in its issue *to just the extent that it is.*

The puzzle here is a deep one, a puzzle that can be traced back to the belief/desire psychology we have inherited from Hume (chapter 4). In order to suppose that deliberation is practical in its issue we have to suppose that we do what we do because we value what we value. And in order to suppose that deliberation fails to be practical in its issue we must suppose that the fact that we value what we value is irrelevant to our doing what we do. But what is it to value something? That is, equivalently, what is it to accept that we have a normative reason to do something? In Hume's terms, is it a matter of *believing?* Or is it a matter of *desiring?* We seem to face a dilemma.

If valuing is a matter of believing then we have an easy explanation of why our values – thought of now as beliefs about our normative reasons – may come apart from our desires. For beliefs and desires are distinct existences. But for that very reason it is then difficult to see how anything we do intentionally could be done *because* we value what we value. If our beliefs cannot produce actions – if, rather, they are simply inert representations of how things are – then how can our beliefs about our normative reasons ever make a difference to what we do? And if valuing is a matter of desiring then our problems are the exact opposite. For though it is then clear how we can act because of our values, given the Humean view of motivation it is difficult to see how there could be the requisite gap between what we value and what we are motivated to do. If accepting that we have a normative reason to do something just is desiring to do it, then how can we fail to be motivated to do what we accept we have a normative reason to do?

What is at issue is thus the very coherence of the idea that deliberation on the basis of our values is practical in its issue to just the extent that it is. As is perhaps evident, this is just the moral problem all over again, redescribed so as to make it explicit that what is at issue is the connection between reason and motivation. And here, accordingly, is where we find the heart of the debate.

In the remainder of this chapter I consider the only two available alternatives: that valuing is a matter of desiring and that valuing is a matter of believing. To anticipate, I will argue that valuing is a matter of believing, not desiring. The solution to the puzzle lies in finding the right content for the belief; an account of the proposition thus believed. Armed with a plausible analysis of our concept of a normative reason I will argue that we can indeed see why our beliefs about our normative reasons are necessarily connected with our desires to just the extent that they are.

5.5   DAVIDSON   ON   VALUING
AS   DESIRING

The most straightforward suggestion is that valuing is desiring: that is, that desires are appropriately expressed as claims about what we have normative reason to do. Such a reduction of valuing to desiring is proposed by Donald Davidson:

> The natural expression of . . . [an agent's] . . . desire . . . [say, the desire to improve the taste of the stew] . . . is . . . evaluative in form; for example, 'It is desirable to improve the taste of the stew'. We may suppose that different pro-attitudes are expressed with other evaluative words in place of 'desirable'.
>
> There is no short proof that evaluative sentences express desires and other pro-attitudes in the way that the sentence 'Snow is white' expresses the belief that snow is white. But the following considerations will perhaps help show what is involved. If someone who knows English says honestly 'Snow is white', then he believes snow is white. If my thesis is correct, someone who says honestly 'It is desirable that I stop smoking' has some pro-attitude towards his stopping smoking. He feels some inclination to do it; in fact he will do it if nothing stands in the way, he knows how, and he has no contrary values or desires. Given this assumption, it is reasonable to generalize: if explicit value judgements represent pro-attitudes, all pro-attitudes may be expressed by value judgements that are at least implicit. (1978: 86)

Simple though it might be Davidson's suggestion is, however, profoundly wrong. For it simply ignores the possibility of the deviant cases already mentioned.

Nor is it difficult to see where Davidson has been misled. In short, he incorrectly assumes that a feature of *rational* evaluators is a feature of *all* evaluators. Thus, by all accounts, a rational evaluator who says honestly 'It is desirable that I stop smoking' does indeed have some pro-attitude towards stopping smoking. But it does not follow from this that someone who is able to say, honestly, 'It is desirable that I stop smoking' may yet have no inclination to stop; and nor does it follow that someone who is unable to say, honestly, 'It is desirable that I smoke', may yet have some inclination to smoke. All that follows is that, if either of these is possible, the agents in question are not rational evaluators. They are depressives or compulsives or whatever whose depression or compulsion has caused them, irrationally, to desire other than what they think they have normative reason to do.

If Davidson's reduction of valuing to desiring is to succeed, then he needs to convince us that these pathologies have no such consequences. That is, he needs to argue that the earlier description of ordinary thought about the differences between valuing and desiring was a *mis*description; that motivating reasons must – for some reason yet to be explained – bring with them the acceptance of corresponding normative reason claims even when agents are compelled, or depressed, or whatever.

In fact, Davidson does provide such an argument in his account of rationalization.

> In the light of a primary reason . . . the agent is shown in his role of Rational Animal. Corresponding to the belief and attitude of a primary reason for an action . . . [i.e. its cause] . . . , we can always construct (with a little ingenuity) the premises of a syllogism from which it follows that the action has some (as Anscombe calls it) 'desirability characteristic'. Thus there is a certain irreducible – though somewhat anaemic – sense in which every rationalization justifies: from the agent's point of view there was, when he acted, something to be said for the action. (1963: 9)

Thus, according to Davidson, when we rationalize an action we give the reason why it was done and thereby come to see the agent in her role as 'Rational Animal'. And what he in effect argues is that this is possible when we cite the desire/belief pair that cause an action only because the desire that causes an action is appropriately expressed in a corresponding normative reason claim. If it were not so expressed then – Davidson seems to be saying – we would not be able to see the agent in her role as Rational Animal.

Michael Woods has much the same idea. Recall his suggestion that 'the concept of a reason for action stands at the point of intersection . . . between the theory of the explanation of actions and the theory of their justification'. Leave out the explanatory dimension and, according to Woods, you don't have a reason for action. For our appreciation of our reasons for action makes a difference to what we do. But leave out the justificatory dimension and, as he sees it, you don't have a reason for action either. For what marks off an explanation of an action in terms of an agent's reasons for action from other sorts of explanations is the fact that an explanation in terms of reasons not only explains but justifies as well.

Davidson's reduction of valuing to desiring is thus a crucial element in an account of how rationalizations can have both the features that he and Woods think rationalizations must have. For, if it works, the reduction shows how it can be that desires both explain and justify what we do. Desires, the psychological states that causally explain our actions, are appropriately expressed in evaluations, claims that permit us to justify our actions.

However, despite the ingenuity of this suggestion, it seems to me once again quite easy to see where it goes wrong. There is an ambiguity in talk of an agent's reasons for action. And, given this ambiguity, there are therefore two different ways in which we might see an agent in her role as Rational Animal. If the woman described by Gary Watson drowns her bawling baby in the bathwater, for example, then, in one sense, we can say that she both has a reason for acting and acts for that reason. For she has a motivating reason and that reason figures in a teleological explanation of what she does. In so far as her motivating reason figures in such an explanation we therefore see the woman in her role as Rational Animal; for what we have here is no mere causal explanation of her behaviour, but rather an explanation that allows us to see the woman as in pursuit of a goal that she has; an explanation that suffices to see her as acting intentionally (Wilson, 1985).

But in another sense, of course, the woman has no reason for acting and what she does is therefore not explicable, even by her own lights, as having been done for a reason. For she acknowledges that there is no rational justification for what she does; acknowledges that the goal she pursues is itself unjustified and unreasonable. What she does is in no way responsive to her thoughts about what it is rational for her to do; in no way responsive to her thoughts about her normative reasons. To this extent we cannot think of her as acting for a reason at all. We cannot see her in her role as Rational Animal.

Davidson's reduction of valuing to desiring overlooks the fact that there are these two different ways in which we can see an agent in her role as Rational Animal. He assumes, wrongly, that seeing an agent in this role requires that we see her as having done something that is rationally justifiable, at least by her own lights, whereas it requires, at most, that we see her as in pursuit of a goal that she has. But if this is right then we have no reason to accept Davidson's reduction of valuing to desiring at all. For such a reduction simply isn't required for an account of how rationalization reveals the agent in her role as Rational Animal.[1]

5.6 GAUTHIER ON VALUING AS A MODE OF DESIRING

David Gauthier suggests that valuing is not desiring *simpliciter*, but rather a mode of desiring (1986: 22–3).

> Practical rationality in the most general sense is identified with maximization ... An objector might agree to identify practical rationality with maximization, but insist that a measure of individual preference is not the appropriate quantity to maximize. It is rational to maximize *value*; the theory of rational choice implicitly identifies value with ... [a precise measure of preference: i.e. with] ... utility, but the objector challenges this identification ... [He might] ... agree that value is a measure, but insist that it does not measure brute preferences, which may be misinformed, inexperienced, or ill-considered. We shall accept this view in so far as it concerns the manner in which preferences are held.

Thus, according to Gauthier, an agent values a certain outcome only if she desires that outcome *in a certain way*: that is, only if her desire passes certain tests of reflection and experience (1986: 29–32). Suppose I prefer white wine to red, but without ever having had either a sip or a sniff of red wine. This preference may not pass the test of experience, for tasting red wine I might find that I prefer red wine to white. Or suppose I have to decide whether to have white wine or red, and that I choose white, so revealing my preference, but without having given the matter any thought whatsoever. This preference may not pass the test of reflection. For, on reflection, I might have found that I prefer red wine to white.

Though these constraints on the mode of desiring appropriate for valuing are not, as they stand, sufficient to rule out the deviant cases we have described, Gauthier could quite evidently enrich his conception of the appropriate mode. Thus he might add: 'valuing is a mode of desiring where the mode in question rules out desires that require support from a psychological complusion, a physical addiction, or a state of emotional distress.' In this way he could agree with ordinary thought that we may desire an outcome without valuing it.

However, while these amendments would suffice to do that, they would fail altogether to show how we may value an outcome without desiring it. Indeed, if valuing is a *mode* of desiring at all, as Gauthier suggests, then valuing without desiring becomes a conceptual impossibility. But as we have seen, ordinary thought tells us that valuing without desiring isn't just possible, it is actual. The 'depressions' Michael Stocker describes sap our desires while leaving our evaluative outlooks in tact.

The problem with any view according to which valuing is even just a *mode* of desiring, then, is that it will only account for the fact that we may desire to do things without thinking that our doing those things is rationally justified. It will rule out of court the very possibility of thinking ourselves rationally justified in acting in a certain ways without having corresponding desires. But given that such cases are evidently possible it follows that we should reject the view that valuing is even just a mode of desiring.

5.7   LEWIS ON VALUING AS DESIRING TO DESIRE

It might be thought that a reduction of valuing to desiring is still on the cards; that we simply need to reconceive the desire in question in a more radical way. For example, both Harry Frankfurt (1971) and David Lewis (1989) suggest that we can reduce valuing to *desiring to desire*. Here is Lewis.

So we turn to desires. But we'd better not say that valuing something is just the same as desiring it. That may do for some of us:

those who manage, by strength of will or by good luck, to desire exactly as they desire to desire. But not all of us are so fortunate. The thoughtful addict may desire his euphoric daze, but not value it. Even apart from all the costs and risks, he may hate himself for desiring something he values not at all. It is a desire he wants very much to be rid of. He desires his high, but he does not desire to desire it. He does not desire an unaltered, mundane state of conciousness, but he does desire to desire it. We conclude that he does not value what he desires, but rather he values what he desires to desire. (1989: 115)

Lewis's reduction of valuing to desiring to desire avoids the problem facing Davidson's. For an agent may certainly first-order desire other than she second-order desires. And his reduction avoids the problem facing Gauthier's as well. For an agent may certainly second-order desire other than she first-order desires.

It might therefore be thought that Lewis's reduction gives us just the distinction we want, the distinction between teleological explicability and rational justifiability. For, the idea might be, we can now say that an action is teleologically explicable if it is explicable in terms of a first-order desire, but that in order to be rationally justifiable an action must in addition be in accordance with an extra second-order desire.

Lewis resists saying this himself however. He denies that action *needs* the backing of a second-order desire in order to be rationally justifiable (Lewis, 1989: 116). It seems to me that he is right to deny this. Let me briefly explain why.

The point that emerged during our discussion of Davidson's and Gauthier's reductions of valuing to desiring was that though a rational agent desires – first-order desires – in accordance with the normative reason claims she accepts, an irrational agent may desire otherwise. This suggests that normative reasons are subject to the following constraint.

C1   If an agent accepts that she has a normative reason to ϕ then she rationally should desire to ϕ.

C1 should look familiar. It is similar to the practicality requirement on moral judgement; similar, that is, to the claim that if an agent judges it right to φ then, absent some form of practical irrationality, she is motivated to φ (chapter 1). If, as I have already argued, our concept of a moral requirement is itself just the concept of a normative reason then this similarity should come as no surprise (chapter 3).

On an intuitive understanding, C1 gives agents relatively clear advice. It tells us that, other things being equal, someone who accepts that she has a normative reason to φ and yet, say, desires not to φ, should get rid of her desire not to φ and acquire the desire to φ instead. The heroin addict, for example, should get rid of his desire for a euphoric daze, and acquire a desire for an unaltered more mundane state of conciousness instead.

But now think about C1 in the context of the proposed reduction of valuing to desiring to desire. If accepting a normative reason claim is the same as valuing, and valuing is just desiring to desire, then it follows that an agent who desires to desire to φ rationally should desire to φ. But is this right? Are our second-order and first-order desires normatively related in this way? Consider again C1 on the intuitive understanding just described. Should an agent who desires to desire to φ, and yet who desires not to φ, get rid of her desire not to φ and acquire the desire to φ instead?

Not necessarily – or rather, not necessarily if we assume, with the Humean, that what it is rational for someone to do is a function of the content and the strength of her various desires; that is, not if we assume, as on the maximizing conception of rationality, that an agent rationally should do what she most wants to do. For everything then depends on which of her two desires is the strongest. If her desire not to φ is stronger than her desire to desire to φ, then the rational thing for her to do is to act on her desire not to φ and to frustrate her desire to desire to φ instead. So, for example, if the heroin addict's desire for his euphoric daze is stronger than his desire to desire an unaltered mundane state of conciousness, then, on the Humean maximizing conception of rationality, what he should do is act so as to satisfy his desire for his euphoric daze and frustrate his desire to desire a mundane state of conciousness. Reason is on the side of the former, not the latter, in violation of C1.

This is bad news for the reduction of valuing to desiring to desire. And the bad news is, of course, directly related to the fact that the reduction is an analysis of valuing in terms of desiring rather than believing. For even if we assume that reason is on the side of a *harmony* between our first-order and second-order desires (though see Smith, 1992), there is simply no reason to assume that reason is on the side of achieving that harmony by changing our first-order desires to suit our second-order desires rather than *vice versa*. On the Humean's maximizing conception of rationality it all depends on which desire is stronger. This sort of problem doesn't arise for analyses of valuing in terms of believing. For then, if any change is to be made at all, there is a principled reason why in cases of disharmony an agent's desires must change so as to match her values: namely, the fact that an agent's contrary first-order desire will not be in any way suggestive of the fact that her evalutive belief is untrue. We will return to this point presently.

It might be thought that what this shows is simply that we need to amend the Humean's maximizing conception of rationality. After all, on that conception desires have two crucial features: content and strength. Perhaps all we need to do is to amend the maximizing conception to take into account the significance of the content of a second-order desire. Perhaps we should add to the maximizing conception the following principle.

D   If an agent desires to desire to ϕ then she rationally should desire to ϕ, and if she desires to desire to ϕ and desires not to ϕ then she rationally should get rid of the desire not to ϕ and acquire the desire to ϕ instead.

In other words, perhaps we should amend the maximizing conception so as to acknowledge the fact that it matters whether our desires are first-order or second-order. Unfortunately, however, this response entirely misses the point.

C1 is supposed to act as a constraint on an adequate account of normative reasons. If we can reduce the acceptance of normative reason claims to desiring to desire then the hope is to be that this reduction, in conjunction with other plausible assumptions, will actually entail this principle. But D is hardly an additional plausible assumption. It is a theoretically motivated principle that we should accept only if we are given an adequate argument. But the only argument we have been given is that it must be true if the reduction of valuing to desiring to desire is correct. And, in this context, that is not a good argument.

Another way of putting the same point is this. The reduction of valuing to desiring to desire in conjunction with D does indeed capture the spirit of C1. But the reduction itself plays no significant role in this. The spirit of C1 is captured by the conjunction of even the most *implausible* reduction with a principle, like D, that stipulates the very connection we want to derive. Things would, of course, be different if we had some independent reason to accept the reduction. But, in the absence of such independent reasons, we simply have no reason to prop up the reduction by accepting D.

In fact, however, I want now to argue that matters are in fact much worse for the reduction of valuing to second-order desiring. For not only are there no independent reasons to accept the reduction of valuing to second-order desiring, such reductions in fact face a decisive objection (Watson, 1975: 107–9). We therefore have every reason to reject the reduction outright.

Those who seek to reduce valuing to higher-order desiring of some sort must come clean and identify valuing with higher-order desiring *at some particular level or other*. Lewis does come clean in this way. He identifies valuing with second-order desiring. But why identify valuing with second-order desiring? Why not third-order, or fourth-order, or . . . ? The question is a difficult one indeed for those proposing the reduction. For each such identification looks to be as plausible as any other. And if each is as plausible as any other then *all* such identifications are equally implausible. For any identification would require an arbitrary choice between levels. Therefore no plausible reduction has been effected at all.

Lewis confronts this objection fairly and squarely, but his response is less than convincing. He tells us that his reason for favouring the second over the first is that 'a thoughtful addict may desire his euphoric daze, but not value it' (1989: 115). And he tells us that his reason for favouring some level other than the highest order at which an agent desires is that 'if we go for the highest order, we automatically rule out the case of someone who desires to value differently than he does, yet this case is not obviously impossible' (1989: 116). So far this line of reasoning seems perfectly sound. Agents may indeed desire to act in ways they do not think they can rationally justify, and they may indeed desire to think that acts that they don't think are rationally justified are. Unfortunately, however, there are no more premises to Lewis's argument. From these premises he concludes that valuing is *second*-order desiring.

The problem isn't just that there is a gap between Lewis's premises and his conclusion – to say a desire isn't first-order and isn't highest-order does not entail that it is second-order, something we see immediately if we imagine someone with four orders of desire – the problem is that his argument demonstrates how formidable the original objection which it is supposed to answer really is. For his conclusion is simply arbitrary, given his premises. He could equally well have chosen any level other than the first or the highest. And if this is right then it follows that we cannot identify valuing with desiring to desire at any level.

5.8   VALUING AS BELIEVING

If we cannot reduce valuing to desiring then we have no alternative but to consider reducing valuing to believing. Lewis, like Davidson, rejects the idea that valuing is believing. By why does he reject this idea? He reasons as follows.

> *What is valuing?* It is some sort of mental state, directed towards that which is valued. It might be a feeling, or a belief, or a desire . . . A feeling? – Evidently not, because the feelings we have when we value things are too diverse. A belief? . . . [I]f valuing something just meant having a certain belief about it, then it seems that there would be no conceptual reason why valuing is a favourable attitude. We might not have favoured the things we value. We might have opposed them, or been entirely indifferent. So we turn to desires. (1989: 116)

Lewis's argument against identifying valuing with believing thus depends crucially on the idea that there is some sort of conceptual connection between valuing and desiring. But does granting this conceptual connection really preclude identifying valuing with believing valuable?

Lewis seems to think it does, but it is not at all clear why. After all, as he himself notes, the addict may desire his euphoric daze, but not value it; and he may value an unaltered, mundane state of conciousness, but not desire it. And to these examples we may add Watson's woman with a bawling baby; his angry, defeated squash player; and Stocker's depressives. In other words, it isn't just a conceptual possibility, *it actually happens*, that we are indifferent, or opposed, to what we value. Whatever the precise nature of the conceptual connection between valuing and desiring, then, it does not obviously preclude the sort of indifference or opposition to what we value that the identification of valuing with believing valuable makes possible.

Everything therefore turns on what, exactly, the nature of the conceptual connection between believing valuable and desiring is. The answer supported by the discussion thus far is that the conceptual connection is simply the *defeasible* connection described in C1. Other things being equal, we rationally should desire what we value. That is, restating C1 now in terms of 'belief' rather than the more neutral 'acceptance', the connection we are after is this.

> C2   If an agent believes that she has a normative reason to φ, then she rationally should desire to φ.

And now we have to face the real problem. How are we to demonstrate the possibility of this kind of conceptual connection between our beliefs and desires? Won't any such demonstration conflict with the Humean view, argued for in the previous chapter, that belief and desire are distinct existences? In my view, in order to answer these questions we must first come up with a plausible analysis of our concept of a normative reason. But can we provide such an analysis?

Certainly there have been attempts. Consider, for example, the following suggestion from Mark Johnston.

> As for securing an internal or conceptual connection between value and the will, *this* at least is true: to the extent that one is not weak-willed one will desire . . . as one judges valuable. So much is part of the definition of weakness of will. As far as making the connection between judging valuable and desiring . . . particularly intelligible, this seems to me achieved by the observation that 'valuable' and 'desire-worthy' are near synonyms. If judging valuable is pretty much judging desire-worthy then it is readily intelligible why judging valuable should lead to desiring. (1989: 161)

Johnston's argument might well be convincing if we were to accept the claim to near synonymy. But should we? Are 'valuable' and 'desire-worthy' 'near synonyms'?

Johnston is right not to say that they are *actual* synonyms. For whereas if φ-ing is valuable then φ-ing is worth *doing*, if φ-ing is desire-worthy then φ-ing is worth *desiring*, but 'worth doing' means something different from 'worth desiring'. However, though not actual synonyms, he might still be right that they are 'near synonyms'. This would be so if, for example, it followed from the fact that something is worth doing that it is worth desiring, and followed from the fact that something is worth desiring that it is worth doing. But even this weaker claim seems quite wrong to me. For, as Derek Parfit has pointed out, it may not be desirable that we desire to do what it is desirable that we do, and it may not be desirable that we do what it is desirable that we desire to do (1984: part I). Consider Parfit's example.

The self-interest theory tells me that the desirability of an action or a desire is a function of the contribution that that action or desire makes to my long-term self-interest. Thus it is desirable that I *do* just one thing: promote my long-term self-interest. However, as Parfit points out, it does not follow that it is desirable that I desire to promote my long-term self-interest. Indeed, it may well be undesirable that I desire to promote my long-term self-interest. It all depends on whether having that desire is necessary in order for me to have the set of desires the having of which will contribute most to my long-term self-interest. And that desire may well not be necessary. For my long-term self-interest may be best served by my desiring to act for the sake of family and friends, write books, advance humanity and so on, without having any direct concern whatever for my own long-term self-interest.

If this is right then it follows that the self-interest theory tells me that it is desirable that I desire to do what it is not desirable that I do. And it also tells me that it is desirable to do what it is not desirable that I desire to do. However unlikely this may seem, the point to emphasize is that the issue is a *substantive* one, and so requires a *substantive* answer. The answer is not to be determined by 'near' conceptual fiat.

The self-interest theory is, of course, just an example. But what is true of the self-interest theory may well be true of other substantive theories of practical rationality, even the correct theory. Johnston's argument overlooks the possibility of this sort of split between what it is desirable that we do and what it is desirable that we desire to do. As such, it fails as an attempt to make 'readily intelligible why judging valuable should lead to desiring'.

However, though Johnston's argument rests on a false claim to 'near synonymy' it is, I think, on exactly the right track. If anything can make intelligible the connection between judging desirable and desiring it is an analysis of our concept of desirability in terms of desiring. Let's therefore see whether we can formulate an argument along his lines in a way that avoids Parfit's objection.

We have seen that to say an action is desirable is to say that we have a reason to do it, where the relevant norms of assessment are the norms of rationality. But now note that we can further explicate this concept, the concept of what we have normative reason to do, though in a way rather different from that suggested by Johnston. For it is a platitude to say that what it is desirable that we do is what we would desire to do if we were fully rational; that what we have normative reason to do is what we would desire that we do if we were fully rational (Korsgaard, 1986). So what we need to do is to turn this platitude into an analysis.

In the next section I show how this can be done. If I am right then this will suffice to show that valuing is a matter of believing. And in the section that follows I show how this analysis, in conjunction with other plausible assumptions, suffices to make readily intelligible why believing desirable should lead to desiring: that is, C2.

5.9   THE ANALYSIS OF NORMATIVE REASONS

In fact the platitude is close to constituting an analysis already. We need simply to remind ourselves of why it is that the platitude is a platitude, and then to refine our understanding of it.

As I see it, the platitude is related to a whole host of platitudes about *advice*. If you are unsure about what to do in some situation, how should you go about deciding what to do? The answer is that you should tap into the wisdom of the folk; you should ask for advice. But you shouldn't just ask any old person for advice. You should ask someone better situated than yourself to know what you should do, someone who knows you well. With this idea as background, a natural interpretation of the platitude suggests itself. For, suitably idealized, we are in fact the best people to give ourselves advice. Let me explain.

The platitude tells us that what it is desirable for us to do is what we would desire that we do if we were fully rational. In other words – and now we really are turning the platitude into an analysis, for we are making explicit distinctions that are at best only implicit in the platitude – it tells us that what it is desirable for us to do in certain circumstances – let's call these circumstances the 'evaluated possible world' – is what we, not as we actually are, but as we would be in a possible world in which we are fully rational – let's call this the 'evaluating possible world' – would want ourselves to do in those circumstances. That is, it tells us that facts about the desirability of acting in certain ways in the evaluated world are constituted by facts about the desires we have *about* the evaluated world *in* the evaluating world.

Typically, of course, the evaluated world will be the actual world. Thus, what it is desirable for us to do in our actual circumstances is what our more rational selves, looking down on ourselves as we actually are from their more privileged position, would want us to do in our actual circumstances. In terms of the background idea, facts about what it is desirable for us to do are constituted by the facts about what we would advise ourselves to do if we were perfectly placed to give ourselves advice.

With this idea of how we are to turn the platitude into an analysis in the background, I want now to refine our understanding of it. I will do so by considering a set of questions about the analysis. As I see it, these questions focus on the key problems that arise for any analysis of normative reasons, and our answers to these questions therefore show how the analysis on offer copes with these key problems.

First question   'The analysis tells us that what it is desirable for us to do in certain circumstances C is what we would desire that we do in C if we were fully rational. But doesn't this analysis, like Johnston's, conflate the fact that φ-ing is worth doing with the fact that φ-ing is worth desiring?'

No it does not. Suppose, for the sake of argument, that what we have reason to do, in our actual circumstances, is to promote our long-term self-interest. According to the analysis this means that, if I were fully rational, I would desire that, in my actual circumstances, I promote my long-term self-interest. But note that this is a desire about what I am to *do* in my actual circumstances. It is not a desire about what I am to desire in my actual circumstances. What it is worth my while to do is thus to promote my long-term self-interest.

However, we may suppose, it is consistent with the fact that I would have this desire if I were fully rational that I would also, if fully rational, desire that, when I find myself in my actual circumstances, I desire to act for the sake of family and friends, write books, advance humanity and so on, without having any direct concern whatever for my own long-term self-interest. This is what I would desire that I *desire* in my actual circumstances. And, accordingly, what it is worth my while to desire is to act for the sake of family and friends, to write books, to advance humanity, and so on.

In short, then, the analysis tells us that whether φ-ing is both worth doing and worth desiring, or only one or the other, depends on whether, if I were fully rational, what I would desire that I *do* in a given set of circumstances and what I would desire that I *desire* in those same circumstances is the same or different. This is a substantive matter, a matter to be determined by the desires of the fully rational person, not a matter to be decided by conceptual fiat.

Second question 'According to the analysis "φ-ing in circumstances C is what we would desire that we do in C if we were fully rational" gives the content of the thought "φ-ing is desirable". But if this were right, wouldn't it follow that thoughts about our values are thoughts about our own desires? And isn't that quite wrong? Value judgements are not introspective claims about our desires, they are claims about a standard against which our introspectible desires may be measured.'

The claim that the analysis turns value judgements into introspective judgements about our own desires is simply mistaken. Rather, it offers us a striking contrast between introspective judgements about our own desires and our value judgements, a contrast which delivers a natural standard against which our introspectible desires can be measured. In order to see why, consider an example.

Suppose Anne very much wants to dance a jig. Recognizing her desire to dance a jig, she asks herself whether this desire is worth having and acting upon. In other words, she deliberates. When Anne deliberates, how does desire figure in her decision making, given the analysis? Desire figures in her decision making in at least two ways. First, introspected, her desire to dance a jig figures as an object of evaluation. She asks herself whether having this desire is desirable. In this case, Anne does indeed focus in on herself and her own desires. However that is hardly surprising given that it is, *inter alia*, her actual desire to dance a jig that is being evaluated. Second, however, a representation of the desires Anne would have if she were fully rational also figures in her decision making. For Anne asks herself, in effect, whether or not if she were fully rational she would desire that she desires to dance a jig in her current circumstances. But is this an introspective judgement? Certainly not. For what makes the judgement true, if it is true, is not an introspectible fact about Anne, rather it is a hypothetical fact about Anne: that is, a fact about what she would want if she were fully rational.

Moreover, whereas the claim that Anne can make about herself by introspection – the claim that she has a certain desire, say the desire to dance a jig – is no ground at all for supposing that this is a desire worth having or acting upon, the claim that, if she were fully rational, she would want that, in the circumstances in which she actually finds herself, she both has the desire to dance a jig and acts upon it, does provide grounds for supposing that her desire is both worth having and acting upon. For it constitutes the grounds of advice that her more perfect self would give her less perfect self about what to desire and do in her current circumstances. This hypothetical fact about Anne's desires, then, offers us a quite plausible standard against which her introspectible desires may be measured, just as the objection insists.

Third question 'What does the analysis tell us about the deviant cases mentioned earlier: Ayer's kleptomaniac, Frankfurt's heroin addict, the mother described by Watson who desires to drown her bawling baby in the bathwater, and Stocker's depressives?'

What these deviant cases show, by all accounts, is that psychological compulsions, physical addictions, emotional disturbances, depression, spiritual tiredness, accidie, illness and the like, have the potential to cause us to desire to do what we believe we have no normative reason to do on the one hand, or not to desire to do what we believe we have normative reason to do on the other. The analysis suggests a straightforward explanation of these splits between our beliefs about our normative reasons and our desires. For, crucially, it is one thing for an agent to believe that she would want herself to act in a certain way in certain circumstances if she were fully rational, but quite another for her actually to desire to act in that way in those circumstances. The various factors mentioned – psychological compulsions, physical addictions, emotional disturbances, and the like – may be causally responsible for the desires an agent actually has. But the effects of these maladies on an agent's desires may quite rightly be imagined away when she forms her beliefs about what she would want if she were fully rational. For such maladies have no constitutive role to play in the psychology of a fully rational agent.

The point is not that agents suffering from such maladies are necessarily irrational: they may or may not be (Stocker, 1979). The point is rather that, if the desires such agents have about what is to be done in various circumstances – including, of course, circumstances in which they suffer from one or another of these maladies (Pettit and Smith, 1993b) – wouldn't be had in the *absence* of such maladies, then those desires are irrational. Desires are irrational to the extent that they are *wholly and solely* the product of psychological compulsions, physical addictions, emotional disturbances and the like; to the extent that they wouldn't be had by someone in a non-depressed, non-addictive, non-emotionally disturbed state.

Thus, for example, the woman who in fact desires to drown her bawling baby in the bathwater may imagine away the effects of her anger and frustration on her desires in forming her beliefs about what, under conditions of full rationality, she would desire that she does to her bawling baby when she is suffering from an emotional disturbance. This is why, even though she desires to drown her baby, she may not believe that she has any normative reason to do so. And the depressive may imagine away the effects of her depression on her desires in forming her beliefs about what, under conditions of full rationality, she would desire that she does when suffering from a crippling depression. This is why, even though she has no desire to get up and get on with her life, she may well believe that she has a normative reason to do so. The analysis thus gives a straightforward and intuitive understanding of the deviant cases.

Fourth question 'The idea of someone's being fully rational plays a crucial role in the analysis. But what exactly does this idea amount to? Can the idea be made more explicit?'

As I see it, the idea of someone's being fully rational is itself a *summary* notion. The role of this idea in the analysis is thus to capture, in summary style, a whole host of more specific platitudes about practical rationality. In effect I have already adverted to some of these. For to say that depression, emotional distress, and the like have no constitutive role to play in the psychology of the fully rational agent is, in effect, to say that there are no platitudes connecting these maladies with our idea of a rational agent.

Note, however, that Bernard Williams makes the idea of a fully rational agent more explicit in his own, similar, analysis of reasons (1980). For, according to Williams, someone has a reason to φ in circumstances C if and only if she would desire that she φs in circumstances C if she were fully rational, where in order to be fully rational an agent must satisfy the following three conditions:

(i)   the agent must have no false beliefs

(ii) the agent must have all relevant true beliefs

(iii) the agent must deliberate correctly

Williams argues that conditions (i) through (iii) must be satisfied by focusing on various examples, examples that will be familiar enough from our earlier discussion of the differences between normative and motivating reasons (chapter 4). In what follows I will briefly explain the idea behind each of these three conditions, and I will then take issue with some of what Williams says in connection with condition (iii). My disagreement with Williams about condition (iii) will prove to be important subsequently.

Williams argues for condition (i) in the following way. Suppose an agent desires to mix some stuff from a certain bottle with tonic and drink it. However he has this desire only because he desires to drink a gin and tonic and believes that the bottle contains gin, whereas in fact the bottle contains petrol. As Williams points out 'it is just very odd to say that he has a reason to drink this stuff, and natural to say that he has no reason to drink it, although he thinks that he has' (1980: 102). Why? Because he would not have the desire if he were fully rational: that is, *if he had no false beliefs.*

Williams then argues for condition (ii) by noting that an agent 'may be ignorant of some fact such that if he did know it he would, in virtue of some element in . . . [his set of desires] . . . , be disposed to φ: we can say that he has a reason to φ, though he does not know it' (1980: 103). Thus, for example, if an agent desires to buy a Picasso and, though she doesn't know it, there is in fact a Picasso for sale very cheap in the local second-hand shop, then we would ordinarily say that she has a reason to buy something from that shop. Why? Because she would desire to do so if she were fully rational: that is, *if she had all relevant true beliefs.*

And, finally, Williams argues for condition (iii) in the following terms. So far we have taken it for granted that desires and beliefs interact in ways that generate new desires. But of course this is a substantive claim about what it is to be rational. Our desires and beliefs only generate new desires if we deliberate and do so correctly. Thus, for example, they generate new desires only if we reason in accordance with the means-ends principle, for only so does a desire for an end turn into a desire for the means.

Moreover, as Williams points out, means-ends reasoning is only one mode of rational deliberation among many. Another example is

> . . . practical reasoning . . . leading to the conclusion that one has reason to φ because φ-ing would be the most convenient, economical pleasant etc. way of satisfying some element in . . . [one's set of desires] . . . and this of course is controlled by other elements in . . . [one's set of desires] . . . if not necessarily in a very clear or determinate way. . . . [And] . . . there are much wider possibilities for deliberation, such as: thinking how the satisfaction of elements in . . . [one's set of desires] . . . can be combined: e.g. by time-ordering; where there is some irresoluble conflict among the elements of . . . [one's set of desires] . . . considering which one attaches most weight to . . . ; or, again, finding constitutive solutions, such as deciding what would make for an entertaining evening, granted that one wants entertainment. (1980: 104)

And he thinks that there are other, more radical, possibilities for deliberation as well.

> More subtly, . . . [an agent] . . . may think he has reason to promote some development because he has not exercised his imagin-

ation enough about what it would be like if it came about. In his unaided deliberative reason, or encouraged by the persuasions of others, he may come to have some more concrete sense of what would be involved, and lose his desire for it, just as positively, the imagination can create new possibilities and new desires. (1980: 104–5)

Thus, according to Williams, the operation of the imagination too must count as a rational deliberative process. Given the wide variety of principles that therefore govern rational deliberation, he concludes that an agent has a reason to φ only if she would desire to φ if she were fully rational: that is, *if she deliberates correctly.*

In general terms, Williams' conditions (i) through (iii) seem to me to constitute a fairly accurate spelling out of our idea of practical rationality. I think that they do require supplementation, however. For one thing, I see no way in which the effects of compulsions, addictions, emotional disturbances, and the like could be precluded by conditions (i) through (iii) – unless some such constraint is supposed to be presupposed by (iii): the condition of correct deliberation. And for another – and more seriously now – it seems to me that Williams omits from his discussion of condition (iii) an account of perhaps the most important form of deliberation. Given the conclusions he wants to draw from his analysis of reasons, conclusions I will discuss presently, this is a serious omission. Let me explain.

Williams admits that deliberation can produce new and destroy old underived desires. For, as he puts it, an agent 'may think he has reason to promote some development because he has not exercised his imagination enough about what it would be like if it came about', and, more 'positively, the imagination can create new possibilities and new desires'. When the imagination does create and destroy desires in these ways Williams tells us that we take its operations to be sanctioned by reason.

Williams is right, I think, that deliberation can both produce new and destroy old underived desires. But he is wrong that the only, or even the most important, way in which this happens is via the exercise of the imagination. For by far the most important way in which we create new and destroy old underived desires when we deliberate is by trying to find out whether our desires are *systematically justifiable.* And, if this is right, then that in turn requires a significant qualification of Williams's claim that reason sanctions the operation of the imagination.

What do I mean when I say that we sometimes deliberate by trying to find out whether our desires are systematically justifiable? I mean just that we can try to decide whether or not some particular underived desire that we have or might have is a desire to do something that is itself non-derivatively desirable. And we do this in a certain characteristic way: namely, by trying to integrate the object of that desire into a more coherent and unified desiderative profile and evaluative outlook. Rawls describes the basics of this procedure of systematic justification in his discussion of how we attempt to find a 'reflective equilibrium' among our specific and general evaluative beliefs (Rawls, 1951; Daniels, 1979). I will restrict myself to saying a little about the way in which achieving reflective equilibrium may also be a goal in the formation of underived desires.

Suppose we take a whole host of desires we have for specific and general things; desires which are not in fact derived from any desire that we have for something more general. We can ask ourselves whether we wouldn't get a more systematically justifiable set of desires by adding to this whole host of specific and general desires another general desire, or a more general desire still, a desire that, in turn, justifies and explains the more specific desires that we have. And the answer might be that we would. For in so far as the new set of desires – the set we imagine ourselves having if we add a more general desire to the more specific desires we in fact have – exhibits more in the way of, say, unity, we may properly think that the new imaginary set of desires is rationally preferable to the old. For we may properly regard the unity of a set of desires as a virtue; a virtue that in turn makes for the rationality of the set as a whole. For exhibiting unity is partially constitutive of having a systematically justified, and so rationally preferable, set of desires, just as exhibiting unity is partially constitutive of having a systematically justified, and so rationally preferable, set of beliefs.

The idea here is straightforwardly analogous to what Rawls has to say about the conditions under which we might come to think that we should acquire a new belief in a general principle given our stock of rather specific evaluative beliefs. For we might find that our specific value judgements would be more satisfyingly justified and explained by seeing them as all falling under a more general principle. The imaginary set of beliefs we get by adding the belief in the more general principle may exhibit more in the way of unity than our current stock of beliefs, just as our imaginary set of desires may exhibit more in the way of unity than our current set of desires.

If we do decide that our more specific desires are better justified, and so explained, in this way, then note that that may itself cause us to have a new, underived, desire for that more general thing. And if it does, it seems entirely right and proper to suppose that this new desire has been arrived at by a rational method. Indeed, the acquisition of the new more general desire will seem rationally required in exactly the same way that the acquisition of the new belief that the object of the desire is desirable will seem rationally required. In fact, if the analysis of desirability being offered here is on the right track, the acquisition of a new evaluative belief will be the cognitive counterpart of the acquisition of the new desire. For – if the analysis is right – an evaluative belief is simply a belief about what would be desired if we were fully rational, and the new desire is acquired precisely because it is believed to be required for us to be rational.

Moreover, note that if this is agreed then we can not only explain how we might come to have new desires as the result of such reflection, but that we can also explain how we might come to lose old desires as well. For, given the goal of having a systematically justifiable set of desires, it may well turn out that, as the attempt at systematic justification proceeds, certain desires that seemed otherwise unassailable have to be given up. Perhaps because we can see no way of integrating these desires into the set as a whole they will come to seem *ad hoc* and so unjustifiable to us. Our belief that such desires are *ad hoc* may then cause us to lose them. And, if so, then it will seem sensible to describe this as a loss that is itself mandated by reason; as again straightforwardly analogous to the loss of an unjustifiable, because *ad hoc*, belief.

As this procedure of systematic justification continues we can therefore well imagine wholesale shifts in our desiderative profile. Systematic reasoning creates new desires and destroys old. Since each such change seems rationally required, the new desiderative profile will seem not just different from the old, but better; more rational. Indeed, it will seem better and more rational in exactly the same way, and for the same reasons, that our new corresponding evaluative beliefs will seem better and more rational than our old ones.

This, then, is what I mean by saying that we can create new and destroy old underived desires by trying to come up with a systematically justifiable set of desires. If what I have said about systematic reasoning seems right, then it should be clear that Williams's claim that reason is on the side of the operation of the imagination requires significant qualification. For though the imagination can indeed produce new and destroy old desires via vivid presentations of the facts, its operations are not guaranteed to produce and destroy desires that would themselves be sanctioned in an attempt at systematic justification of the kind just described. In fact, quite the opposite is true, for the imagination is liable to all sorts of distorting influences; influences that it is the role of systematic reasoning to sort out. For example, vividly imagining what it would be like to kill someone, I might find myself thoroughly averse to the prospect no matter what the imagined outcome. But, for all that, I might well find that the desire to kill someone, given certain outcomes, is one element in a systematically justifiable set of desires. (For similar criticisms see Mark Johnston's (1989) comments on David Lewis's (1989) account of the role of the imagination in deliberation.)

The role played by attempts at systematic justification is thus what is crucially required for an understanding of how deliberation creates new and destroys old underived desires, not the role played by the imagination. From here on I will therefore take it that Williams's condition (iii), the condition of correct deliberation, is understood accordingly.

Fifth question 'Can the analysis be made fully reductive and explicit?'

The analysis of normative reasons on offer so far – the analysis in terms of facts about what we would desire under conditions of full rationality – is evidently a non-reductive, summary style analysis of our concept of a normative reason. It is a summary style analysis because the idea of being fully rational is itself a summary idea; indeed, we have just seen some of what it summarizes. And it is a non-reductive analysis because in spelling out our idea of what it is to be fully rational we have had to use normative concepts. This was evident in our description of systematic reasoning; for in giving that description we said that we aim to find a more 'unified' desiderative profile, and this is itself, of course, a normative notion.

The question, then, is whether we can turn the analysis into a thoroughly explicit and reductive analysis; what I earlier called a 'network' analysis (chapter 2). But before attempting to answer this question it seems to me that we would do well to remind ourselves that, whether or not it is possible to turn the analysis on offer into a network analysis, it simply isn't required – at least not in so far as our goal is simply to give an analysis. For there is simply no requirement that analyses be thoroughly explicit and reductive. However, with that understood, let's consider the question in its own right.

In order to construct a network analysis of our concept of a normative reason we would have to be able to do three things. First, we would have to be able to write down all of the platitudes constitutive of our idea of being fully rational as a long conjunction. None of these could themselves be summary style descriptions, as for example Williams's condition (iii) is, his condition of 'correct deliberation'. Second, we would have to be able to strip out all mention of normative terms from these platitudes, replacing them with bound variables. And then third, we would have to be able to use this abstract description of a set of relations to give simultaneous definitions of all our normative concepts, a set of definitions of our normative concepts in terms of the relations the various normative features stand in to each other and to the world.

However, as we saw earlier, when a set of concepts is *largely* interdefined – that is, when the concept is in part learned through the presentation of paradigms and there is therefore very little outside the circle of concepts being analysed playing a role in the explicit definition of any single one of them, as, for example, we saw to be the case with our colour concepts – then, when we attempt to give such a network analysis a permutation problem looms. For, to focus in on the case at hand, the possibility looms that when we remove *all* normative concepts from the statement of the platitudes and replace them with bound variables, we will not have *sufficient* information left to get the extensions of the normative concepts we want to analyse right. We may have an abstract description of a set of relations, a set of relations that may be instantiated equally by, say, a set of reasonable beliefs and desires and a set of unreasonable beliefs and desires. To this extent, then, we may be unable to use this abstract description of a set of relations to correctly fix the extension of the reasonable.

Now let me confess that I do not know for certain whether network analyses of our normative concepts are vulnerable to a permutation problem or not. For that would require a demonstration one way or the other, and not only has there never been such a demonstration, given that it would be a superhuman task just to write down an explicit, non-summary style, statement of the platitudes that capture our idea of what it is to be fully rational, there is good reason to think that there never will be such a demonstration either. However, for much the same reasons I gave when we considered the parallel question in the case of our moral concepts, if I were forced to speculate, my own assessment would have to be that network analyses of our normative concepts are indeed vulnerable to a permutation problem. My reasons are two. Again they are the same as my reasons in the moral case.

First, what the discussion of colour concepts shows is that permutation problems arise when a set of concepts, acquired *inter alia* via the presentation of paradigms, is therefore largely interdefined. Permutation problems arise when there are very few concepts outside the circle of concepts to be defined playing a significant role in the platitudes we use to state an explicit definition of those inside the circle. And, of course, this is precisely what we find with our normative concepts; they are indeed *largely* interdefined. Very little outside the sphere of the normative is required to define the normative. And again, as with our colour concepts, this is because we learn our normative concepts by being presented with paradigms – paradigms of good arguments,

of what it is for one proposition to support another, and so on –
from which we learn to generalize.

Second, it seems to me that we have other inductive reasons for
thinking that network analyses of our normative concepts are
vulnerable to a permutation problem as well. For it is a remarkable fact about the history of philosophy that analyses of normative concepts in non-normative terms have been such spectacular
failures. It seems that any such analysis is vulnerable to a 'So
what?' objection (Johnston, 1989; Gibbard, 1990: chapter 1).
What is needed to explain this remarkable fact is some principled
reason why normative concepts elude non-normative analysis.
The obvious conjecture is that network analyses of our normative
concepts are vulnerable to a permutation problem. For this is
precisely the sort of principled reason that is needed.

I conclude, then, that the analysis on offer of a normative
reason is, and will forever remain, a non-reductive, summary style
analysis. But it is none the worse for that. For, as we have seen,
there is simply no requirement that our analyses be reductive and
explicit.

Sixth question 'Does the analysis deliver a relative or a non-
relative conception of normative reasons?'

I said I want to take issue with a consequence Williams draws from
his own analysis of normative reasons. The consequence he draws
is that his analysis supports a *relative* conception of reasons. He
puts the point this way.

> [T]he truth of the sentence . . . ['A has a reason to φ'] . . . implies,
> very roughly, that A has some motive which will be served or
> furthered by his φ-ing, and if this turns out not to be so the
> sentence is false: there is a condition relating to the agent's aims,
> and if this is not satisfied it is not true to say . . . that he has a reason
> to φ. (1980: 101)

And again later:

> Basically, and by definition, . . . [an analysis of reasons] . . . must
> display a relativity of . . . [a] . . . reason statement to the agent's
> *subjective motivational set* . . . (1980: 102)

But why does Williams say this? For, as we have seen, even according to his analysis the claim that an agent has a normative reason
to φ is not a claim about her *actual* desires, but rather a claim
about her *hypothetical* desires. The truth of the sentence 'A has a
reason to φ' thus does not imply, not even 'very roughly', that A
has some motive which will be served or furthered by his φ-ing,
what it implies is rather that he *would* have some such desire if he
were fully rational.

Williams might concede this. But, he might say, it doesn't show
that he is wrong when he says that an analysis of reasons must
display a relativity of an agent's reasons to her actual desires, it
simply shows that the sort of relativity at issue requires more
careful formulation. The crucial point is that the desires an agent
would have if she were fully rational are themselves simply functions from her actual desires, where the relevant functions are
those described in conditions (i) through (iii). An agent's reasons
are thus relative to her actual desires, he might say, because we
cannot expect that, even under conditions of full rationality,
agents would all converge on the same desires about what is to be
done in the various circumstances they might face. Even if it is
rational for each of us to change our actual desires by trying to
come up with a set of desires that can be systematically justified –
in the manner captured by conditions (i) through (iii) – such
changes will always fall short of making us have the same desires
as our fellows; they will always reflect the antecedent fact that we
have the actual desires that we have.

As I see it, this is the best interpretation of Williams's claim that
our reasons are all relative. This explains why he is quite right to
insist that he is defending a 'Humean' conception of normative
reasons (1980: 102). For his conception of reasons, like Hume's
own, is predicated on scepticism about the scope for reasoned
change in our desires (Korsgaard, 1986); predicated on denying
that, through a process of rational deliberation – through attempting to give a systematic justification of our desires, for example
– we could ever come to discover reasons that we all share. For
what we have reason to do is given by the content of the desires we
would have if we were fully rational, and these differ in content
from agent to agent. Williams's Humean view is thus in opposition
to the anti-Humean or Kantian view that under conditions of full

rationality we would all reason ourselves towards the same conclusions as regards what is to be done; in opposition to the view
that via a process of systematic justification of our desires we could
bring it about that we converge in the desires that we have.

The question to ask is therefore whether Williams is right that
our concept of a normative reason presupposes such scepticism
about the scope for reasoned change in our desires. Does our
concept of a normative reason presuppose that there will, or
alternatively that there will not, be a convergence in the desires
that we would have under conditions of full rationality? If it
presupposes that there will not be such a convergence then our
concept of a normative reason is relative. If it presupposes instead
that there will be such a convergence then our concept of a
normative reason is, by contrast, non-relative.

In terms of the distinction introduced earlier, note that we are
asking a *conceptual* question, not a *substantive* question (chapter 3).
We are asking what we mean when we talk of people being fully
rational; whether it is part of what we mean by 'rational' that fully
rational people converge in their desires, or whether this is no
part of what we mean by 'rational'. However, though we are asking
a conceptual question, note that we are not thereby begging any
substantive questions. Even if our concept of a normative reason
is itself non-relative – even if our concept optimistically presupposes that we would all converge on the same desires under
conditions of full rationality – the world might disappoint us.
Entrenched and apparently rationally inexplicable differences in
what we desire might make it impossible to believe, substantively,
that there are any such non-relative normative reasons. We will
return to this idea in the next chapter.

Let's, then, confront the conceptual question head on. Is our
concept of a normative reason relative or non-relative? The relativity of a claim should manifest itself in the way we talk. Consider,
for example, the schematic claim 'It is desirable that p in circumstances C'. On the non-relative conception of normative reasons –
at least if we abstract away from some complications to be dealt
with presently – this claim has a straightforward truth condition: it
is desirable that p in C just in case we would all desire that p in C
if we were fully rational. There is, then, a sense in which we can

talk about rational justification or desirability *simpliciter*. When you and I talk about the reasons that there are for acting, we are therefore talking about the same thing. We are talking about reasons *period*.

On the relative conception, however, matters are quite different. For in order to give a truth condition for the schematic claim 'It is desirable that p in C' we need first to know from whose perspective the truth of the claim is to be assessed. For while 'It is desirable that p in C' as assessed from A's perspective is true if and only if A would desire that p in C if A were fully rational, 'It is desirable that p in C' as assessed from B's perspective is true if and only if B would desire that p in C if B were fully rational, and so on and so forth. There is thus no such thing as desirability or rational justification *simpliciter*, but only desirability$_A$, desirability$_B$, . . . ; rational-justifiability-from-A's-perspective, rational-justifiability-from-B's-perspective, . . . and so on. If I say to you 'There is a reason for ϕ-ing', and you deny this, we are therefore potentially talking about quite different things: reasons$_{me}$ and reasons$_{you}$. The question to ask is therefore whether the way in which we talk about reasons for action and rational justification reflects a relative or a non-relative conception of truth conditions.

One reason for thinking that it reflects the non-relative conception comes from the broader context in which the question is being asked. For it is important to remember that we have a whole range of normative concepts: truth, meaning, support, entailment, desirability, and so on. Between them these concepts allow us to ask all sorts of normative questions, questions about what we should and should not believe, say and do. But how many of these other normative concepts are plausibly thought to give rise to claims having relativized truth conditions? As I understand it, none of them do.

Consider our concept of support, by way of example. It seems quite implausible to suppose that the truth of claims about which propositions support which others is implicitly relative to the individual; that when A says 'p supports q' and B says 'p does not support q' they are potentially talking about quite different things: that A is talking about what supports$_A$ q and B is talking about what supports$_B$ q, for instance. For if this were the case then we should expect to find that we are sometimes able to dissolve apparent disagreements by finding that both parties are speaking truly. It should be permissable for B to say 'A said "p supports q" and what she said is true, but p does not support q'. However it is a striking feature of our talk about which propositions support which others that we *never* dissolve apparent disagreements in this way. Propositions have normative force *simpliciter*, not just normative-force-relative-to-this-individual or relative-to-that. When one individual says 'p supports q' and the other says 'p does not support q' they thus express their disagreement about whether p supports q in a *non-relative* sense.

If our concept of desirability were implicitly relativized, then, it seems that this would mark a significant difference between this concept and our other normative concepts. We should expect to find that with claims about what is desirable, unlike claims about which propositions support which, we *are* able to dissolve apparent disagreements in the way just described. But do we find this?

It might be thought that we do. After all, aren't there all sorts of familiar cases in which we say things like 'That may be a reason for you, but it isn't for me', 'Desirable for you maybe, but not desirable for me', and the like? But though there are indeed such cases, it is important to note that the sort of relativity we signal when we say such things is quite different from the kind just described; quite different from the kind of relativity Williams has in mind. For, in the familiar cases, 'That may be a reason for you, but it isn't for me' signals the fact that there is a relativity built in to the *considerations* that we use to rationally justify our choices. It does not signal the fact that our concept of rational justification is itself relative to the individual; that there is no such thing as which considerations, relative or not, rationally justify our choices, but only which considerations rationally-justify-relative-to-this-person or rationally-justify-relative-to-that-person. Here, then, we come to the complications abstracted away from earlier.

Sometimes what we have in mind when we say 'That may be a reason for you, but it isn't for me' is that the considerations that rationally justify our choices are, to use Parfit's terms, *agent-rela-*

tive, rather than *agent-neutral* (Parfit, 1984). Suppose you are standing on a beach. Two people are drowning to your left and one is drowning to your right. You can either swim left and save two, in which case the one on the right will drown, or you can swim right and save one, in which case the two on the left will drown. You decide to swim right and save the one and you justify your choice by saying 'The one on the right is my child, whereas the two on the left are perfect strangers to me'.

In one sense, of course, I may well say 'That may be a reason for you, but it isn't for me'. For if the three people drowning are all perfect strangers to me then, had I been standing on the beach instead of you, I would not have been able to justify the choice of swimming right and saving the one. But in another sense it seems that what is a reason for you may indeed be a reason for me. For if I had been standing on the beach instead of you, and if the one on the right had been my child, then surely I too would have been able to justify the choice of swimming right and saving the one by saying 'The one on the right is my child'. Indeed, if we think that a parent who fails to save their child in such circumstances fails to act on a reason available to her – as it seems to me that we do – then we are in fact obliged to say this; obliged to assume the non-relative conception of normative reasons.

What this sort of example shows is therefore that, even if reasons are non-relative in the crucial sense at issue here, among the considerations that may rationally justify our choices are both considerations that are properly given a *de dicto* formulation and considerations that are properly given a *de se* formulation (see also Lewis, 1989). That is there are both *de dicto* and *de se* normative reasons. We can each express the content of the *de dicto* reason relevant in this case by using the words 'There is a reason to save people quite generally' and we can each express the content of the *de se* reason by using the words 'There is a reason to save my child in particular'. In these terms we can then say that what is a reason for you, in this case, is not a reason for me in the sense that, if it had been me standing on the beach rather than you, and if the same people had been drowning, then the only consideration that would have been relevant to my choice is the *de dicto* reason. The *de se* reason would not have been relevant to my choice because the people who are in fact drowning are all perfect strangers to me. But in another sense what is a reason for you is indeed a reason for me. For if I had been standing on the beach and the one person on the right had been my child, as the one on the right is your child, then both the *de se* and the *de dicto* reason would have been relevant to my choice in just the way they are both relevant to yours.

I said that this sort of relativity is different from the kind that Williams has in mind, and it should now be plain why this is so. For, in terms of the analysis, even if some of the considerations that rationally justify our choices are relative because *de se*, the existence of such *de se* reasons may still require a convergence in the desires that we would all have if we were fully rational. That is, the existence of reasons with *de se* contents may still require that, under conditions of full rationality, we would each have desires whose contents we would express by using words like 'to help my children', 'to promote my welfare', and the like. The mere existence of *de se* reasons is thus quite different from the relativity Williams has in mind. For his claim is that reasons are relative in the sense of requiring no such convergence; that the fact that my act helps my child may rationally-justify-relative-to-me even though the fact that your act helps your child does not rationally-justify-relative-to-you.

There is another familiar sort of relativity in our claims about the reasons we have as well, a sort that derives from the fact that what we have reason to do is relative to our circumstances, where our circumstances may include aspects of our own psychology. Suppose, for example, that you and I differ in our preferences for wine over beer. Preferring wine, as you do, you may tell me that there is a reason to go to the local wine bar after work for a drink, for they sell very good wine. But then, preferring beer, as I do, I may quite rightly reply 'That may be a reason for you to go to the wine bar, but it is not a reason for me'.

Now while this might initially look like the claim that our reasons are relative to our desires in something like the sense Williams has in mind, it isn't really. For the crucial point in this case is that a relevant feature of your circumstances is your preference for wine, whereas a relevant feature of my circumstances is my preference for beer. That this is a relevant feature of our circumstances is manifest from the fact that I can quite happily agree with you that if I were in your circumstances – if I preferred wine to beer – then the fact that the local wine bar sells very good wine would constitute a reason for me to go there as well, just as it constitutes a reason for you.

This sort of relativity is thus completely different from the kind that Williams has in mind as well. For, in terms of the analysis, even if an agent's preferences may enter into a specification of the circumstances that she faces it may still be the case that whether or not she is rationally justified in taking her own preferences into account, and the way in which she is justified in taking them into account if she is, depends on whether fully rational agents would all converge on a desire which makes the preferences she has relevant to her choice, and, if they do, the way in which the desire they converge upon makes her preferences relevant to her choice (Pettit and Smith, 1993b). The fact that in rationally justifying our choices our preferences may sometimes be a relevant feature of our circumstances thus does nothing to support Williams's view that rational justification is itself a relative matter; that really there is only rational-justification-relative-to-this-person or rational-justification-relative-to-that.

In order to find support for the sort of relativity Williams has in mind, we therefore need to look for cases in which it is permissable to make much more radically relativized claims about what there is reason to do. But in fact, as far as I can tell, we find no such claims. Suppose someone tells me that she has a reason to take a holiday and that I think I would have no reason to take a holiday in the circumstances she faces. Provided we have taken proper account of the *de se* considerations that might be relevant to her choice, and provided we have taken proper account of the way in which her preferences may constitute a relevant feature of her circumstances, it seems that I straightforwardly disagree with her about the rational justifiability of her taking a holiday in the circumstances she faces, a disagreement I can express by saying 'She thinks that there is a reason to take a holiday in her circumstances, but there is no such reason'. If she cites a consideration in support of her taking a holiday that I think fails to justify, then I do not conclude that it may justify-relative-to-her, though not justify-relative-to-me, I conclude that it fails to justify *simpliciter*.

The point is important, for it suggests that when we talk about reasons for action we quite generally take ourselves to be talking about a common subject matter. We are thus potentially in agreement or disagreement with each other about what constitutes a reason and what doesn't. This is why, when we find ourselves in disagreement – as for example in the case of disagreement about whether or not there is a reason to take a holiday in certain circumstances – we always have the option of engaging in argument in the attempt to find out who is right and who is wrong. Other people's opinions about the reasons that there are thus constitute potential challenges to my own opinions. I have something to learn about myself and my own reasons by finding out about others and their reasons. This is why books and films are so engaging. All of this is flat out inconsistent with the claim that our concept of a reason for action is quite generally relative to the individual; that it typically means reason$_{me}$ out of my mouth, reason$_{you}$ out of your's, reason$_{her}$ out of her's and so on. It suggests rather that our concept of a normative reason is stubbornly non-relative.

Indeed, it seems to me that we have no choice but to think this; for if normative reasons were indeed relative, then mere reflection on that fact would suffice to undermine their normative significance. For on the relative conception it turns out that, for example, the desirability$_{me}$ of some consideration, p, is entirely dependent on the fact that *my* actual desires are such that, if *I* were to engage in a process of systematically justifying *my* desires, weeding out those that aren't justified and acquiring those that are, a desire that p would be one of the desires *I* would end up having. But what my actual desires are to begin with is, on this relative conception of reasons, an entirely *arbitrary* matter, one without any normative significance of its own. I might have had any old set of desires to begin with, even a set that delivered up the desire that not p after a process of systematic justification. The desirability$_{me}$ of the fact that p thus turns out to be an entirely arbitrary fact about it. But arbitrariness is precisely a feature of a consideration that tends to undermine any normative significance it might initially appear to have (Smith, 1989; Darwall, Gibbard and Railton, 1992).

On the non-relative conception, by contrast, reflection on our concept of desirability reveals no such arbitrariness. For on that conception everyone can reason themselves to the same desires if they engage in a process of systematic justification of their desires. Which desires *I* would end up with, after engaging in such a process, thus in no way depends on what *my* actual desires are to begin with. Reason itself determines the content of our fully rational desires, not the arbitrary fact that we have the actual desires that we have. Reflection on the concept of desirability thus leaves the normative significance of facts about what is desirable and undesirable perfectly intact.

I have been arguing that the truth of a normative reason claim requires a convergence in the desires of fully rational agents. However note that the convergence required is not at the level of desires about how each such agent is to organize her own life in her own world. In their own worlds fully rational agents will find themselves in quite different circumstances from each other, circumstances that are conditioned by their different embodiments, talents, environments and attachments in their respective worlds. Their desires about how to organize their own lives in their own worlds will therefore reflect these differences in their circumstances. The convergence required is rather at the level of their hypothetical desires about what is to be done in the various circumstances in which they might find themselves.

The mere fact that a convergence in the hypothetical desires of fully rational creatures is required for the truth of normative reason claims does nothing to guarantee that such a convergence is forthcoming, of course. In defending the non-relative *conception* of normative reasons we have therefore said nothing to suggest that, *substantively*, there are any such reasons. But what we have said does suggest that, in order to discover whether there are any normative reasons, and if so what they are, we have no alternative but to give the arguments and see where they lead. Substantive convergence is always assumed to be available, in so far as we converse and argue about the reasons that we have. But whether or not this assumption is true is always *sub judice*; something to be discovered by the outcome of those very conversations and arguments (compare Pettit on rule-following 1993: especially 96–7).

Seventh question 'Are normative reason claims categorical imperatives or hypothetical imperatives?'

Foot claims that the requirements of practical reason are hypothetical imperatives. For, she tells us, claims about what an agent has normative reason to do must be withdrawn 'if we find that the right relation does not hold between the action and the end – that it is either no way of getting what he wants (or doing what he wants to do) or not the most eligible among possible means'; or again because she tells us that the agent can rebut a normative reason claim 'by showing that the action is not ancillary to his interests or desires' (Foot, 1972: 159). None of this would be possible if normative reason claims were categorical imperatives. For then the truth of the reason claim would be a function of the circumstances in which the agent finds herself quite irrespective of whether or not she has a desire or interest in what she is supposed to have a reason to do.

But, as should now be clear, the idea that reason claims are hypothetical imperatives – at least as Foot characterizes the hypothetical imperative – simply flies in the face of commonplaces about the ways in which normative reasons and motivating reasons may come apart. For it is a commonplace that, for example, depressives have reasons to do all sorts of things. But these are not reasons to do things that they desire or take an interest in, for the effect of their depression has been precisely to destroy any desire or interest they have in anything, even the things that they believe they have reason to do. Claims about the reasons depressives have are therefore not to be withdrawn simply because depressives lack relevant desires.

At best, then, in order for an agent to rebut the claim that she has a normative reason to act in a certain way what she has to show is that acting in that way is not ancillary to her *hypothetical* desires: the desires she would have, if she were fully rational, about what she is to do in the circumstances she in fact faces. However, as we have seen, because our concept of a normative reason is non-relative, in assessing the truth of such claims we presuppose that fully rational agents would all have the same desires about what is to be done and desired in various circumstances. On this account, normative reason claims are therefore categorical imperatives, for agents who face the same circumstances all have the same reasons.

We must therefore reject Foot's claim that reason claims are hypothetical imperatives. The non-relative character of normative reasons entails that normative reason claims are categorical imperatives after all.

Eighth question 'What are the epistemological consequences of the fact that normative reason claims are categorical imperatives?'

Consider again the earlier discussion of deliberation. We saw then that one of the ways in which we can decide what we have normative reason to do – that is, what we would desire that we do under conditions of full rationality – is by attempting to find a set of desires that is systematically justifiable. For such a set of desires will be our best assessment of the desires we would have under conditions of full rationality. However now that we have seen that the truth of a normative reason claim presupposes that fully rational agents would all have the same desires about what is to be done in the various circumstances they might face, this task of finding a systematic justification of our desires starts to take on a distinctively social dimension. Let me explain why.

Since other people's opinions about what is and is not desirable are not just either the same as or different from our own, so it follows that they potentially confirm or disconfirm our own opinions – depending, of course, on the quality of the arguments they can offer in their support. It is therefore not just important to them, but also important to us, which of their desires they think of as appropriate starting points for this process of systematic justification described earlier, not just because where they end up will be a function of where they begin, but because their judgements about the appropriateness of the desires from which to begin are themselves potentially in conflict with our own judgements about the desires from which it would be appropriate to begin. For, if there are any non-relative facts about what is desirable, then the desires from which it is appropriate for anyone to begin in engaging in systematic reasoning in the attempt to find out what these facts are can only be those from which we are able to build a substantive convergence in our desires.

Unsurprisingly, then, argument about what is and is not desirable thus becomes just like argument about what supports what. The epistemology of value, like the epistemology of what supports what, requires the individual to see herself as one among a group of individuals who are trying to answer a common set of questions, questions whose formulation does not require reference to any one of them in particular. She must admit that, other things being equal, no one is better placed than any one else to answer these questions simply in virtue of being the person they are: no one is infallible about such matters and no one is incapable of having an opinion worth listening to. Other things being equal, the individual must therefore have a proper sense of humility when she finds herself in disagreement with the group. She must admit that she can rationally take a stand against the group only when she can construct a plausible story about why her own opinion is more credible than the opinion of her fellows. And, on plausible assumptions, that will in general be no easy task.

Rawls was himself well aware of all these implications. As I see it, this is why he formulated reflective equilibrium in social terms rather than individualistic terms; why, for example, he insists that the appropriate judgements with which to begin our attempts at systematic justification are our 'considered judgements', which he defines *inter alia* as follows.

> It is required that the judgement be stable, that is, that there be evidence that at other times and at other places competent judges have rendered the same judgement on similar cases, understanding similar cases to be those in which the relevant facts and the competing interests are similar. The similarity must hold, by and large, over the class of competent judges and over their judgements at different times. (Rawls, 1951: 182)

In deciding which desires to begin from in the attempt to find a systematic justification of our desires, then, we have no choice but to look for desires that are similarly widely shared. We have no choice given two key assumptions: first, that the goal is to find a single set of desires that all rational creatures would acknowledge to be systematically justifiable, and second, that none of us has any special epistemic gifts that would justify us in privileging our own desires and judgements over the desires and judgements of others in advance; justify us in advance in writing off their contrary desires and opinions as having no epistemic significance for us.

5.10   THE PUZZLE SOLVED

Let's return to the main line of argument. I said that an analysis of desirability in terms of what we would desire if we were fully rational allows us to make sense of C2; the claim that if I believe that I have a normative reason to φ then I rationally should desire to φ. We are now in a position to explain why that is so.

C2 tells us that if we believe we have a normative reason to φ then we rationally should desire to φ. According to the analysis, the belief that we have a normative reason to φ, or that it is desirable that we φ, can be represented as the belief that we would desire to φ if we were fully rational. But now, suppose we believe that we would desire to φ if we were fully rational and yet fail to desire to φ. Are we irrational? We most certainly are. And by our own lights. For we fail to have a desire that we believe it is rational for us to have. In other words, if we believe that we would desire to φ if we were fully rational then we rationally should desire to φ. And that is just C2.

In this way we capture the letter of C2, but can we capture its spirit? If we believe that we would desire to φ if we were fully rational, and yet desire not to φ, can we see why we should get rid of the desire not to φ and acquire the desire to φ instead, rather than, for example, change our evaluative belief? (Here we recall the problem facing the reduction of valuing to desiring to desire.) We certainly can.

Our φ-ing is desirable just in case we would desire to φ if we were fully rational. Now, by hypothesis, what we believe is that we would desire to φ if we were fully rational. We do not believe that we would desire *not* to φ if we were fully rational. And the mere fact that we actually desire not to φ gives us no reason to change this belief; it gives us no reason to reevaluate the truth of our belief. Believing what we believe it therefore follows that we rationally should get rid of the desire not to φ and acquire the desire to φ instead.[2]

This argument is admittedly very simple. As with many simple arguments, its real power may therefore be overlooked; it might be thought *too* simple. So let me add further support for this argument by showing that a structurally similar argument allows us to explain a similar phenomenon in the case of belief.

Note that the following principle, itself much like C2, governs our beliefs:

C3   If an agent believes she has (most) reason to believe that p then she rationally should believe that p.

And note, furthermore, that we can explain C3 via an argument that strictly parallels the argument just given to explain C2. That argument trades on a platitude about reasons for action. So consider a platitude about reasons for believing. Just as, if we have a reason for φ-ing we can say that φ-ing is desirable, where desirability is fixed by norms of rationality, if we have (most) reason to believe p we can say that p is (most) credible, where credibility too is fixed by norms of rationality. But now note that just as it is a platitude to say that if φ-ing is desirable then φ-ing is what we would desire if we were fully rational, it is also a platitude to say that if p is (most) credible then p is what we would believe if we were fully rational. Equipped with these platitudes, we have enough to explain C3.

Suppose an agent believes that she would believe that p if she were fully rational and yet fails to believe that p. Is she irrational? She certainly is. And by her own lights! For she fails to believe something she believes she has (most) reason to believe. Indeed, this must surely be a paradigmatic case of irrationality. Moreover, note that we can also explain why someone who believes that p is (most) credible, but who also finds herself believing that not p, rationally should get rid of her belief that not p and acquire the belief that p instead. For p is (most) credible just in case she would believe that p if she were fully rational. And, by hypothesis, that is what she believes. She does not believe that she would believe that not p if she were fully rational. And the mere fact that she actually believes that not p gives her no reason to change her belief. Thus she rationally should get rid of her belief that not p and acquire the belief that p instead. And that is just C3.

Given the structural similarity between this argument and the argument for C2, and given the success of the argument in the case of belief, I conclude that both arguments are successful. The platitude that desirability is a matter of what we would desire if we were fully rational suffices to show how it can be that our beliefs about our reasons rationally require us to have corresponding desires.

The truth of C2 has obvious repurcussions for the nature of deliberation. Suppose an agent who does not yet desire to φ deliberates and, as a result, comes to believe that she has a normative reason to φ. And suppose further that her coming to have this belief then causes her to desire to φ. Given C2 it follows that we should redescribe this causal transition between belief and desire in normative terms. For her having that belief causes her to have a desire that it is rational for her to have, given her belief. The causal transition between this belief and desire is thus on all fours with the causal transition between, say, the beliefs that p and that p → q and the belief that q; or between the belief that all the evidence supports q, or it is (most) credible that q, and the belief that q.

Moreover, note the fact that our beliefs and desires may bear such normative relations to each other is not inconsistent with the Humean theory of motivating reasons defended earlier. Indeed, this whole discussion has been premised on the Humean theory. All actions are indeed produced by desires, just as the Humean says; no actions are produced by beliefs alone or by besires. But, if what we have said here is right, some of these desires are themselves produced by the agent's beliefs about the reasons she has, beliefs she acquires through rational deliberation.

We are now in a position to pull the threads of the discussion together. It seemed difficult to reconcile the claim that deliberation on the basis of our values is practical in its issue to just the extent that it is with two further claims, the claim that deliberation normally reflects our evaluative beliefs and the claim that our actions are produced by our desires. However we have seen that these claims are not in conflict. Instead they reflect a substantive fact about human agents: namely, that we are rational creatures who are sometimes more rational, sometimes less. Deliberation on the basis of our evaluative beliefs is practical in its issue to just the extent that it is because *that* is precisely the extent to which we are rational.

The point is not that this answer is in any way surprising. It was always the only answer available. For if, when we deliberate, we try to decide what we have reason to do, and to the extent that we are rational we will either already have corresponding desires or our beliefs about what we have reason to do will cause us to have corresponding desires, then nothing else but the contingent fact that we are rational to just the extent that we are could explain the resulting matches and mismatches between our beliefs about what we have reason to do and our desires. Our contingent rationality is the only variable. The point is simply that now we know *why* our being rational plays this role. It plays this role because what we have normative reason to do is a matter of what we would desire that we do if we were fully rational.

It thus follows that there is no conflict in the two perspectives on the explanation of action described at the outset: the intentional and the deliberative. All intentional actions are indeed explicable from the intentional perspective in terms of our underlying desires and beliefs. But, to the extent that we are rational, our actions are also explicable from the deliberative perspective, for our desires are themselves sensitive to our beliefs about our reasons. Our substantive rationality thus explains why the connection between deliberation and action is not entirely contingent and fortuitous.

5.11   SUMMARY AND PREVIEW

The aim of this chapter has been to provide a radically anti-Humean analysis of normative reasons. According to the analysis, to say that we have a normative reason to φ in certain circumstances C is to say that, if we were fully rational, we would want that we φ in C. The analysis is radically anti-Humean in four respects.

First, it makes our normative reasons the object of our beliefs, and so allows our beliefs about our normative reasons a proper causal role in the production of action. Second, it affords us a critical perspective on even our underived desires, showing us why we may have reason to get rid of them and reason to acquire other, new, underived desires instead. Third, it is a non-relative conception of normative reasons – what is to count as a reason for you in your circumstances must also count as a reason for me in mine if our circumstances are the same – and so claims about our normative reasons are thus categorical rather than hypothetical imperatives. And fourth, it forces us to admit that the epistemology of normative reason claims is itself therefore a social matter: other things being equal, each person is as well placed to come up with an answer to the question 'What is there normative reason to do?' as any other person. The analysis itself does not entail that there are any normative reasons of course – why should we think it would? – but it does allow us to set about asking whether there are with a clearer understanding of what we are looking for.

In the next chapter I show how these considerations allow us to solve the moral problem of the book's title. I also consider the substantive question whether there are any normative reasons. To anticipate: I argue that we have good reason to believe that there are.

6

How to Solve the Moral Problem

6.1 AN ANALYSIS OF RIGHTNESS IN TERMS OF FACTS ABOUT OUR NORMATIVE REASONS

We said that an analysis of rightness must capture various core platitudes about morality, platitudes concerning the objectivity and practicality of moral judgement, the supervenience of the moral on the natural, the distinctive substance of moral requirements, and the various procedures via which we come by moral knowledge (chapter 2). Moreover, we said that even if such an analysis is not a thoroughly reductive naturalistic definition, even if it is merely a non-reductive analysis, we must still be able to use it to square morality with a broader naturalism. Moral features must turn out to be natural features, if there are any moral features at all; morality must not require anything non-natural for its realization (chapter 2). And finally, we said that, according to such an analysis, it must turn out that facts about rightness have the character of categorical requirements of reason (chapter 3).

Now we have already seen that we can analyse our concept of a normative reason quite generally in congenial, radically anti-Humean, categorical imperative terms. To say that we have a normative reason to ϕ in certain circumstances C is to say that we would want ourselves to ϕ in C if we were fully rational. If there is a normative reason for some agent to ϕ in certain circumstances C then there is a like normative reason for all those who find themselves in circumstances C to ϕ. Such an analysis thus already captures platitudes about objectivity, practicality, supervenience, and procedure. However facts about the normative reasons we have quite generally are not themselves *identical* with facts about which acts it is right for us to perform. For even though all claims about what it is right for us to do entail corresponding claims about what we have normative reason to do, not all claims about what we have normative reason to do entail corresponding claims about what it is right for us to do. Consider some examples by way of illustration.

It seems easy to imagine that I have a normative reason to drink beer rather than wine while relaxing after work. For anyone in relevantly similar circumstances to mine – which in this case includes the fact that I enjoy beer rather than wine – this may be the perfect way of relaxing. To suppose otherwise would be mistaken. If I drink wine to relax after work then I am not doing what I have normative reason to do. But even admitting that this is so, it is hard to believe that I am *morally required* to drink beer rather than wine while relaxing after work; that it would be *immoral* for me to drink wine. For even though reasons are at stake, the reasons at stake are not themselves *moral* reasons.

Or again, consider the life of someone who is moved wholly and solely by considerations of rightness. Perhaps she devotes her life to the common good, never giving her own welfare a single thought, except in so far as her welfare is part of, or implicated in, the common good. Such a life certainly seems to have something important missing from it. For a life that is perfect from the moral point of view may lack much of what makes a life personally fulfilling. It may lack much that is significant, not from the moral point of view, but from the point of view of the person whose life it is: the point of view of *personal perfection* (Wolf, 1982). Reasons are at stake but, again, they are not moral reasons.

What needs to be addressed is thus how precisely we are to demarcate the province of the moral, as opposed to the non-moral, reasons. And the answer is plain enough. For what the analysis of normative reasons quite generally leaves out of account – and rightly so, of course – is the distinctive *substance* or *content* of reasons that makes them into moral reasons as opposed to non-moral reasons. The fact that there is such a distinctive substance or content is, you will recall, evident from the platitudes concerning substance that we find amongst the platitudes constitutive of the moral. These are platitudes like 'Right acts are often concerned to promote or sustain or contribute in some way to human flourishing', 'Right acts are in some way expressive of equal concern and respect', and the like (chapter 2). These platitudes need not and should not be thought of as fixing a unique content or substance for moral reasons all by themselves, rather they simply serve to tell us when we are in the ballpark of moral reasons, as opposed to the ballpark of non-moral reasons (Dreier 1990). It is these platitudes about substance that need to be added in and captured if we are to turn our analysis of normative reasons quite generally into an analysis of rightness in particular.

My suggestion then, in schematic form at least, is that our φ-ing in circumstances C is right if and only if we would desire that we φ in C, if we were fully rational, *where φ-ing in C is an act of the appropriate substantive kind*: that is, it is an act of the kind picked out in the platitudes about substance. There is clearly further work to be done here in filling out this idea of an 'appropriate substantive kind' in detail, but the schematic form of the analysis will suffice for our purposes.

6.2   THE SOLUTION TO THE
MORAL PROBLEM

We now have a solution to the moral problem at hand. That is, we can now explain why the following three propositions:

1   Moral judgements of the form 'It is right that I φ' express a subject's beliefs about an objective matter of fact, a fact about what it is right for her to do.

2   If someone judges that it is right that she φs then, *ceteris paribus*, she is motivated to φ.

3   An agent is motivated to act in a certain way just in case she has an appropriate desire and a means-end belief, where belief and desire are, in Hume's terms, distinct existences.

are both consistent and true. Let me briefly explain why.

If our concept of rightness is the concept of what we would desire ourselves to do if we were fully rational, where this is a desire for something of the appropriate substantive kind, then it does indeed follow that our moral judgements are expressions of our beliefs about an objective matter of fact. For our moral judgements are expressions of our beliefs about what we have normative reason to do, where such reasons are in turn categorical requirements of rationality. (1) is thus true. Moreover, as we have seen, such beliefs do indeed connect with motivation in the manner of (2). And, again as we have seen, their doing so does not in any way compomise the claim that motivation is to be explained in Humean terms: that is, in terms of belief and desire, where belief and desire are distinct existences. (3) too is thus true. So far so good. But does the analysis allow us not only to solve the moral problem, but to do so in a way that allows us to square morality with a broader naturalism? It seems to me that it does.

The analysis tells us that the rightness of acts in certain circumstances C – using our earlier terminology, let's call this the 'evaluated possible world' – is the feature that we would want acts to have in C if we were fully rational, where these wants have the appropriate content – and, again, using our earlier terminology, let's call this world, the world in which we are fully rational, the 'evaluating possible world'. Now though, for reasons already given, this does not itself constitute a naturalistic definition of rightness – though it is merely a non-reductive, summary style analysis (chapter 5) – it does provide us with the materials to construct a two-stage argument of the following kind.

Conceptual claim: Rightness in circumstances C is the feature we would want acts to have in C if we were fully rational, where these wants have the appropriate content

Substantive claim: Fness is the feature we would want acts to have in C if we were fully rational, and Fness is a feature of the appropriate kind

Conclusion: Rightness in C is Fness

And this argument is, in turn, broadly naturalistic in two respects. First, it is naturalistic in so far as the features that we would want our acts to have under conditions of full rationality, the features that we would want acts to instantiate in the evaluated possible world, are themselves all natural features whenever the evaluated world is itself naturalistic. Our non-reductive, summary style definition of rightness, in conjunction with a substantive claim of the kind described, thus allows us to identify rightness with a natural feature of acts in naturalistic worlds like the actual world: for example, in this case, with Fness.

And second, even though the analysis is not itself naturalistic – even though it defines rightness in terms of full rationality where this may not itself be definable in naturalistic terms – fully rational creatures in the evaluating possible world are themselves naturalistically realized. For a fully rational creature is simply someone with a certain psychology and, as you will recall, a natural feature is simply a feature that figures in one of the natural or social sciences, *including psychology* (chapter 2). Of course, the psychology of a fully rational creature is an idealized psychology, but such an idealization requires nothing non-natural for its realization. Thus, if we wanted to, we could construct non-reductive analyses of the key normative concepts we use to characterize the normative features of such an idealized creature's psychology – the unity, the coherence, and the like, of its desires – and then use these analyses to construct two-stage arguments, much like that just given, in order to identify these normative features of a fully rational creature's psychology with natural features of its psychology (for an analogy, see note 9 to chapter 2). Coherence and unity, though not naturalistically definable are therefore themselves just natural features of a psychology. The evaluating possible world is therefore naturalistic in the relevant respect as well.

The analysis of rightness provided thus makes the legitimacy of moral talk depend ultimately upon the possibility of identifying moral features, like rightness, with natural features of acts. Absent such identifications, we would have to conclude that moral features are simply not instantiated at all; that moral talk is, much as Mackie thought, based on an error of presupposition.

But can we say more? Can we say whether moral talk is or is not legitimate?

6.3 ARE THERE ANY MORAL FACTS?

The substantive claim in the two-stage argument described above tells us that moral talk is legitimate just in case a certain condition is met. My handing back a wallet I found in the street in such and such circumstances is right, for example, only if, under conditions of full rationality, we would all want that if we find a wallet in the street in such and such circumstances, then we hand it back. Of course, if this is indeed true, then it is an *a priori* truth. The fact that we would have such a desire under conditions of full rationality will be a consequence of the theory that systematically justifies our desires, and this task of theory construction is itself a relatively *a priori* enterprise; it is a task that requires reflection and conversation, not empirical investigation. However that does not mean that it is an *obvious* truth. For it might not only take a good deal of reflection and conversation for any individual to discover this to be true, it might also take time and effort to convince anyone else. And of course, even after all of that time and effort, it might turn out that we are wrong. What we thought was an *a priori* truth might have been no truth at all. In deciding whether or not moral talk is legitimate, then, it seems to me that we have no alternative but to admit that we are venturing an opinion on something about which we can have no cast-iron guarantee.

However, for all that, it seems to me that we should none the less have some confidence in the legitimacy of moral talk. For, in short, the empirical fact that moral argument tends to elicit the agreement of our fellows gives us reason to believe that there will be a convergence in our desires under conditions of full rationality. For the best explanation of that tendency is our convergence upon a set of extremely unobvious *a priori* moral truths. And the truth of these unobvious *a priori* moral truths requires, in turn, a convergence in the desires that fully rational creatures would have.

Now this argument is likely to meet with some resistance. After all, isn't there currently much entrenched moral disagreement?

And don't such disagreements constitute profound obstacles to a convergence in our desires in fact emerging? This is true, but it does not count against the force of the argument. Indeed, once we remember the following three points, such disagreements can be seen to add to the force of the argument.

First, we must remember that alongside such entrenched disagreements as we in fact find we also find massive areas of entrenched agreement. As I see it, this is the real significance of the fact that we have and use the so-called 'thick' moral concepts, concepts that at once both describe some naturalistic state of affairs and positively or negatively evaluate it: concepts like courage, brutality, honesty, duplicity, loyalty, meanness, kindness, treachery, and the like (Williams, 1985: 129). For what the prevalence of such concepts suggests is that there is in fact considerable agreement about what is right and wrong: acts of brutality, duplicity, meanness and treachery are wrong, at least other things being equal, whereas acts of courage, honesty, loyalty, and kindness are right, again, other things being equal. What the prevalence of such concepts suggests is therefore that moral agreement is in fact *so* extensive that our language has developed in such a way as to build an evaluative component into certain naturalistically descriptive concepts.[1]

Second, when we look at current areas of entrenched disagreement, we must remember that in the past similarly entrenched disagreements were removed *inter alia* via a process of moral argument. I am thinking in particular of the historical, and in some places still current, debates over slavery, worker's rights, women's rights, democracy and the like. We must not forget that there has been considerable moral progress, and that what moral progress consists in is the removal of entrenched disagreements of just the kind that we currently face.

And third and finally, we must remember that where entrenched disagreements currently seem utterly intractable we can often explain why this is the case in ways that make them seem less threatening to the idea of a convergence in the opinions of fully rational creatures. For example, one or the other parties to the disagreement all too often forms their moral beliefs in response to the directives of a religious authority rather than as the result of

the exercise of their own free thought in concert with their fellows. But beliefs formed exclusively in this way have dubious rational credentials. They require that we privilege one group's opinions about what is to be done – those of the religious authority – over another's – those of the followers – for no good reason. The fact that disagreement persists for this sort of reason thus casts no doubt on the possibility of an agreement if we were to engage in free and rational debate.[2]

In light of these points it seems to me that, notwithstanding such disagreements as there are and will perhaps remain, we should therefore in fact be quite optimistic about the possibility of an agreement about what is right and wrong being reached under more idealized conditions of reflection and discussion. We might eventually come to be pessimistic, of course. Our epistemic situation might deteriorate, widespread disagreements might emerge, disagreements that seem both unresolvable and inexplicable. And if that were to happen, then we might well quite justifiably come to think that Mackie was right after all, that there are no moral facts, though there would still be room for doubt. The point is simply that this *is not* our current epistemic situation.[3]

6.4 HOW THE ANALYSIS OF RIGHTNESS ENABLES US TO REPLY TO STANDARD OBJECTIONS TO RATIONALISM

The argument so far has been that, given our analysis of rightness, it follows that we should accept both the rationalist's conceptual claim and the rationalist's substantive claim. Our concept of a right act is the concept of a categorical requirement of reason and, substantively, there are indeed such categorical requirements of reason – or so we should think. In this next to final section I want briefly to consider how the analysis of rightness enables us to reply some of the standard objections to rationalism. I consider objections put forward by Hume, Foot, Harman, Gauthier and Mackie.

Hume's Objection

Perhaps the most famous objection to rationalism is to be found in the following passage from Hume's *Treatise*.

> In every system of morality which I have hitherto met with, I have always remarked that the author proceeds for some time in the ordinary way of reasoning, and establishes the being of a god, or makes observations concerning human affairs; when of a sudden I am surpised to find that instead of the usual copulations of propositions is and is not, I meet with no proposition that is not connected with an ought or an ought not. This change is imperceptible, but is, however, of the last consequence. For as this ought or ought not expresses some new relation or affirmation, it is necessary that it should be observed and explained; and at the same time that a reason should be given for what seems altogether inconceiveable, how this new relation can be a deduction from others which are entirely different from it. (1888: 469)

Hume is right that an explanation is needed. But an explanation is also easy enough to provide.

Consider an analogy. Suppose we discover that a certain surface reflectance property, α, is the property that causes objects to look red to normal perceivers under standard conditions. Familiarly enough, we are then in a position to assert that an object's having surface reflectance property α entails that that object is red. But how can this be? How can facts about an object's colour 'be a deduction' from, or entailed by, facts about its surface reflectance properties? For these two sorts of fact are 'entirely different' from each other, at least in the sense that they are not definitionally equivalent.

The answer is that, even though it is not true by definition that being red is a matter of having surface reflectance property α, it is true by definition that being red is a matter of having the property that *actually* causes objects to look red to normal perceivers under standard conditions.[4] The entailment therefore follows from the fact that the following inference can be known to be valid merely by knowing the meanings of words.

First premise: Object x has surface reflectance property α

Second premise: Surface reflectance property α is the property
                             that actually causes objects to look red to nor-
                             mal perceivers under standard conditions

Conclusion: Object x is red

For then, since the second premise is a necessary truth – that is,
since every possible world in which surface reflectance property α
exists is a possible world in which the property that causes objects
to look red to normal perceivers under standard conditions *in the
actual world* exists – it can be removed without affecting the argument's validity. For it is impossible for the first premise to be true
and the conclusion false. The first premise thus entails the conclusion all by itself.

The transition from 'is' to 'ought' is in some respects the same.
Suppose we discover that, in certain circumstances C, giving to
famine relief is the feature we would want acts to have in C if we
were fully rational. Then we are in a position to assert that someone's giving to famine relief in certain circumstances C entails
that they do the right thing in C. True enough, the fact that
someone does the right thing in C is 'entirely different' from
the fact that she gives to famine relief in C, at least in the sense
that the two are not definitionally equivalent. But, none the less,
the appropriateness of the entailment claim follows from the
fact that the following inference is one that we can know to be
valid merely by knowing the meanings of words.

First premise: An agent gives to famine relief in circum-
                             stances C

Second premise: Giving to famine relief in circumstances C is the
                             feature that we would want acts to have in C if
                             we were fully rational, where such a want is of
                             the appropriate substantive kind

Conclusion: Giving to famine relief in circumstances C is the
                             right thing to do in C

For, again, since the second premise is a necessary truth it too can be omitted without affecting the argument's validity. But in that case it follows that the first premise entails the conclusion all by itself. For the first premise cannot be true and the conclusion false. We have therefore derived an 'ought' from an 'is'.

There is, of course, a point of disanalogy between the two arguments just given, and it is worthwhile making this explicit. Whereas, in the moral case, the second premise of the argument is not just necessary, but also knowable *a priori*, the second premise of the argument in the colour case, though necessary, is itself only knowable *a posteriori*. However this feature of disanalogy should not hide the more striking features of analogy already mentioned. For in neither case is the second premise a matter of definitional equivalence. Knowledge of the second premise of the argument in the moral case requires substantive work in the form of reflection on which of our desires would survive a process of reflective equilibrium, and even if this is a relatively *a priori* enterprise, unlike the attempt to discover *a posteriori* which surface reflectance properties of objects cause the appropriate visual experiences, it is arguably just as difficult and problematic, perhaps even more so. This is why the truth of the entailment claim comes as such a surprise in both cases.

Not everyone will be entirely happy with this explanation of the transition from 'is' to 'ought'. Barry Stroud, for example, tells us that Hume's real concern in the famous 'is-ought' passage is that though we

> . . . undoubtedly do make transitions from beliefs about the way things are to the judgement that things ought to be a certain way . . . if we understand the peculiar nature of these 'conclusions' – if we recognize their 'active' or motivational force – we see that the transitions by which they are reached are not ones that reason determines us to make. Once we come to have certain beliefs about the way things are, then, because of natural human dispositions we come to feel certain sentiments which we express in moral judgements. (1977: 187)

But the previous discussion suffices to show why, if this was Hume's concern, it too can be laid to rest.

The active or motivational force of an 'ought' judgement is captured by the practicality requirement on moral judgement: if an agent judges that an act is right then either she is motivated to act accordingly or she is irrational. But now, contrary to Hume, we have seen that there is no tension involved in accepting this requirement while thinking of moral judgements as expressions of beliefs rather than expressions of our 'sentiments'. Indeed, the very analysis of rightness in terms of facts about normative reasons, the analysis that allows us to explain why the transition from 'is' to 'ought' is one that reason determines us to make, itself allows us to explain why moral beliefs are subject to the practicality requirement. For, very roughly, if we believe that φ-ing in certain circumstances C has the feature that we would want acts to have in C if we were fully rational then, on the one hand, to the extent that we are rational either we will already want to φ in C or our belief will cause us to have this want, and, on the other, to the extent that we do not want to φ in C and our belief does not cause us to have this want we will not be fully rational. And that is, of course, just what the practicality requirement on moral judgement would lead us to expect about the connection between our moral beliefs and motivations.[5]

Foot's and Harman's Objection

Foot's main objection to rationalism is that we can give no content to the idea that the immoral person is irrational.

> Attempts have sometimes been made to show that some kind of irrationality is involved in ignoring the 'should' of morality: in saying 'Immoral – so what?' as one says 'Not *comme il faut* – so what?' But as far as I can see these have rested on some illegitimate assumption, as, for instance, of thinking that the amoral man who agrees that some piece of conduct is immoral but takes no notice of that, is inconsistently disregarding a rule of conduct that he has accepted; or again of thinking it inconsistent to desire that others will not do to one what one proposes to do to them. The fact is that the man who rejects morality because he sees no reason to obey its rules can be convicted of villainy but not inconsistency. (1972: 161)

Foot's objection here is, in effect, that there is no way of rationally criticizing the desires of those who reject morality, so the
rationalist who claims that there is must be making some 'illicit
assumption'.

Gilbert Harman objects to rationalism – or, as he calls it, 'ab-
solutism' – in a similar vein.

> [T]here are people, such as the successful criminal, who do not
> observe the alleged requirement not to harm or injure others and
> this is not due to inattention, failure to consider or appreciate
> certain arguments, ignorance of relevant evidence, errors in
> reasoning, irrationality, unreasonableness, or weakness of will . . .
>
> The absolutist might argue that the criminal must be irrational
> or at least unreasonable. Seeing that a proposed course of action
> will probably cause serious injury to some outsider, the criminal
> does not treat this as a reason not to undertake that course of
> action. This must be irrational or unreasonable, because such a
> consideration simply is such a reason and indeed is an obvious
> reason, a basic reason, not one that has to be derived in some
> complex way through arcane reasoning. But then it must be ir-
> rational or at least unreasonable for the criminal not to care suf-
> ficiently about others, since the criminal's lack of concern for
> others is what is responsible for the criminal's not taking the
> likelihood of harm to an outsider to be a reason against a proposed
> course of action . . .
>
> The relativist's reply to such an argument is that, on any plaus-
> ible characterization of reasonableness and unreasonableness (or
> rationality and irrationality) as notions that can be part of the
> scientific conception of the world, the absolutist's claim is just false.
> Someone can be completely rational without feeling concern and
> respect for outsiders. (1985: 39–40)

In effect, then, both Harman and Foot challenge the rationalist to
explain an uncontroversial sense in which the successful criminal
is being irrational. Contrary to both, however, it seems to me easy
to meet this challenge.

The successful criminal must begin his deliberations from some
evaluative premise or other. Let's imagine that he begins from the
premise that he has a normative reason to gain wealth no matter
what the cost to others. Now, given this premise we can certainly

imagine that he is not inconsistent, that he does not disregard a rule of conduct that he has himself already accepted, that he is not inattentive, that he does not suffer from weakness of will and so on and so forth . . . But all that that shows is that the flaw in his reasoning lies in the premise from which he begins: that he has a normative reason to gain wealth no matter what the cost to others. For, as we have seen, this is equivalent to the claim that fully rational creatures would want that, if they find themselves in the circumstances of the successful criminal, then they gain wealth no matter what the cost to others. And the successful criminal's opinion notwithstanding, it seems quite evident that we have no reason to believe that this is true. Fully rational creatures would want no such thing.

Note what I have not said. I have not said that the fact that we all disagree with the successful criminal entails that he is wrong. Perhaps we are all mistaken about what fully rational creatures would want. But the mere fact that it is logically possible that we are wrong gives us no more reason to endorse the opinions of the successful criminal and doubt our own convictions than the mere fact that it is logically possible that we are wrong when we think that the sun will rise tomorrow gives us reason to endorse the opinions of the prophets of doom.

Harman tells us that the fact that the successful criminal does not observe the moral requirement not to harm others cannot be traced to a 'failure to consider or appreciate certain arguments'. But it seems to me that that should now seem quite wrong. After all, the successful criminal thinks that he has a normative reason to gain wealth no matter what the cost to others, and he sticks with this opinion despite the fact that virtually everyone disagrees with him. Moreover, he does so without good reason. For he can give no account of why his own opinion about what fully rational creatures would want should be privileged over the opinion of others; he can give no account of why his opinion should be right, others' opinions should be wrong. He can give no such account because he rejects the very idea that the folk possess between them a stock of wisdom about such matters against which each person's opinions should be tested. And yet, ultimately, this is the only court of appeal there is for claims about what we have normative reason to do. The successful criminal thus seems to me to suffer from the all too common vice of *intellectual arrogance*. He therefore does indeed suffer from a 'failure to consider or appreciate certain arguments', for he doesn't feel the force of arguments that come from *others* at all.

Gauthier's Objections

In *Morals by Agreement* David Gauthier contrasts two competing conceptions of rationality and two competing strategies for demonstrating the rationality of morality.

> Let it . . . be agreed that in so far as the interests of others are not affected, a person acts rationally if and only if she seeks her greatest interest or benefit. This might be denied by some, but we wish here to isolate the essential difference between the opposed conceptions of practical rationality. And this appears when we consider rational action in which the interests of others are involved. Proponents of the *maximizing* conception . . . insist that essentially nothing is changed . . . On the other hand, proponents of the *universalistic* conception . . . insist that what makes it rational to satisfy an interest does not depend on whose interest it is. Thus the rational person seeks to satisfy all interests . . .
>
> The main task of our moral theory – the generation of moral constraints as rational – is thus easily accomplished by proponents of the universalistic conception of practical reason. For them the relation between reason and morals is clear. Their task is to defend their conception of rationality, since the maximizing and the universalistic conceptions do not rest on equal footings. The maximizing conception possesses the virtue, among conceptions, of weakness. Any consideration affording one a reason for acting on the maximizing conception, also affords one such a reason on the universalistic conception. But the converse does not hold. On the universalistic conception all persons have in effect the same basis for rational choice – the interests of all – and this assumption, of the impersonality or impartiality of reason, demands defence. (1986: 6–7)

Since Gauthier embraces the maximizing conception of rationality, he therefore sees his own problem in achieving the 'main task of moral theory' to be the opposite. He thinks he doesn't have to defend his own views about practical rationality at all. Rather he has to show how it could be that the maximizing conception underwrites the rationality of morality.

Gauthier's two competing conceptions of practical rationality are supposed to represent what would be characterized in more traditional terms as the rationalist's and the anti-rationalist's conceptions. Gauthier is firmly in favour of the anti-rationalist's maximizing, or Humean, conception of practical rationality. He has two fundamental criticisms of the rationalist's conception. First, he objects that the rationalist makes all the same assumptions about practical rationality as the anti-rationalist *plus more*, so that the rationalist's view of practical rationality is related to the anti-rationalist's as a stronger view is to a weaker. And second, he objects that what the rationalist adds to the anti-rationalist's assumptions about practical rationality is, in effect, the assumption that it is irrational not to have concern for other people. The rationalist thus hands herself the conclusion that rationality is on the side of morality on a plate.

However the analysis of normative reasons offered here, and the interpretation of rationalism, suggests that Gauthier's criticisms are radically misplaced. For, to begin with and most fundamentally, Gauthier is simply wrong to assume that the maximizing conception of practical rationality is uncontroversial. Indeed, as we have seen, no one should accept the maximizing conception of rationality. Rationalists and anti-rationalists alike should reject the view that what we have most reason to do in certain circumstances is whatever we happen to desire most to do in those circumstances, in favour of the view that what we have most reason to do, in certain circumstances, is whatever we would desire most that we do in those circumstances if we were fully rational. And once this crucial point is agreed, we see immediately what the flaws are in Gauthier's two criticisms of rationalism.

Consider his first criticism. Once it is agreed that the rationalist and anti-rationalist both have to accept an analysis of reasons in terms of what would be desired under conditions of full rationality it becomes quite clear that the rationalist isn't just saying everything the anti-rationalist says plus more. Rather, the rationalist and anti-rationalist can agree about something fundamental, while yet still disagreeing about something fundamental. They can both agree that practical rationality is to be defined in terms of the uncontroversial procedures via which we justify our desires; that only so can we characterize what full rationality consists in. Each may therefore be said to accept a 'reflective equilibrium' conception of practical rationality. But they still disagree about something fundamental because they disagree about the scope for reasoned change in our desires via the process of reflective equilibrium. The rationalist thinks that the existence of reasons presupposes that under conditions of full rationality we would all have the same desires about what we are to do in the various circumstances we might face; that absent such a convergence we should say that there are no reasons at all. And the anti-rationalist denies this, claiming instead that reasons may exist even if what any particular agent would desire under conditions of full rationality depends crucially upon what her actual desires were to begin with. The rationalist thus accepts a *non-relative* reflective equilibrium conception of practical rationality, whereas the anti-rationalist accepts a *relative* reflective equilibrium conception of practical rationality. Gauther is therefore wrong that rationalism and antirationalism are related as a stronger doctrine is to a weaker. Rather they disagree fundamentally about whether normative reasons are to be analysed in relative or non-relative terms (see again the discussion in chapter 5).

Now consider Gauthier's second objection. He tells us that the rationalist hands herself the conclusion that it is irrational not to have concern for other people on a plate, for she simply defines practical rationality in these terms. This is the so-called 'universalistic' conception of practical rationality. But, as we have just seen, the rationalist need not and should not define practical rationality in these terms. Rather, like the anti-rationalist, she can and should define practical rationality in terms of reflective equilibrium, and she should then distinguish herself from the anti-rationalist by insisting that, on her conception, the existence of reasons presupposes a convergence in the desires of fully rational creatures. In other words, she should distinguish herself from the anti-rationalist by insisting that, as she sees things, reasons are non-relative. For once the rationalist has so defined her conception of practical rationality, she can then insist that it is irrational not to have concern for other people if and only if, when we engage in the method of reflective equilibrium in order to justify our desires, a concern for other people turns out to be among the desires that are themselves rationally justifiable; one of the desires any person would have under conditions of full rationality. In this way, not only does she not have to make the conclusion that it is irrational not to have concern for others a trivial consequence of her definition of practical rationality, but she can insist that it may well be hotly contested whether or not it is irrational not to have concern for other people. For it is controversial what the outcome of the method of reflective equilibrium would be. Indeed, on the rationalist's non-relative conception of reasons, it may well be hotly contested whether there are any reasons at all.

Mackie's Objections

John Mackie tells us that

> ... Kant himself thought that moral judgements are categorical imperatives ... So far as ethics is concerned, my thesis that there are no objective values is specifically the denial that any such categorically imperative element is objectively valid. (1977: 29)

Mackie's two famous objections to the claim that there exist objective values are thus directed quite specifically against the rationalist.

Consider his first argument.

> If there were objective values, then they would be entities or qualities or relations of a very strange sort, utterly different from anything else in the universe. Correspondingly, if we were aware of them, it would have to be by some special faculty of moral perception or intuition, utterly different from ordinary ways of knowing everything else. (1977: 38)

But can Mackie really lay a charge of strangeness against rightness, at least as that feature of acts has been analysed here? It
seems not.

To say that performing an act of a certain sort in certain
circumstances is right is, I have argued, to say *inter alia* that there
is a normative reason to perform it. And this, in turn, is simply to
say that fully rational creatures would desire that such an act
be performed in such circumstances, where such a desire is of
the appropriate substantive kind. On this account, moral features
like rightness thus simply are not 'entities or qualities or relations
of a very strange sort'; no 'special faculty of moral perception of
intuition' is required in order to gain knowledge of them. All that
is required is the ability to think about what a more rational
person would want. And this, in turn, just requires the ability to
engage in an attempt to find a systematic and unified justification
of the various desires that we have; to engage in a process of
reflective equilibrium. The charge of strangeness is thus entirely
misplaced.

Consider now Mackie's second argument. The idea here is that

> . . . radical differences between first order moral judgements make
> it difficult to treat those judgements as apprehensions of objective
> truths. But it is not the mere occurrence of disagreements that tells
> against the objectivity of values. Disagreement on questions in
> history or biology or cosmology does not show that there are no
> objective issues in these fields for investigators to disagree about.
> But such scientific disagreement results from speculative infer-
> ences or explanatory hypotheses based on inadequate evidence,
> and it is hardly plausible to interpret moral disagreement in the
> same way. Disagreement about moral codes seems to reflect
> people's adherence to and participation in different ways of life.
> (1977: 36)

Mackie thus agrees that the availability of a rational procedure for
resolving moral disagreement would render the 'mere occur-
rence' of moral disagreements harmless, from the rationalist's
point of view. But he suggests that the idea that there exists such
a procedure is 'hardly plausible'. His actual arguments for this
claim are, however, hardly convincing.

Mackie tells us that moral disagreement cannot plausibly be interpreted as resulting from 'speculative inferences or explanatory hypotheses based on inadequate evidence'. But, in many ways, this is just false. For, as we have seen, when we construct moral theories we are trying to find out what we have normative reason to do, and when we try to find out what we have normative reason to do we are trying to find out what fully rational creatures would want, and when we try to find out what fully rational creatures would want we embark on a procedure of justification of our various desires that is very similar indeed to the enterprise of theory construction in science in response to observational evidence. Both are simply applications of the idea of reflective equilibrium.

Of course, perhaps Mackie is saying that this attempt to provide our desires with a systematic justification is doomed to failure; that no such justification will be forthcoming; that there is no *single* thing that fully rational creatures would all want us to do in the various circumstances in which we find ourselves. Perhaps that is the real point of his argument from relativity. But if so then the reply is again simple enough. For though it is certainly logically possible that no systematic justification of our desires is forthcoming, in light of the remarks we made in the previous section about the power of moral argument to elicit agreement, it seems more reasonable to think that such a justification is forthcoming.

This is not to deny, of course, that the real test of Mackie's argument from relativity lies in the ultimate outcome of debate in normative ethics. The real question is whether we will, by engaging in such debate, come up with answers to moral questions that secure the free agreement of those who participate. If we do not, then our confidence that such agreement is to be had may be undermined, and quite rightly so. But that gives us no reason for scepticism *now*. We must give the arguments and see what their outcome is.

6.5 CONCLUSION

The task in this chapter has been to provide an analysis of our concept of rightness in terms of our concept of a normative reason. The analysis provided has many advantages.

First, the analysis allows us to solve the moral problem. For it gives us a way of thinking about our moral beliefs as beliefs about an objective matter of fact, and it explains why these beliefs connect with motivation, but it does each of these things while all the while taking it for granted that Hume was right that our motivations are to be explained in terms of beliefs and desires, where beliefs and desires are distinct existences. Second, the analysis allows us to square morality with a broader naturalism. For it allows us to see why the rightness of an act just is a natural feature that that act possesses. And third, and finally, in conjunction with some plausible assumptions about the potential that moral argument has to bring about agreement, the analysis also allows us to think that our moral talk is in fact legitimate. For it is plausible to suppose that through moral argument we can in fact discover what the reasons that we all share really are.

At the beginning of this book I said that, as I see things, debate in normative ethics is crucial for the final resolution of meta-ethical questions. It should now be clear why I said this. For, given the analysis of rightness argued for here, the justifiability of our commitment to morality is itself a hostage to the fortune of debate in normative ethics. As I see it we are justified in thinking that there are moral facts, and so in engaging in ordinary moral debate, but our justification is defeasible, and may itself be defeated by the outcome of those very debates. If we are interested in the final resolution of meta-ethical questions – in whether or not there *really are* any moral facts – then it seems to me that we therefore have little alternative but to engage in normative ethical debate and to see where the arguments that we give ultimately lead us.

Notes

NOTES TO CHAPTER 1   WHAT IS THE MORAL PROBLEM?

1   Crispin Wright (1992) and Paul Horwich (1992) have both recently argued that on a minimal theory of truth, we have no choice but to regard moral claims as apt for assessment in terms of truth and falsehood. If they were right then, on the minimal theory of truth, we would have to regard moral claims as expressions of belief. A preference for the expressivists' solution to the moral problem would then have to depend on taking a non-minimal view of truth. However, as I have argued elsewhere, contrary to both Wright and Horwich, expressivists need not take a non-minimal view of truth. Minimalism about truth is neutral with regard to solutions to the moral problem. For relevant discussion see Smith, 1994a, 1994b; Divers and Miller, 1994; Horwich, 1994; Jackson, Oppy and Smith, 1994.

NOTES TO CHAPTER 2   THE EXPRESSIVIST CHALLENGE

1   Here I follow Wiggins (1987: 193 note 12), who reminds us that Moore himself gave the following useful account of naturalism: 'By nature then I do mean . . . that which is the subject matter of the natural sciences, and also of psychology' (Moore, 1903: 183 and note 40). This certainly seems to be what Ayer has in mind by the term 'naturalism' as well. Note two points, however. First, for this to be a good way of defining 'natural' we must assume that ethical facts are not themselves part of the subject matter of a natural or social science. The assumption might seem harmless enough once we note that, even so, *the making of ethical claims* may still be part of the

subject matter of a natural or a social science. And second, note that when 'natural' is defined in this way, it turns out that a natural feature of the world may or may not be a physical feature (Jackson, 1992: 481). A possible world in which there are creatures with certain psychological traits has natural features, according to this definition, but it may or may not be a world with physical features. The creatures may all be non-physical beings: angels, for example. A naturalist in ethics thus need not be a physicalist.

2   Moore expresses his reluctance to posit a perceptual faculty of moral intuition in these terms: 'I would wish it observed that, when I call such propositions "Intuitions", I mean merely to assert that they are incapable of proof; I *imply nothing whatever as to the manner or origin of our cognition of them*' (1903, x).

3   For discussion of the general question whether moral features have an explanatory role see Harman, 1977; Sturgeon, 1985, 1986; Harman, 1986; and, especially, Sayre-McCord, 1988.

4   Note that though, according to this story, we know which natural features we have our pro- and con-attitudes towards on the basis of mere reflection, and though we are thereby able to explain how we can make moral judgements in accordance with particular supervenience conditionals on the basis of mere reflection, it isn't the case we know a *priori* that objects having certain natural features have certain moral features. In other words, we have not crossed an 'is-ought gap'. For, very roughly, though we know on the basis of reflection what the contents of our pro- and con-attitudes are, this is not knowledge a *priori*, but only a *posteriori*. Reflection here is thus not to be thought of as entailing a *priori* access. Reflection in this case is more like inner perception of our own non-cognitive states.

5   Though Hare is, I think, rightly described as an expressivist, his views are in fact rather complicated (1981). In his view moral judgements have both an expressive function, which is primary, and a descriptive function, which is secondary. When someone judges an act to be right she is both describing it as having the natural features that, for her, makes prescribing it appropriate, and she is also prescribing it or expressing her pro-attitude towards it. In Hare's view, the prescriptive or expressive function of moral judgements is best captured semantically by ascribing to them the linguistic form of an imperative.

6   Note that the dispositional analysis has here been formulated so as to make it transparent that we can identify a disposition with its categorical base (Evans, 1980). Though this view is controversial (see, for example, McGinn, 1982), I adopt it in order to make the

points that follow easier to state. Everything that follows could still be said, though they would have to be said somewhat differently, if we took instead the view that dispositions are constituted by, but not identical with, their categorical bases.

7 An analogy might be helpful. The view that 'right' refers to the cause of our uses of the word 'right' might usefully be compared to a related view about natural kind terms; indeed, one way of understanding it is as the view that 'right' is a natural kind term. Suppose our word 'water' refers to whatever natural kind is the cause of our use of the word 'water'. Then, as Putnam (1981) famously points out, there may well be another community which uses a word, 'water*' say, a word which plays a role in their language just like the role 'water' plays in our language – they may use it to refer to the stuff that comes from rivers, lakes and streams, is good to drink, and so on – but whose reference differs from the reference of our word 'water'. For whereas the causal history of our word 'water', given that it is a natural kind term, ensures that it refers to H_2O, the causal history of their word 'water*', given that it is a natural kind term, ensures that it refers to XYZ. Thus, even though our words 'water' and 'water*' play the same role – they are each used to refer to the natural kind that is found in rivers, lakes and streams, is good to drink, and so on – this will not by itself guarantee that we would be disagreeing if we said, of certain stuff, 'That stuff is water' and they said, of the same stuff, 'That stuff is not water*'. In these terms, the objection to the view that the word 'right' refers to the cause of our uses of the word 'right' stated in the text may now be put like this. Whereas the possibility of explaining such disagreements away is acceptable in the case of two communities who use natural kind terms – like 'water' and 'water*' – to play the same role in their lives, the possibility of explaining such disagreements away is unacceptable in the case of two communities who use a word to play the same role in their lives as the word 'right' plays in our lives. Yet metaphysical-but-not-definitional naturalism leaves open the possibility that we should explain such disagreements away.

8 I owe this useful term to Philip Pettit.

9 It might be thought that we don't yet have an argument that would allow us to square colour talk with a broader physicalism *per se*, as the argument just given has no bearing on whether a subject's experience of having something look red to her is itself a physical state. But the foregoing discussion suggests an obvious strategy for squaring talk of colour experience with physical talk as well. The first step would be to construct an analysis of our concept of a colour experi-

ence. The second stage would be to show how these analyses allow us to identify colour experiences with, say, states of the brain. If, as seems plausible, our concept of a colour experience is the concept of a state of a subject that, in conjunction with a relevant desire, causally explains our bodily movements – for example, our picking out red objects from objects of other colours – then it should be clear enough how the attempt at vindication would go, and why it should be deemed likely to be successful (compare Lewis, 1972).

NOTES TO CHAPTER 3   THE EXTERNALIST CHALLENGE

1 To my knowledge this point is never admitted by the externalists themselves, largely because the problem to which admitting this point is the solution is never explicitly addressed: that is, the problem of explaining the reliability of the connection between moral judgement and motivation in the good and strong-willed person. Indeed, both Brink and Foot seem to think that externalism offers a *better* explanation of the connection between moral judgement and motivation than that offered by defenders of the practicality requirement (Brink, 1989: 49; Foot, 1972: 165–7). Whether they would still think so if they were to think about the point currently under discussion I do not know.

2 For this reason I am not convinced that Hart's insitutional account of law adequately captures the normativity of law either. For – absent a defence of the claim that all those who live inside a legal system have tacitly agreed to obey the law – on Hart's institutional account, there can be no legitimate expectation that all those who are inside a legal system will act in accordance with it; no legitimate grounds for disapproving of their acts of disobedience; no reason for rejecting the image of 'us' versus 'them'. If indeed the law has normative content, then it seems to me that we have no alternative but to derive that content from the normativity of morality, and so to reject the very fundamentals of positivism.

NOTES TO CHAPTER 4   THE HUMEAN THEORY OF MOTIVATION

1 Normative reasons are the subject matter of what Philip Pettit and I elsewhere call the theory of 'foreground' rationality (Pettit and

Smith, forthcoming). A theory of foreground rationality will spell out the considerations that rationally justify action. But note that we can, under the name of a 'theory of rationality', describe something else as well. We can describe the psychology of the perfectly rational agent; someone who embraces such foreground reasons. Pettit and I call this the theory of 'background' rationality. Will a theory of background rationality tell us about the motivating reasons an agent has? Only if the agent in question is perfectly rational. For more on this, see chapter 5.

2   In suggesting that the requirement is 'in the broad sense' a requirement of rationality I am following Williams (1980: 102–3) and Parfit (1984: footnote 2a to part I; 117–20). Both think that a theory of practical rationality would tell us what an agent has reason to do, and both think that this in turn depends, *inter alia*, on what is the case, rather than merely on what the agent believes to be the case.

3   Note that we can distinguish the two claims being made here in terms of the distinction made in footnote 1. To say that agents are rationally required to promote their future interests, or that there is a normative reason of rationality to do so, is to make a claim about the theory of *foreground* rationality (a claim about the considerations that rationally justify action), whereas to say that agents are rationally required to have a desire to promote their future interests is to make a claim about the theory of *background* rationality (a claim about the psychology of the perfectly rational agent). Relatedly, note that the Humean who thinks that agents have and act upon a desire to promote their future interests need not, and perhaps should not, think that that desire has to be appealed to in justifying their actions (Pettit and Smith, 1990: 589–91).

4   Indeed, it seems to me that there are more mundane counter-examples to the principle left to right. Consider cases in which you go to the refrigerator convinced that there is something in particular that you want, though you aren't quite sure what it is. Then, while looking at the contents you suddenly, as we should put it, 'realize what it was that you wanted all along'. If we wish to respect this commonsense description of such occurrences then we should reject the principle left to right.

5   I say McDowell rejects a phenomenological conception. He nowhere says that he rejects such a conception. But given that he thinks that 'consequentially ascribed desires are indeed desires' (1978: 25), he must. For the point of consequentially ascribed

desires is that there may be no phenomenological ground for their ascription. I discuss this idea towards the end of this chapter.

6   Thus, I contend that a subject's *false* belief that she desires to φ is not a state that is potentially explanatory of her behaviour. Everyday experience supports this contention. Reflect on occasions when you stand at the edge of a cold swimming pool thinking that you desire to jump in. On some such occasions your body is totally unresponsive to the desires that you profess to have. As you stand there motionless you sometimes come to the conclusion that, contrary to what you thought, you didn't really want to go swimming after all. Thus, just as we would expect if this contention were true, there are cases in which a subject believes that she desires to φ right up until the time that she is supposed to act only to discover that she in fact has no such desire when her body fails to respond to her desire.

Of course, we can construct cases in which it might *appear* that an agent's false beliefs about what she wants motivate her. The example of John the musician discussed earlier who pursues a career as a musician even though he does not want to, though he falsely believes he does, may perhaps be such a case. But it seems to me that we are obliged to think that in cases like this the false belief itself does no motivational work; that that work is done by other desires that are present: for example, in this case, John's desire to please his mother. We are obliged to construe matters in this way in order to explain the motivational *difference* between two ways John's case might have turned out. It could have turned out as described. Or it could have turned out like the case of the agent at the swimming pool. John might have found that he was unable to bring himself to engage in musical pursuits. His inability might have brought home to him the fact that he does not want to be a musician after all.

7   Why have I said that this is very rough and somewhat simplified? Because where 'p' is a proposition about the past, or a proposition to the effect that something happens though not through the agent's own doing, it will not be true that the desire that p is a disposition to bring p about. A more accurate and fully general characterization of the functional role of desire would therefore need to be given along the lines suggested in decision theory. A desire that p is a state that disposes a subject to make certain sorts of bets when faced with lotteries where the outcome is *inter alia* that p. On this account, it is still true that the difference between desire and belief is given by their differential roles in the explanation of action, though in this case the action is all betting behaviour.

Though rough and simplified, the suggestion in the text will do for present purposes, however. For our interest here is in explaining the nature of motivating reasons, and the desires that constitute motivating reasons are therefore desires for states of affairs that *are not* in the past, and that *are* to be brought about through the agent's own doing. As I understand it, this constitutes a reply to G. F. Schueler's (1991) more pressing criticisms of an earlier presentation of these ideas (Smith, 1987). For further discussion of directions of fit see Humberstone (1992) and Velleman (1992).

8 Philip Pettit distinguishes between two kinds of state which are such that the world must fit with their content: *desires* and *habits of inference* (1993: 18–19). Thus, for example, he argues that the *modus ponens* habit of inferring is a state that produces the output of believing that q when the input is a belief that p and a belief that p → q, and, he claims, this is therefore just as much a state with which the world must fit as a desire; for it requires that our psychology be a certain way, and our psychology's not being that way is not a reason for changing the habit of inference, but rather a reason for changing our psychology. Pettit claims that we therefore need to distinguish desires from habits of inference, and that considerations of direction of fit are inadequate to this task.

His positive suggestion about how we might make this distinction is that desires, unlike habits of inference, are 'belief-channelled': that is, he suggests that the belief that the response is suitable for realizing the content of the desire must channel the impact of the desire, whereas the belief that the response is suitable for realizing the content of the habit of inference need not channel the impact of the habit of inference. Someone who, desiring to ψ, φs, φs only because her belief that she can ψ by φ-ing channels the impact of her desire to ψ. But someone who has the *modus ponens* habit of inferring need not have the impact of her habit channelled in this way in order to end up believing that q when she believes that p and that p → q. There need be no role played by the belief that believing q is a way of believing something that follows by *modus ponens* from her other beliefs.

I am, however, unconvinced by Pettit's claim that we need to distinguish desires from habits of inference in the way he suggests. What the example of habits of inference seems to me to show is just how much slack there is in the phrase 'direction of fit', and that, for certain purposes, we do better to talk directly in terms of patterns of dispositions, where these get spelled out in functionalist terms. For it seems plain enough that, for example, the *modus ponens* habit of inference must itself be *internal* to the dispositions of believing that p, believing that p → q, and the like, not, as Pettit's way of setting things up seems to suggest, a separate disposition that *combines with* the dispositions constitutive of these beliefs to produce other beliefs. After all, what would the dispositions constitutive of believing p be if they did not already include dispositions like the disposition to believe q when you believe p → q, and other similar dispositions? Indeed, it seems plain enough that habits of inference must be thought of in this way, because they are themselves criticizable if they do not fit the world. Someone who has the gambler's fallacy habit of inference, for example, should get rid of that habit and acquire a different habit instead; a habit that better allows her to derive truths from truths. And this seems to me best understood as a claim about the dispositions constitutive of being a believer at all. Someone who has the gambler's fallacy habit of inference is a defective *believer.*

When I talk of states having directions of fit, I therefore have in mind whole packages of dispositions constitutive of desiring and believing, not states that might be so described more loosely. I therefore ignore habits of inference in what follows.

9   What about having truth as a goal? Does this amount to desiring truth? And if it does, then since believers have truth as a goal, does it follow that believers must be desirers of the truth? I do not think so. As I see it, talk of believers having truth as a goal is best understood more loosely. To say that a believer has truth as a goal is not to credit her with dispositions *in addition* to the dispositions constitutive of being a believer. Rather, the dispositions constitutive of having truth as a goal are themselves *internal* to the dispositions constitutive of being a believer at all. Thus, as I see it, it is wrong to suppose that there may be a believer who does not have truth as a goal. Someone who does not have truth as a goal is not a kosher *believer* at all. That is the cash value of the claim that beliefs are states that must fit the world. See again footnote 8 for relevant discussion.

10   Must the anti-Humean concede that beliefs and desires have only one direction of fit? As I have argued elsewhere, in one way this issue is entirely terminological (Pettit, 1987; Smith, 1988a). However in order to ask the question discussed next in the text, 'Are there psychological states that are both belief-like and desire-like?', we must take a stand on the terminological issue. I interpret this as asking whether there is some third kind of psychological state –

besires (Altham, 1986) or *quasi-beliefs* as I have called them elsewhere (1986: 56) – not whether any beliefs are also desires. Note, however, that if we did choose to ask this question in these latter terms then we would have to restate the Humean's P1 as the claim that motivating reasons are constitutued, *inter alia*, by desires-that-are-not-beliefs (Smith, 1988a).

11 David Lewis argues that the concept of an instrumental besire is incoherent because inconsistent with the tenets of Bayesian decision theory (1988). A version of Lewis's argument for non-quantitative decision theory is developed by John Collins (1988). However, even if Lewis and Collins are right about this (see Huw Price's reply (1989)), that wouldn't be enough to show that there are no besires at all. For in order to argue for that conclusion we require an additional argument, an argument to the effect that there are no non-instrumental besires either. Lewis does attempt to give such an argument, but the argument he gives is unconvincing (1989: footnote 1). Non-instrumental besires are, he tells us, 'impervious to change under the impact of experience'. But why he thinks this I do not know. Surely, if there are non-instrumental besires, all that follows is that they change under the impact of experience in the manner of an ordinary belief, not an instrumental desire. Thus experiences that suffice for getting rid of the belief-like part will also suffice for getting rid of the desire-like part; and experiences that suffice for acquiring the belief-like part will also suffice for acquiring the desire-like part.

12 As I understand it, Nagel's view is similar to McDowell's. Nagel thinks that certain propositions with impersonal and tenseless contents are such that, if they are entertained at all, then the entertainer is disposed to act in a certain way. Thus, for example, Nagel thinks that if I now entertain the proposition that A is in pain at t – entertain it while fully appreciating the reality of other people and times – then I am now disposed to relieve A's pain at t. However Nagel also thinks that simply in virtue of being so disposed we can say that an agent has a 'motivated desire' to pursue the act in question. For this reason he thinks that we should concede P2 to the Humean: motivation does indeed entail the presence of desire. But, as he puts it, 'if the desire is a motivated one the explanation of it will be the same as the explanation of the pursuit, and it is by no means obvious that a desire must enter into this further explanation' (1970: 29). The pursuit may rather be properly explained by the presence of a besire, not a desire. And, if it is, then we should

deny P1. Motivations may be constituted by besires; they are not only constituted by desires. So says Nagel. And our reply to Nagel is the same as our reply to McDowell in the text.

NOTES TO CHAPTER 5   AN ANTI-HUMEAN THEORY OF NORMATIVE REASONS

1   Michael Stocker puts the point this way. 'It is often held that something's being good or believed good – its being rational, given the agent's values and beliefs – makes intelligible (explains) why a person seeks or desires it. If what I have said . . . is correct, then this is mistaken . . . [J]ust as the person may well not seek or desire the (believed) good, so, were that person to do what would produce (believed) good, that fact might well not make intelligible why the person so acted. If I am known to be sunk deeply into despair or some other depression or to have long ago ceased caring about someone's welfare, then citing the (believed) goodness of my act will not make intelligible my act which benefits that other person' (Stocker, 1979: 746). And again later: 'Thus rationality in the sense of value maximization against the background of an agent's beliefs is not the form of all action, nor even all intelligible action. Nor is the correspondingly rational person the form of all people, nor even all intelligible people. Trying to understand people as if they were such rational beings involves inadequate moral psychologies' (Stocker, 1979: footnote 12).

2   Is this argument consistent with the earlier argument against Johnston? It is. Indeed, it helps to explain why a theory like the self-interest theory may be self-effacing (Parfit, 1984: 23–4). Suppose it is rational for me to do just one thing: promote my long-term self-interest. And suppose further that it is not rational for me to desire to promote my long-term self-interest; that my long-term self-interest would be best served by my desiring to act for the sake of family and friends, write books, advance humanity and so on, without having any direct concern whatever for my own long-term self-interest. What it is desirable that I do is, in this case, not what it is desirable that I desire that I do. But now suppose I come to believe the self-interest theory. I come to believe that it is desirable to promote my long-term self-interest and undesirable to desire to promote my long-term self-interest. From the argument just given, having these beliefs makes it rational for me to desire to promote my long-term self-interest and to desire not to desire to promote my

own long-term self-interest. Since the reason I have the desire to promote my long-term self-interest, something we know independently that I rationally shouldn't desire, is that I believe the self-interest theory, it is no surprise to learn that I rationally shouldn't believe the self-interest theory. The theory is thus self-effacing. And since I desire not to desire to promote my long-term self-interest, it is no surprise that I am motivated to get rid of that belief. I am indeed moved to do what the theory tells me it is rational to do.

3 Once we have accepted C2 we have no reason to deny that our beliefs about our reasons play a causal role in the production of our desires. However, note that the argument I have given for C2 does not depend at all on accepting the *non-relative* conception of normative reasons I myself favour. It goes through as well on the *relative* conception favoured by Williams. If this is right, then it follows that even those who accept a Humean, relative conception of reasons should admit that our beliefs about our reasons can play a causal role in the production of our desires. This suggests that one of the issues that is supposed standardly to divide Humean from anti-Humean theorists of normative reasons does not divide them at all. According to Christine Korsgaard for instance (1986), anti-Humeans assert, and Humeans deny, that reason can produce a motive. But, as we have seen, what is at issue is not this, but rather whether the reasons that produce motives are themselves relative, as the Humeans suppose, or non-relative, as the anti-Humeans suppose.

NOTES TO CHAPTER 6   HOW TO SOLVE THE MORAL PROBLEM

1 Note that I am merely saying that the existence of these concepts shows the extent to which we agree in our evaluations, not that these evaluations are correct. As I see it, many of these evaluations – those implicit in the use of our concepts of chastity, promiscuity, piety, frugality, self-reliance and the like – are or may well be incorrect. For I do not think it at all obvious that we would desire people to act in these ways if we were fully rational. For this reason, I (perhaps mistakenly) take myself to be endorsing what Susan Hurley calls 'centralism', not 'non-centralism' (1985).

2 James Rachels has an excellent discussion of this point in his account of the Biblical story in which God asks Abraham to sacrifice Isaac (1971). You will recall that, in that story, Abraham is supposed

to be conflicted. He believed that it would be wrong for him to kill his own son, but he also believed in God's perfect goodness; that God would not ask him to do something wrong. Yet how could Abraham rationally maintain his belief in God's perfect goodness if he genuinely believes both that it would be wrong for him to kill Isaac and that this is what God is asking him to do? The point that the story drives home is that there is no escaping forming your own moral beliefs – in Abraham's case, beliefs about the rightness or wrongness of killing Isaac, and beliefs about the perfect or imperfect goodness of God. The only question is whether you will form these beliefs via an exercise of your own rational capacities, in the light of the evidence, or whether you will form them without exercising your rational capacities, simply in response to the directives of an authority.

3   I thus find myself in substantial agreement with Derek Parfit when he writes at the end of *Reasons and Persons*: 'There could clearly be higher achievements in the struggle for a wholly just world-wide community. And there could be higher achievements in all of the Arts and Sciences. But the progress could be greatest in what is now the least advanced of these Arts or Sciences. This, I have claimed, is Non-Religious Ethics. Belief in God, or in many gods, prevented the free development of moral reasoning. Disbelief in God, openly admitted by a majority, is a very recent event, not yet completed. Because this event is so recent, Non-Religious Ethics is at a very early stage. We cannot yet predict whether, as in Mathematics, we will all reach agreement. Since we cannot know how Ethics will develop, it is not irrational to have high hopes.' (1984: 454)

4   For an explanation of why we should use 'actually' in this definition, and how that helps to facillitate the entailment claim, see Davies and Humberstone, 1980. The point is also discussed in Smith, 1986b; Wiggins, 1987; Wright, 1988; Lewis, 1989; Johnston, 1989.

5   Suppose that we discover that our desires are out of line with our evaluative beliefs when we deliberate, and that we are not rational. Our evaluative beliefs do not cause us to have the desires that they can and should cause us to have. What happens then? The answer is: many different things might happen (Pettit and Smith, 1993a, 1993b; Kennett and Smith, forthcoming). We might employ some technique of self-control we have at our disposal and thereby get ourselves to do what we believe desirable none the less: that is, we might manage to be continent. Alternatively, though we have some technique of self-control at our disposal, we might not exercise it:

that is, we might suffer from weakness of will. Or alternatively, we might have no technique of self-control at our disposal, and so go on to act on a desire that we have, but a desire that causes us to act in a way that we do not value: that is, we might suffer from compulsion.

References

Altham, J. E. J. 1986: 'The Legacy of Emotivism' in Graham Macdonald and Crispin Wright, eds, *Fact, Science and Morality: Essays on A. J. Ayer's Language, Truth and Logic.* Basil Blackwell. 275–88.

Anscombe, G. E. M. 1957: *Intention.* Basil Blackwell.

Ayer, A. J. 1936: *Language, Truth and Logic.* Gollancz. Second Edition 1946.
    1954: 'Freedom and Necessity' reprinted in Gary Watson, ed., *Free Will.* Oxford University Press, 1982. 15–23.

Blackburn, Simon 1971: 'Moral Realism' in John Casey, ed., *Morality and Moral Reasoning.* Methuen. 101–24.
    1984: *Spreading the Word.* Oxford University Press.
    1985a: 'Errors and the Phenomenology of Value' in Ted Honderich, ed., *Morality and Objectivity.* Routledge and Kegan Paul. 1–22.
    1985b: 'Supervenience Revisited' in Ian Hacking, ed., *Exercises in Analysis: Essays by Students of Casimir Lewy.* Cambridge University Press.
    1986: 'Morals and Modals' in Graham Macdonald and Crispin Wright, eds, *Fact, Science and Morality: Essays on A. J. Ayer's Language, Truth and Logic.* Basil Blackwell. 119–42.
    1987: 'How to Be an Ethical Antirealist' in Peter A. French, Theodore E. Uehling, Jr. and Howard K. Wettstein, eds, 1987: *Midwest Studies in Philosophy Volume XII: Realism and Anti-Realism.* University of Notre Dame Press. 361–75.
    1994: 'Circles, Finks, Smells, and Biconditionals' in James Tomberlin, ed., *Philosophical Perspectives: Volume VII, Language and Logic.* Ridgeview Press. 259–81.
    forthcoming: 'Flight from Reality' in Rosalind Hursthouse, Gavin Lawrence and Warren Quinn, eds, *Virtues and Reasons, a Festschrift for Philippa Foot.*

Boyd, Richard 1988: 'How to be a Moral Realist' in Geoffrey Sayre-McCord, ed., *Essays on Moral Realism.* Cornell University Press. 181–228.

Brink, David O. 1984: 'Moral Realism and the Skeptical Arguments from Disagreement and Queerness', *Australasian Journal of Philosophy.* 111–25.

——— 1986: 'Externalist Moral Realism', *Southern Journal of Philosophy* Supplement. 23–42.

——— 1989: *Moral Realism and the Foundations of Ethics.* Cambridge University Press.

Campbell, John 1993: 'A Simple View of Colour' in John Haldane and Crispin Wright, eds., *Reality, Representation and Projection.* Oxford University Press. 257–68.

Carnap, Rudolf 1963: 'Replies and Systematic Expositions' in P. A. Schilpp, ed., *The Philosophy of Rudolf Carnap.* Open Court.

Collins, John 1988: 'Belief, Desire and Revision', *Mind.* 333–42.

Dancy, Jonathan 1993: *Moral Reasons.* Basil Blackwell.

Daniels, Norman 1979: 'Wide Reflective Equilibrium and Theory Acceptance in Ethics' *Journal of Philosophy.* 256–82.

Darwall, Stephen 1983: *Impartial Reason.* Cornell University Press.

Gibbard, Allan and Railton, Peter 1992: 'Toward *Fin de siècle* Ethics: Some Trends', *Philosophical Review.* 115–89.

Davidson, Donald 1963: 'Actions, Reasons and Causes' reprinted in Davidson 1980. 3–20.

——— 1970: 'How is Weakness of the Will Possible?' reprinted in Davidson 1980. 21–42.

——— 1978: 'Intending' reprinted in Davidson 1980. 83–102.

——— 1980: *Essays on Actions and Events.* Oxford University Press.

Davies, Martin and Humberstone, Lloyd 1980: 'Two Notions of Necessity', Philosophical Studies. 1–30.

Divers, John and Miller, Alex 1994: 'Why Expressivists about Value Should Not Love Minimalism about Truth', *Analysis.*

Dreier, James 1990: 'Internalism and Speaker Relativism', *Ethics.* 6–26.

Dworkin, Ronald 1977: *Taking Rights Seriously.* Duckworth.

Evans, Gareth 1980: 'Things Without the Mind – A Commentary on Chapter Two of Strawson's *Individuals*' in Zak van Straaten, ed., *Philosophical Subjects: Essays Presented to P. F. Strawson.* Clarendon Press. 76–116.

Falk, W. D. 1948: ' "Ought" and Motivation', *Proceedings of the Aristotelian Society.* 111–38.

Foot, Philippa 1958: 'Moral Arguments' reprinted in Foot 1978. 96–109.

——— 1972: 'Morality as a System of Hypothetical Imperatives' reprinted in Foot 1978. 157–73.

——— 1977: 'Approval and Disapproval' reprinted in Foot 1978. 189–207.

1978: *Virtues and Vices.* University of California Press.

Frankena, William 1958: 'Obligation and Motivation in Recent Moral Philosophy' in A. I. Melden, ed., *Essays on Moral Philosophy*. University of Washington Press.

Frankfurt, Harry 1971: 'Freedom of the Will and the Concept of a Person' reprinted in Gary Watson, ed., *Free Will*. Oxford University Press, 1982. 81–95

Gauthier, David 1975: 'Reason and Maximization', *Canadian Journal of Philosophy*. 411–34.

1986: *Morals by Agreement.* Clarendon Press.

Gibbard, Allan 1990: *Wise Choices, Apt Feelings.* Clarendon Press.

Hale, Bob 1986: 'The Compleat Projectivist', *Philosophical Quarterly*. 65–84.

1993: 'Can There Be a Logic of Attitudes?' in John Haldane and Crispin Wright, eds., *Reality, Representation and Projection*. Oxford University Press. 337–63.

Hare, R. M. 1952: *The Language of Morals.* Oxford University Press.

1981: *Moral Thinking.* Oxford University Press.

Hart, H. L. A. 1961: *The Concept of Law.* Clarendon Press.

Harman, Gilbert 1973: *Thought.* Princeton University Press.

1975: 'Moral Relativism Defended', *Philosophical Review*. 3–22.

1977: *The Nature of Morality.* Oxford University Press.

1985: 'Is There a Single True Morality?' in David Copp and David Zimmerman, eds, 1985: *Morality, Reason and Truth*. Rowman and Allanheld.

1986: 'Moral Explanations of Natural Facts – Can Moral Claims Be Tested Against Moral Reality?', *Southern Journal of Philosophy* Supplement. 69–78.

Horwich, Paul 1992: 'Gibbard's Theory of Norms', *Philosophy and Public Affairs*. 67–78.

1994: 'The Essence of Expressivism', *Analysis*.

Humberstone, I. L. 1992: 'Direction of Fit', *Mind*. 59–83.

Hume, David 1888: *A Treatise of Human Nature.* Clarendon Press, 1968.

Hurley, S. L. 1985: 'Objectity and Disagreement' in Ted Honderich, ed., *Morality and Objectivity*. Routledge and Kegan Paul.

Jackson, Frank 1992: 'Critical Notice of Susan Hurley's *Natural Reasons: Personality and Polity*', *Australasian Journal of Philosophy*.

forthcoming: 'Armchair Metaphysics' in Michaelis Michael and John O'Leary Hawthorne, eds, *Philosophy in Mind*. Kluwer Press.

and Pargetter, Robert 1987: 'An Objectivist's Guide to Subjectivism about Colour' in *Review Internationale de Philosophie*. 127–41.

and Pettit, Philip 1988: 'Functionalism and Broad Content', *Mind*. 381–400.

Oppy, Graham and Smith, Michael 1994: 'Minimalism and Truth-Aptness', *Mind*.

Johnston, Mark 1989: 'Dispositional Theories of Value', *Proceedings of the Aristotelian Society* Supplementary Volume. 139–74.

Kant, Immanuel 1786: *Foundations of the Metaphysics of Morals*. Library of Liberal Arts, 1959.

Kennett, Jeanette forthcoming: 'Mixed Motives', *Australasian Journal of Philosophy*.

and Smith, Michael forthcoming: 'Philosophy and Commonsense: The Case of Weakness of Will' in Michaelis Michael and John O'Leary Hawthorne, eds, *Philosophy in Mind*. Kluwer Press.

Korsgaard, Christine 1986: 'Skepticism about Practical Reason', *Journal of Philosophy*. 5–25.

Kripke, Saul 1980: *Naming and Necessity*. Basil Blackwell.

Kymlicka, Will 1989: *Liberalism, Community and Culture*. Clarendon Press.
1990: *Contemporary Political Philosophy*. Oxford University Press.

Lewis, David 1970: 'How to Define Theoretical Terms', *Journal of Philosophy*. 427–46.
1972: 'Psychophysical and Theoretical Identifications', *Australasian Journal of Philosophy*. 249–58.
1988: 'Desire as Belief', *Mind*. 323–32.
1989: 'Dispositional Theories of Value', *Proceedings of the Aristotelian Society* Supplementary Volume. 113–37.

Loar, Brian 1981: *Mind and Meaning*. Cambridge University Press.

McDowell, John 1978: 'Are Moral Requirements Hypothetical Imperatives?', *Proceedings of the Aristotelian Society* Supplementary Volume. 13–29.
1979: 'Virtue and Reason', *The Monist*, 331–50.
1981: 'Non-Cognitivism and Rule-Following' in Steven Holtzman and Christopher Leich, eds, *Wittgenstein: To Follow a Rule*. Routledge. 141–62.
1985: 'Values and Secondary Qualities' in Honderich 1985. 110–29.

McGinn, Colin 1982: *The Character of Mind*. Oxford University Press.
1983: *The Subjective View*. Oxford University Press.

Mackie, J. L. 1976: *Problems from Locke*. Clarendon Press.
1977: Ethics: *Inventing Right and Wrong*. Penguin.

McNaughton, David 1988: *Moral Vision*. Basil Blackwell.

Monro, D. H. 1967: *Empiricism and Ethics*. Cambridge University Press.

Moore, G. E. 1903: *Principia Ethica*. Cambridge University Press.

Nagel, Thomas 1970: *The Possibility of Altruism*. Princeton University Press.

1986: *The View from Nowhere.* Oxford University Press.

Nozick, Robert 1981: *Philosophical Explanations*. Harvard University Press.

Parfit, Derek 1984: *Reasons and Persons*. Oxford University Press.

Peacocke, Christopher 1979: *Holistic Explanation*. Oxford University Press.

1985: *Sense and Content*. Oxford University Press.

Pettit, Philip 1987: 'Humeans, Anti-Humeans and Motivation', *Mind*. 530–3.

1993: *The Common Mind*. Oxford University Press.

and Smith, Michael 1990: 'Backgrounding Desire', *Philosophical Review*. 565–92.

and Smith, Michael 1993a: 'Practical Unreason', *Mind*. 53–79.

and Smith, Michael 1993b: 'Brandt on Self-Control' in Brad Hooker, ed., *Rationality, Rules and Utility*. Westview Press. 33–50.

and Smith, Michael forthcoming: 'Parfit's P' in Jonathan Dancy, ed., *Reading Parfit*. Basil Blackwell.

Platts, Mark 1979: *Ways of Meaning*. Routledge and Kegan Paul.

1981: 'Moral Reality and the End of Desire' in Mark Platts, ed., *Reference, Truth and Reality*. Routledge and Kegan Paul. 69–82.

Price, Huw 1988: *Facts and the Function of Truth*. Basil Blackwell.

1989: 'Defending Desire-as-Belief', *Mind*. 119–27.

Prior, Elizabeth W., Pargetter, Robert and Jackson, Frank 1982: 'Three Theses About Dispositions', *American Philosophical Quarterly*. 251–7.

Putnam, Hilary 1981: *Reason, Truth and History*. Cambridge University Press.

Rachels, James 1971: 'God and Human Attitudes', reprinted in Tom L. Beauchamp, Joel Feinberg and James M. Smith, eds, *Philosophy and the Human Condition*. Prentice Hall, 1989. 509–16.

Railton, Peter 1986: 'Moral Realism', *Philosophical Review*. 163–207.

1993a: 'What the Noncognitivist Helps Us to See the Naturalist Must Help Us to Explain' in John Haldane and Crispin Wright, eds., *Reality, Representation and Projection*. Oxford University Press. 279–300.

1993b: 'Reply to David Wiggins' in John Haldane and Crispin Wright, eds., *Reality, Representation and Projection*. Oxford University Press. 315–28.

Ramsey, Frank P. 1931: 'Theories' in his *The Foundations of Mathematics*. Routledge and Kegan Paul.

Rawls, John 1951: 'Outline of a Decision Procedure for Ethics', *Philosophical Review*. 177–97.

Sayre-McCord, Geoffrey 1988: 'Moral Theory and Explanatory Impotence' reprinted in Geoffrey Sayre-McCord, ed., *Essays on Moral Realism.* Cornell University Press. 256–81.

Scanlon, Thomas 1982: 'Contractualism and Utilitarianism' in Amartya Sen and Bernard Williams, eds, *Utilitarianism and Beyond.* Cambridge University Press. 103–28.

Schueler, G. F. 1991: 'Pro-Attitudes and Directions of fit', *Mind.* 277–81.

Sidgwick, Henry 1907: *The Methods of Ethics.* Hackett Publishing Company. 1981.

Singer, Peter 1973: 'The Triviality of the Debate over "Is-Ought" and the Definition of "Moral"', *American Philosophical Quarterly.* 51–6.

Smart, J. J. C. 1975: 'On Some Criticisms of a Physicalist Theory of Colour' reprinted in his *Essays Metaphysical and Moral.* Basil Blackwell. 1987.

Smith, Michael 1986a: 'Peacocke on Red and Red′', *Synthese.* 559–76.

1986b: 'Should We Believe in Emotivism?' in Graham Macdonald and Crispin Wright, eds, *Fact, Science and Morality: Essays on A. J. Ayer's Language, Truth and Logic.* Basil Blackwell. 289–310.

1987: 'The Humean Theory of Motivation', *Mind.* 36–61.

1988a: 'On Humeans, Anti-Humeans and Motivation: A Reply to Pettit', *Mind.* 589–95.

1988b: 'Reason and Desire', *Proceedings of the Aristotelian Society.* 243–56.

1989: 'Dispositional Theories of Value', *Proceedings of the Aristotelian Society* Supplementary Volume. 89–111.

1991: 'Realism' in Peter Singer, ed., *A Companion to Ethics.* Basil Blackwell. 399–410.

1992: 'Valuing: Desiring or Believing?' in David Charles and Kathleen Lennon, eds, *Reduction, Explanation,* and *Realism.* Oxford University Press. 323–60.

1993a: 'Objectivity and Moral Realism: On the Significance of the Phenomenology of Moral Experience' in John Haldane and Crispin Wright, eds, *Reality, Representation and Projection.* Oxford University Press. 235–6.

1993b: 'Colour, Transparency, Mind-Independence' in John Haldane and Crispin Wright, eds, *Reality, Representation and Projection.* Oxford University Press. 269–78.

1994a: 'Why Expressivists about Value Should Love Minimalism about Truth', *Analysis.* 1–12.

1994b: 'Minimalism, Truth-Aptitude and Belief', *Analysis.* 21–6.

Stocker, Michael 1979: 'Desiring the Bad: An Essay in Moral Psychology', *Journal of Philosophy.* 738–53.

Stroud, Barry 1977: *Hume*. Routledge and Kegan Paul.

Sturgeon, Nicholas 1985: 'Moral Explanations' in David Copp and David Zimmerman, eds, *Morality, Reason and Truth*. Rowman and Allanheld. 49–78.

— 1986: 'What Difference Does It Make Whether Moral Realism Is True?', *Southern Journal of Philosophy* Supplement. 115–41.

Tawil, Nathan 1987: *Reference and Intentionality*. Ph.D. Dissertation, Princeton University.

Velleman, J. David 1992: 'The Guise of the Good', *Noûs*. 3–26.

Wallace, Jay 1983: *Motivation and Moral Reality*. Bachelor of Philosophy thesis. Oxford University.

— 1990: 'How to Argue about Practical Reason' in *Mind*. 267–97.

Watson, Gary 1975: 'Free Agency' reprinted in Gary Watson, ed., *Free Will*. Oxford University Press. 1982. 96–110.

— 1987: 'Responsibility and the Limits of Evil' in Ferdinand Schoeman, ed., *Responsibility, Character and the Emotions: New Essays in Moral Psychology*. Cambridge University Press. 256–86.

Wiggins, David 1987: 'A Sensible Subjectivism' in his *Needs, Values, Truth*. Basil Blackwell. 185–214.

— 1993a: 'Cognitivism, Naturalism, and Normativity: A Reply to Peter Railton' in John Haldane and Crispin Wright, eds., *Reality, Representation and Projection*. Oxford University Press. 301–314.

— 1993b: 'A Neglected Position?' in John Haldane and Crispin Wright, eds., *Reality, Representation and Projection*. Oxford University Press. 329–36.

Williams, Bernard 1976: 'Persons, Character and Morality' reprinted in Williams 1981. 1–19.

— 1980: 'Internal and External Reasons' reprinted in Williams 1981. 101–13.

— 1981: *Moral Luck*. Cambridge University Press.

— 1985: *Ethics and the Limits of Philosophy*. Harvard University Press.

Wilson, George 1985: 'Davidson on Intentional Action' in Ernest LePore and Brian McLaughlin, eds., *Actions and Events: Perspectives on the Philosophy of Donald Davidson*. Basil Blackwell. 29–43.

Wolf, Susan 1982: 'Moral Saints', *Journal of Philosophy*. 419–39.

Woods, Michael 1972: 'Reasons for Action and Desire', *Proceedings of the Aristotelian Society* Supplementary Volume. 189–201.

Wright, Crispin 1988: 'Moral Values, Projection and Secondary Qualities', *Proceedings of the Aristotelian Society* Supplementary Volume. 1–26.

— 1992: *Truth and Objectivity*. Harvard University Press.

Index